Advance Praise

These essays on the current state and evolution of India's banking industry, and its future trajectory, are topical and enlightening. The general as well as the expert reader will find much in them that is engaging and provocative. Most importantly, the author overlays decades of hands-on banking experience on a rigorous economics base.

Dr Sudhir Shah, *Head of Department, Professor,*
Delhi School of Economics

Mr Madan Sabnavis does an admirable job walking the reader through the ins and outs of this very crucial piece of the economic puzzle—has Indian Banking come of age in these nearly three decades. Not surprisingly, the answer about the success of Indian banking sector reforms is filled with shades of grey. What is particularly noteworthy is Mr Sabnavis' analytical and communicative ability to do so in a non-ideological fashion.

Dr Sunder Ramaswamy, *Vice Chancellor,*
Krea University, Sri City, Andhra Pradesh

A long-awaited book covering all contemporary issues of banking. The book is not merely a narration of events; deep analysis and unfolding of new dimensions make it different from other texts. Mr Madan Sabnavis likes to call a spade a spade and his views and inferences in this book once again demonstrate that trait. A scholarly writing presented in a lucid manner—a must read for all who are interested in banking.

Dr J. N. Misra, *Chief Executive Officer,*
Indian Institute of Banking and Finance (IIBF)

I have known Madan for over two and a half decades. I have always respected him for fearlessly speaking out his point of view, particularly with reference to banking and allied sectors. I have always paid attention to his views even if I might have disagreed with him. What always impressed me has been the clarity of his thoughts and that he has been well-grounded. I have no doubt that, as in the past, his candid speaking would be reflected in these essays.

P. H. Ravikumar, *Director of Aditya Birla Capital and former MD and CEO, NCDEX*

This book is a much-needed study of an extremely complex subject. Drawing on his nearly 35 years of experience in financial and applied economic fields, Madan has written the most comprehensive book on the evolution of the Indian banking sector post-financial sector reforms. The coverage of topics and the analytical treatment strongly reflect his theoretical intelligence and deep practical insights.

Dr Rupa Rege Nitsure, *Group Chief Economist, L&T Financial Services Limited*

This book will surely promote informed debates on the economic outcomes of reforms in the financial sector and the essential road ahead. There are no more lucid accounts than this book on this vital cog for successful reforms. There are a few to match Sabnavis in clarity when it comes to analysing economic topics that concern us day to day. In this work, he has captured the essence of financial sector evolution since reforms, dissecting major initiatives. The potential as well as the pitfalls have been brought out very crisply.

V. Kumaraswamy, *CFO (JK Paper), Author and Columnist*

Madan uses his training as an economist and his experience of being a participant in India's financial system to discuss key trends in a sector which is key to our economy and the centre of attention at the moment. He touches on a number of topics where there are differing views and provokes the reader to think about these topics both deeply and differently.

Ajay Srinivasan, *Chief Executive, Aditya Birla Capital Limited*

This book provides numerous unbiased insights into bringing the moribund Indian banking system into a new mode. While dwelling in basic economic theory, Madan has always brought in a fresh practical perspective being a good lateral thinker that is easily understood by most readers and not just specialists. Honest in his analysis, Madan does not shy away from expressing his views which perhaps is the best way to begin any discussion. I would strongly recommend this book for its 360-degree review of the Indian banking system.

Dr Manju Ghodke, *Consultant and former Chief Economist, L&T Limited*

For some, history is a nightmare from which they try to awaken. However, Madan Sabnavis' book wakes us up gently, without allowing history to become a nightmare. He explains economic policies with gentleness and understanding that is rare among economists. Yet he pushes for governance, accountability and the need to protect customers and depositors. His ability to explain the 'why' and firmly, yet almost softly, suggest what should be done is what makes the book special.

R. N. Bhaskar, *Consulting editor with Free Press Journal*

Sabnavis combines the skills of an economist with the speed of a journalist, and that's what makes this book so important. It examines all the questions people have about banks: Do bank mergers make sense? Are we serious about the Insolvency and Bankruptcy Code? What is wrong with the government telling its banks what to do if a private sector owner can call the shots in a bank? and so on. A 'two-handed' approach is a bit disappointing, but that's because there are no unalloyed truths. The lay reader will certainly benefit from the book; the specialist may also learn a trick or two.

Sunil Jain, *Managing Editor,* Financial Express

The book chronicles the evolution of Indian banking since economic liberalization and attempts to figure out whether things have changed—they haven't. This is primarily because India has not been able to separate politics from economics. Economist Madan Sabnavis doesn't impose his view on the readers but kicks off a much-needed debate.

Tamal Bandyopadhyay, *Consulting Editor,*
Business Standard, *Author and Columnist*

Over the last few years, Indian banking, and especially the public sector part, has been lurching from one crisis to another. Madan Sabnavis' book on the sector's Hits and Misses is thus not only timely, but something policymakers, regulators and bankers should grab with both hands if they want a dispassionate opinion on what has worked, and what has not. Frank, independent and unbiased, Sabnavis tells it like it is.

Raghavan Jagannathan, *Author, Editorial Director,* Swarajya

This is a refreshingly different book about the evolution of Indian banking since liberalization. It is different because it doesn't shy away from discussing the politics of banking reforms, the clash of ideologies and the numerous controversies that have hobbled Indian banking. Madan Sabnavis brings years of experience with his usual clarity, insight, depth and objectivity to the debate.

Manas Chakravarty, *Group Consulting Editor, Moneycontrol*

This book is a must-read for those interested in knowing what worked and what did not work in the three decades since the country chose to trudge down the path of reforms. Sabnavis has both the benefit of being closely associated with the sector and at the same time a position where he can take a dispassionate view. Sabnavis has identified how ideology often continues to be a barrier for reform despite policymakers knowing the right answers. With the banking sector at yet another inflection point because of the economic crisis brought about by the pandemic, this is a timely publication.

Mayur Shetty, *Senior Editor,* The Times of India

Madan Sabnavis was among the first economic analysts in the mid-1990s to provide—through a commissioned newspaper column—a cogent, informed and layered critique of the banking sector reforms process. He remained immune to the reforms hysteria that was sweeping through the financial services sector and was able to pinpoint with great accuracy the structural, sequential or regulatory flaws in the entire process. This book adds a political economy angle to that critical gaze, making his evaluation of banking sector reforms more comprehensive, and definitely more readable.

Rajrishi Singhal, *Policy Consultant and Consulting Editor with* Mint

It is no secret that India is grappling with its worst banking crisis ever, though we are still discovering how and why we landed here and, most importantly, whether we can prevent it from happening again. Madan Sabnavis brings in his vast experience to bear on this important question and also answers the more fundamental one: Is my money safe?

Govindraj Ethiraj, *Founder of IndiaSpend & BOOM*

Hits & Misses

Hits & Misses

The Indian Banking Story

Madan Sabnavis

Los Angeles | London | New Delhi
Singapore | Washington DC | Melbourne

First published in 2021 by

SAGE Publications India Pvt. Ltd
B1/I-1 Mohan Cooperative Industrial Area
Mathura Road, New Delhi 110 044, India
www.sagepub.in

SAGE Publications Inc
2455 Teller Road
Thousand Oaks, California 91320, USA

SAGE Publications Ltd
1 Oliver's Yard, 55 City Road
London EC1Y 1SP, United Kingdom

SAGE Publications Asia-Pacific Pte Ltd
18 Cross Street #10-10/11/12
China Square Central
Singapore 048423

Published by Vivek Mehra for SAGE Publications India Pvt. Ltd. Typeset in 11/14 pt Californian FB by Fidus Design Pvt. Ltd, Chandigarh.

Library of Congress Control Number: 2020948612

ISBN: 978-93-5388-686-8 (PB)

SAGE Team: Neha Pal, Shruti Gupta, Parul Prasad and Rajinder Kaur

For Charu and Ragini

Yet be most proud of that which I compile
Whose influence is thine, and born of thee
In others' works thou dost but mend the style,
And arts with thy sweet graces graced be;
But thou art all my art, and dost advance
As high as learning my rude ignorance

—Shakespeare's Sonnet (78)

Thank you for choosing a SAGE product!
If you have any comment, observation or feedback,
I would like to personally hear from you.

Please write to me at **contactceo@sagepub.in**

Vivek Mehra, Managing Director and CEO, SAGE India.

Bulk Sales

SAGE India offers special discounts
for purchase of books in bulk.
We also make available special imprints
and excerpts from our books on demand.

For orders and enquiries, write to us at

Marketing Department
SAGE Publications India Pvt Ltd
B1/I-1, Mohan Cooperative Industrial Area
Mathura Road, Post Bag 7
New Delhi 110044, India

E-mail us at **marketing@sagepub.in**

Subscribe to our mailing list
Write to **marketing@sagepub.in**

This book is also available as an e-book.

Contents

List of Abbreviations

ALM	Asset liability management
AQR	Asset quality review
ARCs	Asset reconstruction companies
BBB	Banking Board Bureau
CAG	Comptroller and Auditor General
CAGR	Compounded average growth rate
CASA	Current and savings account deposits
CBI	Central Bureau of Investigation
CDR	Corporate debt restructuring
CDs	corporate deposits
CDS	Credit default swap
CEO	Chief executive officer
CMD	Chairman and managing director
CP	Commercial paper
CPI	Consumer price index
CRAR	Capital to risk-weighted assets ratio
CRR	Cash reserve ratio
CTC	Cost to company
CVC	Central Vigilance Commission
DFI	Development Financial Institution
ECB	External commercial borrowing
FDI	Foreign direct investment
FIs	Financial institutions
GST	Goods and services tax

IBA	Indian Banks Association
IBC	Insolvency and Bankruptcy Code
ICA	Inter-creditor agreement
LAF	Liquidity adjustment facility
MCLR	Marginal cost lending rate
MFI	Microfinance institution
MLR	Minimum lending rate
MPC	Monetary Policy Committee
NBFCs	Non-banking financial companies
NDTL	Net demand and time liabilities
NPA	Non-performing asset
OMOs	Open market operations
PCA	Prompt Corrective Action
PLR	Prime lending rate
PMC	Punjab and Maharashtra Cooperative Bank
PPA	Power purchasing agreements
PPF	Public Provident Fund
PSB	Public sector bank
RBI	Reserve Bank of India
RP	Resolution plan
RRB	Regional Rural Bank
RTGS	Real-time gross settlement
S4A	Scheme for sustainable structuring of stressed assets
SBI	State Bank of India
SDR	Strategic debt restructuring
SLR	Statutory liquidity ratio
SME	Small and medium enterprise
VRS	Voluntary retirement scheme

Foreword

Banking in India has evolved over the last 25 years from being a staid sector dominated by public sector banks (PSBs), working on a template set by the wholesale nationalization of the industry, to its current vibrant and varied landscape. This remarkable transformation has powered economic growth, helped drive consumption, produced stock market multibaggers as well as more than its fair share of prima donnas, scandals and tales of hubris.

The change was triggered in the 1990s by the Narasimham Committee in its first and second reports, a two-part tour de force, which not only changed the direction of the industry but also its vocabulary and lexicon. It brought in new competitive energy which not only produced new institutions that are household names today but also revitalized PSBs which responded to competition by reinventing themselves.

Madan, therefore, very appropriately takes the Narasimham Committee Report in 1993 as the starting point of mapping this transformation, beginning, first, with an assessment of the recommendations that have been implemented including fundamental propositions like the asset quality framework, minimum capital requirements, as well as entry of new private banks, an assessment of what did not change or only partially changed and others like consolidation, which have only recently been set in trend.

What is particularly interesting is, how through a juxtaposition of facts and figures of the 1990s, against the current position, Madan illustrates the extent of dramatic changes like the increase in share of private banks, less appreciated ones like the increase of bank branches in metropolitan centres, as the economy boomed post liberalization, as well as busts some myths like the relative compensation of staff in public sector and private sector banks. All of us suffer from a recency bias. It, therefore, comes as a surprise when we are told that, notwithstanding the inevitable erosion in market share, once new competitive elements are introduced, the business of PSBs grew at a compounded average growth rate (CAGR) of 14.6 per cent during this period, just shy of the industry growth rate of 15.8 per cent.

Having laid down the context, in the second part of the book Madan proceeds to grapple with issues that concern us all—current as well as contentious—including tackling non-performing assets (NPAs), the pros and cons of Prompt Corrective Action (PCA), challenges around governance, chief executive officer (CEO) tenure and compensation, and the role of non-banking financial companies (NBFCs). While, Madan, self-deprecatingly, does speak of the two hands of the economist, what stands out is not equivocation but a rare ability to see both sides of the argument, as well as an unhesitating willingness to lay out his position clearly thereafter. The issues which benefit from this balanced perspective, particularly include the influence of the government in determining policies of PSBs as well as the adequacy of private ownership in resolving issues around governance.

The third part of the book which dwells on the role of the central bank and ruminates on issues around monetary policy is possibly the one which most clearly demonstrates Madan's command over his subject benefiting from both his skills as a trained economist, as well as his perspective as a long time watcher of the Reserve Bank of India (RBI). Readers will find his take on relations between the central bank and the government, the functioning of the Monetary Policy Committee (MPC), the appointment and tenure of the Governor—informed, balanced as well as original.

The book is a magisterial survey of the transformation of banking in India over the last quarter century, and Madan's inimitable candour and forthright style will make it a rewarding and enjoyable read for both, the lay reader as well as the professional banker.

Sanjiv Chadha, *Managing Director & CEO, Bank of Baroda*

Preface

This book is all about banking and how it has evolved post financial sector reforms. Financial sector reforms were a cut-off point as there was a metamorphosis in the way in which the system worked, as there was not just a transformational change but also reorientation of mindset which was important as banking was looked as a business rather than just a set of transactions involving taking deposits and lending money.

The narrative, hence, starts with a series of chapters which analyses if statistically the structure of banking has changed over a period of a little over a quarter of a century along with reasons for this change which include the way in which banking was conducted.

But have things changed really? Here, it is actually a shoulder shrug as there are certain areas which remain intractable as there are strong ideologies which are hard to dislodge and even though successive governments have made the right sounds, these shibboleths remain undisturbed and probably will remain so until such time we are able to separate politics from economics, which arguably is not easy.

These subjects have been discussed in a fairly dispassionate manner and while a specific view has been taken, the reader could differ and argue otherwise. Fomenting further discussion is the idea of this book and strong dissent from the reader would also measure the success of this discourse.

Acknowledgements

My interest in banking began in the late-1980s when I was not a banker but an employee in a development financial institution (DFI) with pretensions of being an economist, when I had a chance to pen down my thoughts in a weekly column in the *Financial Express* called 'Banker to Banker', where I was able to convey my rather amateurish views on the sector speaking as an economist, with little practical knowledge and only theory to guide my interpretation. It evolved over time when I was fortunate to have a column quite regularly in the *Economic Times* on the 'Finance' page. I had my first exposure as economist in ICICI Bank which was a different entity prior to the reverse merger with ICICI Limited. This was probably my first learning experience in banking where I understood what I wrote and, as financial sector reforms were the core, managed to understand the broad contours and probably some finer points too by sitting through asset and liability committee meetings and understanding how things worked.

Being a critic has its advantage and the business newspapers gave me the front to express my views, and taking a contrarian stance always clicked with the Editors. Banking is always topical because so many things keep happening all the time and there are always interpretations to give to any policy or development. As banking became more complex and policies controversial, I took a chance in commenting on them with a critical eye which helped a lot to gain attention as few corporate economists or bankers preferred to take this path. This provided more scope to express views which, though critical, steered clear of personalizing the institution. That's a lesson one should imbibe where we critically analyse the policy without commenting on the institution.

The controversies that have been debated here use the infamous two hands of economists but does present the contrarian view quite forcefully to convince the reader that we need not take things at face value. We should not shy away from talking of compensation for private bankers just because they are considered to be too sacred to even express a different view. We should be aware that changing the rules of the game to extract profit from the central bank is not in the right spirit, though perfectly legitimate, or we should not hesitate to say that criticizing public sector bankers is not right as one can do no better if the government interferes every time. More importantly, we should not get swayed by monetary policy stance and interest rates as they are looking at only one side of the cube. The reader need not agree with the author but, hopefully, will appreciate the argument.

The tryst of being in a position to write a book on subjects which have been dealt in some form by the author in the newspapers in the past could not have been possible without a lot of support from various newspaper editors who saw value in what was conveyed to be acceptable to readers. Here, I am thankful to R. N. Bhaskar (former *Financial Express*, *DNA* and now *The Free Press Journal*), Rajrishi Singhal (former *The Economic Times* and now *Mint*), Govardhana Rangan and Gayatri Nayak (*The Economic Times*), T. N. Ninan and Kanika Datta (*Business Standard*), Raghuvir Srinivasan and A. Srinivas (*Business Line*), R. Jagannathan and Dinesh Unnikrishnan (*Firstpost*) and Sarthak Ray (*Financial Express*), and above all I am grateful to Sunil Jain of the *Financial Express* to give me an opportunity to write almost on a weekly basis for the last 10 years on any subject without objecting to any view even though he may have had a very different take on the subject.

This book would not have been possible without the support from Neha Pal of SAGE Publications whose perseverance and most meaningful comments have made this treatise much better than what it was on submission. The title that is carried is entirely the creation of Neha Pal which would otherwise have been as odious as one which can be expected from economists. The same holds for some of the chapter titles which make them more appealing to read on.

Introduction

When one looks at the state of banking today, the picture emerging is ambivalent just as is the case with any other structure of the economy. In terms of business numbers, the picture is impressive as banking has spread across not just geography but also economic activity. However, there is also a fair degree of discomfort when looking closer at the system especially in the area of practices which has been gradually exposed over the last five years, which has called for a review. In fact, the recent developments regarding Punjab and Maharashtra Cooperative Bank (PMC) and Yes Bank have raised fresh concerns about the banking sector. These episodes came just after the government had taken some firm action to rein in the NPAs of PSBs which gave the sense that the worst was behind us and that the system was back on the rails.

Until around 2015 or so, it did appear that all was well and that the sector was evolving satisfactorily against the background of the so-called 'policy paralysis' which had hampered investment and led to the creation of stalled projects. In fact, post the financial crisis in 2007 and 2008, we had taken pride in the fact that the Indian banking system was a cut above the rest as we were well-ring fenced by prudential regulation and best practices.

When the fissures appeared in our system in the form of NPAs and capital scarcity, it was a kind of revelation because it involved not just the banks and bankers but also the regulator. All regulatory forbearance was in place and somewhere it appeared that the banks went overboard in understating their NPAs which went unnoticed by the regulator in regular inspections.

It has been over two and a half decades of financial sector reforms when this sector was opened up and at this point it could be said that there is still some scepticism on the strength of the system as there is a sense of déjà vu which goes back to the 1990s when the cleaning up operation of the banking system really began. It is true that the RBI has brought in several reforms that have changed the architecture of banking in these years, but at the end of the day if we are still not sure of what is a bad asset or what should be done about it, serious issues get flagged. This was also the case two decades back when the system grappled with accounting norms and balance sheets that looked sturdy, suddenly appeared fragile and needed repair. We appear to be going through the same cycle as questions regarding the accounting practices have been raised for a number of banks. Quite clearly, banking regulation is an evolutionary process and cycles of deviation are bound to be when the system is questioned quite sharply.

Also, the challenge of capital remains where every bank has to fend for itself and the government has to let go of its ownership now much so reluctant it may be. More importantly, the PSBs in particular are as shaky as ever and it does seem that all the problems that we thought had been addressed have actually been swept below the carpet rather than countered to reach a solution. Interestingly, even today there is an incentive to side-step rules and make exceptions which while prima facie can be justified, nonetheless casts a shadow on the commitment we have to prudence. Hence, while we do have an impressive structure and access to technology, the internals continue to be uncertain. While nationalization had ushered in a distinct form of banking in the country which was run with socialist ideals, the model has developed fissures that need to be repaired which in a way had pushed the clock back.

Also, several ideas that were put forward at the beginning of reforms have probably not moved at all for various reasons. This is another thought which comes to mind when one looks back on reforms and the changes that have come about. One reason can be that the government, irrespective of which party is in power, is not keen to let it happen as the system ensures a symbiotic relationship between all the components with the government benefiting the most. It is not just the statutory liquidity ratio (SLR) which is being alluded to but also populism and the dividend when things go well. Hence, while the Finance Minister talks tough when it comes to recapitalizing banks, there is quite a bit of dependence on the banks for dividend which helps the government when formulating the budget. There is, hence, a two-way relationship here. When there are political agendas to be adhered to, banks are an integral part of the story whether it relates to loan waivers or inclusive banking or small and medium enterprise (SME) lending and so on. Hence, banking is an important lever for any government in power which is an instrument for delivery of a political agenda.

The purpose of this book is to examine how things have changed in the last 25 years for the banking system. There are evidently a lot of good stories to take away which cannot be ignored but the deep-rooted challenges which are there today are not new and also existed in the period prior to 1991. Take for instance, the infamous loan melas which were held by various state governments. The idea was to focus on giving loans to certain groups ostensibly for political gains. Banks did not have a choice and lent money which was never returned. This picture has not changed even today as bankers would attest that often there are 'orders from above' to give loans which probably would never have been given under normal circumstances. They may not be called loan melas but were euphemistically 'orders from above'.

The culture remains the same. Politicians who have a nexus with corporates still call the shots, and hence it looks like the world has not changed. Earlier these loans were of small magnitude and covered farmers where the ticket sizes were small. But now these are the large NPAs which reside in some of the leading industries.

One of the big success stories for India has been the implementation of financial sector reforms from 1991 to 1992 onwards, which did change the way in which the sector operated. From being a large behemoth dominated by PSBs under the continuous pressure of nationalistic ideology, the sector was transformed more under the compulsions of globalization and prudence. The landscape of banking changed especially with global concepts in terms of accounting coming into our lexicon which was implemented quite relentlessly by the RBI over the last 25 years and this can be interpreted as being transformational in nature. In a way, these reforms acted as a mirror which reflected the true picture of banking. While challenges still exist in this sphere, there has been a lot of learning along the way, both in terms of suggestions made by internal committees as well as through global experiences which have played a significant role in shaping the sector.

It is always believed that banking reform is a continuous process as there are always global developments which shape the broad contours of policy while specific domestic issues pre-dominate the mind of the regulator when planning for the future. The present issue of NPAs is primarily a home-grown one while the conceptual framework that came in on the relatively new area of structured products was more a result of the developments that took place during the global financial crisis of 2007–2008 when central banks all over the world took special interest in addressing the issue of financial engineering. Handling the present NPA crisis comes along with meeting the Basel III standards that has posed additional challenges to the banking system.

In the same length, the changing appearance of the financial sector called for different approaches to banking as disintermediation, in particular, took off quite decisively in the last decade as market-based financial instruments caught the fancy of both buyers and sellers of credit given the regulatory differences caused by differing structures. During this phase, there was also a change in ideology where there have been committees set up to look at integrating the financial structure which really means that there is still a lot of work in progress.

The approach here is to look at two aspects of banking as it has evolved over this time period. The first aspect is looking through the prism of 25 years to gauge the transformation that has taken place which is compared at two different points of time. This is data driven and hence is factual with certain explanations being provided on the reasons behind the change in the trends today compared with those in the past. Going through these aspects of Indian banking, one can actually see major changes that have taken place in the banking structure over the years with various innovations actually changing the architecture quite sharply. This is not just in terms of physical structures but also ideology where the advent of latest technology has brought about quite a transformation. Also, banking became a business from a rather sleepy activity where bankers took deposits and lent the money.

There are other aspects of banking which are also interesting to track in terms of physical numbers. As we are dealing with just over 25 years of banking reforms which made their mark with the implementation of the recommendations of the Narasimham Committee, it may be expected that there would be a sea change in the banking canvas. Do we have more branches in rural areas? Are banks still preferred to other modes of borrowing? Has universal banking made banks the main source for term loans? Is there a change in the structure of bank deposits and credit? Have new private banks made a big difference to the architecture of banking in the country?

These questions and more are posed and answered along the way so that over this span of 25 years one can see whether or not things have changed significantly. There is hence some bit of number comparison made between two points of time which are taken to be indicative of the period at the time of reforms and the present situation. Data are taken from the RBI site and when data are not available for the 1991–1993 period, the earliest year for which information is presented has been chosen. The important thing is that the starting point does not matter as we are comparing figures over a long period of time and the absolute ratio value may not be as important as the trend that is signalled.

This book hence looks at various facets of the banking sector over the years to ascertain whether or not there has been a major transformation in specific areas. The various developments that took place during this evolution would throw light on how adjustments were made by the players. Today, there is a fair distinction made between the PSBs and private banks. The latter is typified by the new private banks which have come up to dominate the banking space and while there were a number of such entities which came up, there was a tendency for some of them to merge with others as their models were not sustainable. But these new banks had ushered in a new brand of technology-driven banking which was a major innovation that has changed the way in which business is conducted, and hence is a positive disruption.

The foregoing thoughts are focused on how this architecture has changed over these two and a half decades under the umbrella of reforms, more specifically bank-oriented ones. This is one part of the story where the above-mentioned regulation has played a role. The response of both the deposit holders and borrowers is also interesting as it tells us more about how the operations of banking have changed. There are several factors which go into decision-making at both ends, but it is interesting to see whether at the end of the day the patterns have changed over the years.

The second part takes a hard look at certain crucial banking issues and puts on the table the issues involved and a perspective on the same. While the general drift of the arguments may be away from the conventional, it is not to disprove the existing thought on the subject. There are evidently two sides to all arguments and the tendency here may be tilted towards the contrarian. This should allow the reader to examine the merits of the points put forward and enable them to take a view. As there are no clear answers, these subjects have been bracketed under controversies that pervade our system where hard decisions need to be taken. For various subjects, certain decisions have been taken not without a strong rationale but then we need to also recognize that there is a different view. We have been eschewing some of them for some time and it does appear that they will have to be tackled head on in the next few years.

Also the fact that banks have become commercial entities in the true sense is an important development because the balance sheet and profit and loss accounts have become as important as it is for a production unit. While reforms have driven them towards working with commercial sense, banks have gotten listed which has also meant that they become an integral part of the system of value creation which is what the stock market measures. Banking stocks have come to occupy important positions in the two benchmark indices (6 of the 30 BSE Sensex list and Nifty) and are also an attractive proposition for investors at both institutional and retail level as it is assumed that this sector has to do well in future notwithstanding the bumps that may exist along the way. This also reflects the change in motivation for banking where the emphasis is more on enhancing shareholder value rather than maintaining the sanctity of the basic principles of the business. Once banking becomes commercial in the true sense, the policies and advocacies are all directed at one goal which is increasing profits.

There is evidently no end to the reform process in banking as it is evolutionary and guided a lot by how the world looks at this business and structures. Prudential regulation today is almost homogenous across the world and the name Basel has caught on with three versions laying down strict standards that are adopted by all central banks to usher in discipline and compliance with the best standards. Further, it is agreed in principle that the government should not be running banks which means that it is only a matter of time before the big reformation takes place wherein these banks move into the private sector and become more market oriented. This also means that the support that is provided by the implicit ownership of the government will disappear and they would be open to takeovers or dissolution in case they are unable to remain profitable or find themselves in a position where their net worth is eroded.

Hence, the lazy banking days could just be getting over and it would be Darwinism in this field too where the force of competition would drive these entities towards working in a more efficient manner.

It is hoped that the data put forward here as well as the issues raised and views provided are useful for the student as well as the practitioner as the financial sector is probably the most dynamic one with several developments taking place almost every day. The banking sector gets involved with almost every policy or decision taken relating to the real sector, and hence is very dynamic in nature. While the discourse in the media tends to be more in the area of the markets as this is where money is made, the banking sector is the field which facilitates all aspects of growth and the RBI as the regulator has a critical role to play everywhere. In fact, the RBI website is one of the most dynamic ones as it has several policies and notifications issued on a continuous basis which are required to closely monitor the system.

Hence, this book would serve two purposes which follow one another. The first one is the delineation of the major trends in banking over this period of over 25 years which though statistical in nature would provide insights into how the business of banking changed. This would serve as a background to the selected issues or controversies that are discussed for which there are two strong views on the opposite side. Where possible there is an attempt made to say which side the author is on. But as you read along you may have your view which is what the aim here really is. If the reader is willing to accept the two sides but opt for one, then the greater purpose of this book would be served as the idea is to foment thinking of the critical variety so that there is a healthy debate. Often most issues are not discussed threadbare because there is a tendency to be politically correct. Neither the practitioners nor the experts would like to say bluntly that the government should not be taking on the profits of the RBI or that the CEO of a bank should not be having a term of more than say 10 years. Doing so may mean antagonizing the concerned persons and often the institution involved is too respected and would be taken negatively. By providing the two sides of the issue, hopefully the non-conventional view would find utterance.

PART I

TRENDS

Banking on Reforms

The Narasimham Committee Report

Why the Narasimham Report? This Report is quite epochal in our context as it did examine in great detail all aspects of banking and suggested the way forward. The Committee had the foresight to visualize most things that we are talking of today. Other studies and committees that have come subsequently have largely mouthed what was already suggested in these two reports (there were two of them in a span of around six–seven years). The Narasimham Committee had formed the backbone of the edifice of financial sector reforms in the country. The template laid down was remarkable as it had been ushered in 1991–1992 when a lot of research had to be done manually to align the recommendations with the best practices in the world. The Committee had made a second set of suggestions in 1997–1998 too.

The thrust was on liberalization of the system with less interference and structured regulation, which was in line with the global best practices. New concepts were brought in so that the accounting practices were aligned with global systems and the balance sheets were more transparent. This was the time when the country also went in for financial sector reforms in a big way and the idea here was to ensure that the financial system which comprised mainly the banks was in sync with these changes so that the two segments, that is, real sector and monetary sector could grow together in an effective manner.

The process of financial sector reforms was, hence, two fold. First, the Committee provided the blueprints to be followed. Second, the RBI took a call on how to implement these reforms and it was done in a phased manner so that the system was able to adapt to the same. The norms on income recognition, provisioning, NPAs, capital adequacy and so on, were brought in for the first time and adhering to the same was a challenge for banks which had followed the earlier principles where prudential regulation was not a part of the deal. Interestingly, most of these terms which are used in banking lexicon today were unheard of in the period before financial sector reforms and the income statements always looked very good and one was rarely able to distinguish between the good and the not-so-good banks. What mattered was the balance sheet where they were to expand keeping in mind the goals of nationalization.

Some of the main recommendations that may not have necessarily been followed fully or were adapted to the prevalent circumstances were the following.

- The creation of a four-tiered hierarchy where there would be three or four large banks, eight to ten national-level banks with a network across the country, local banks for regional operations that would be niche in nature and rural banks at the bottom mainly engaged in financial inclusion and would focus on agriculture and other priority sector areas. This has come in a modified form and if one views the recent announcement of the government to merge PSBs, it can be seen that the system has gravitated towards the same. Prior to this move, the government and the RBI have also brought in the concept of small banks which are basically those which focus on priority sector lending. The multi-pronged approach to be followed by banks was hence very much a part of what was advocated three decades ago.

- Interest rates had to be deregulated to reflect emerging market conditions and there was no direct action taken by the RBI or government to fix rates on both the deposit and lending sides. They had to be market determined. While this has been followed to a large extent, it will be seen later that there have been strong attempts made to regulate them through market techniques and suasion. But theoretically, the RBI uses the repo rate as the benchmark and banks have to adjust to the same. But officially, banks have to fix their interest rates and are not determined by statute which was the case earlier. Of late with the central bank asking banks to fix their rates to benchmarks, there are signs of intervention through the back door again.

- There should be no attempt made ever for nationalization of the private banks which was done earlier and the private banks had to be treated on par with the PSBs. Clearly, the message was to ensure that the field for private banks would never be impinged by attempts to nationalize them which was required as the Committee also recommended the lifting of the bar on setting up new private banks. This went with the move to abolish the licensing procedure for branch expansion of existing banks. The policy of licensing new private banks (other than local area banks) would continue. The start-up capital requirements of ₹100 crore were set in 1993 and these could be reviewed. The Committee would recommend that there should be well-defined criteria and a transparent mechanism for deciding the ability of promoters to professionally manage the banks, and no category should be excluded on a priori grounds. The question of a minimum threshold capital for old private banks also deserved attention and mergers could be one of the options available for reaching the required capital thresholds. The Committee would also, in this connection, suggest that as long as it is laid down (as now) that any particular promoter group cannot hold more than 40 per cent of the equity of a bank, any further restriction of voting rights by limiting it to 10 per cent may be done away with. But interestingly as will be revealed in the discussions in the following chapters while nationalization has not been on cards of private banks, failure of banks has led to PSB actually taking it over which probably was the best solution given that the ideology of banking in India has been that deposit holders should not lose money irrespective of the circumstances that have led to the bank failing.

- The issue of quality of assets was discussed in detail and some suggestions made were that in case of doubtful debts, provisions should be created to the extent of 100 per cent of the security shortfall. Further loss of assets had to be fully written off. Also, modalities had to be worked out for taking off from the balance sheet of banks and financial institutions (FIs) part of the bad and doubtful debts. This would enable banks to better make use of their capital which would be freed on this score. *The Committee was of the firm view that in any effort at financial restructuring in the form of hiving off the NPA portfolio from the books of the banks or measures to mitigate the impact of a high level of NPAs must go hand in hand with operational restructuring. Cleaning up the balance sheets of banks would thus make sense only if steps were taken simultaneously to prevent or limit the re-emergence of new NPAs which could only come about through a strict application of prudential norms and managerial improvement.* It will be seen later in the book that this remains contentious as the Insolvency and Bankruptcy Code (IBC) which was implemented in this spirit has been made more flexible in course of time.

- Foreign banks were to be allowed to open more branches as part of the liberalization package which went along with the rules set down for foreign direct investment (FDI) in the country where the limits for foreigners in Indian banks were increased in a phased manner. The Committee was of the view that foreign banks may be allowed to set up subsidiaries or joint ventures in India. Such subsidiaries or joint ventures should be treated at par with other private banks and subject to the same conditions with regard to branches and directed credit as these banks. Here, while foreign banks are definitely more entrenched in the country, the bone of contention has been the method of operating in the country which could be a branch or subsidiary. The former does impose constraints while the latter gives scope to operate like domestic banks but comes with the clause of adherence to norms of priority sector lending which is applicable to all other banks. Banks have not chosen this route as this would also mean getting into farm lending which is out of their purview. Therefore, on this score there has been no change in structure of ownership and this is why they seem to be fairly niche in operations.

- The reserve requirements that banks had to keep with the RBI in the form of cash reserve ratio (CRR) and liquid assets which were mainly government securities as SLR, were to be progressively brought down from 1991 to 1992 levels. The thought process was that the SLR should be used for maintaining prudence in liquidity management and not as a tool to finance government budgets. Interestingly, today banks prefer to hold government paper beyond the SLR limit as such investments are safe and can yield a good return besides saving on capital.

- Introduction of the norm of 90 days for income recognition in a phased manner.

- The case of priority sector lending was recognized as being important. However, it was felt that such directed credit programme had to be revisited and redefined to cover small and marginal farmers, micro and small industry, small business operators and other weaker sections of society. The Committee had noted the reasons why the government could not accept the recommendation for reducing the scope of directed credit under priority sector from 40 per cent to 10 per cent. The Committee recognized that the small and marginal farmers and the tiny sector of industry and small businesses have problems with regard to obtaining credit and some earmarking may be necessary for this sector. Under the present dispensation, within the priority sector 10 per cent of net bank credit is earmarked for lending to weaker sections. A major portion of this lending is on account of government-sponsored poverty alleviation and employment generation schemes. The Committee recommended that given the special needs of this sector, the current practice may continue. The branch managers of banks should, however, be fully responsible for the identification of beneficiaries under the government-sponsored credit-linked schemes. The Committee proposed that given the importance and needs of employment-oriented sectors like food processing and related service activities in agriculture, fisheries, poultry and dairying, these sectors should also be covered under the scope of priority sector lending. *The Committee recommended that the interest subsidy element in credit for the priority sector should be totally eliminated and even interest rates on loans under ₹2 lakh should be deregulated for scheduled commercial banks as has been done in the case of Regional Rural Banks (RRBs) and co-operative credit institutions. The Committee believes that it is the timely and adequate availability of credit rather than its cost which is material for the intended beneficiaries.* This is one recommendation that has not found favour with successive governments as farm loans do carry interest rate subvention which is around 2 per cent and could go higher if the payment record is made timely.

- The process for recruitment of staff should be left to the banks and the common entrance exams concept had to be dispensed with. Appointments to the key posts had to be kept out of the political circle and be based on merit. Here too, there has been virtually no change and where it has, as will be discussed later, another layer of government appointees have taken over the Board that is to decide on such appointments.
- PSBs had to set up a rural subsidiary which would take over all the rural branches and be kept at par with the RRBs.

- Privatization of PSBs was a goal in the long run where a part of the equity had to be divested just like was done for other PSUs. This has been done partly more in action than spirit as the government is not willing to go below 50 per cent owner-ship. This has been dealt with in the section on controversies.
- Full autonomy to be given to banks in their operations which would ensure autonomy in operations and adherence to the principles of commerce. This is yet to materialize and the reasons for the same will be discussed later.
- The job of supervision of banks should ideally be hived off to another quasi autonomous body sponsored by the RBI. This has become a recent bone of contention in the central bank where the staff associations are not in congruence with this new set up.
- The DFIs had hitherto followed a consortium approach where all of them were involved in every loan that was given. The Committee had suggested that they follow a syndicating approach instead. Also, they had to raise capital in line with global practices to ensure that they had healthy capital adequacy ratios. The two large DFIs have become universal banks, and hence the concept remains quite irrelevant today.
- IDBI should retain only its refinancing role and delegate its direct lending to a separate corporate body.
- Provision to make for proper classification of assets and full disclosure and also for transparency of accounts of bank and other FIs.
- The entire portfolio of government securities should be marked to market and this schedule of adjustment should be announced at the earliest. It would be appropriate that there should be a 5 per cent weight for market risk for government and approved securities.
- The risk weight for a government-guaranteed advance should be the same as for other advances. To ensure that banks do not suddenly face difficulties in meeting the capital ade-quacy requirement, the new prescription on risk weight for

government-guaranteed advances should be made prospective from the time the new prescription is put in place.

- The Committee believed that it would be appropriate to go beyond the earlier norms and set new and higher norms for capital adequacy. The Committee accordingly recommended that the minimum capital to risk assets ratio be increased to 10 per cent from its present level of 8 per cent. It would be appropriate to phase the increase as was done on the previous occasion. Accordingly, the Committee recommended that an intermediate minimum target of 9 per cent be achieved by the year 2000 and the ratio of 10 per cent by 2002. The RBI should also have the authority to raise this further in respect of individual banks if in its judgement the situation with respect to their risk profile warrants such an increase. The issue of an individual bank's shortfalls in the capital to risk-weighted assets ratio (CRAR) needs to be addressed in much the same way that the discipline of reserve requirements is now applied, viz., of uniformity across weak and strong banks.

- Banks and FIs should avoid the practice of 'evergreening' by making fresh advances to their troubled constituents only with a view to settling interest dues and avoiding classification of the loans in question as NPAs. The Committee noted that the regulatory and supervisory authorities are paying particular attention to such breaches in the adherence to the spirit of the NPA definitions and are taking appropriate corrective action. At the same time, it is necessary to resist the suggestions made from time to time for a relaxation of the definition of NPAs and the norms in this regard. This is a significant statement made as the present NPA problem had its genesis in the phenomenon of evergreening where the system permitted corporate debt restructuring (CDR) for several years which led to a pile-up of impaired assets. While this was the idea, we have made several compromises along the way starting with the concept of restructured assets and tweaking of the definition for specific sectors which has resulted in dilution of such resolution.

- Mergers between banks and between banks and DFIs and NBFCs need to be based on synergies and locational and business-specific complementarities of the concerned institutions and must obviously make sound commercial sense. Mergers of PSBs should emanate from management of banks with government as the common shareholder playing a supportive role. Such mergers, however, can be worthwhile if they lead to rationalisation of workforce and branch network; otherwise the mergers of PSBs would tie down the managements with operational issues and distract attention from the real issue. It would be necessary to evolve policies aimed at 'rightsizing' and redeployment of the surplus staff either by way of retraining them and giving them appropriate alternate employment or by introducing a voluntary retirement scheme (VRS) with appropriate incentives. This would necessitate the co-operation and understanding of the employees and towards this direction, managements should initiate discussions with the representatives of staff and would need to convince their employees about the intrinsic soundness of the idea, the competitive benefits that would accrue and the scope and potential for employees' own professional advancement in a larger institution. Mergers should not be seen as a means of bailing out weak banks. Mergers between strong banks/FIs would make for greater economic and commercial sense and would be a case where the whole is greater than the sum of its parts and have a 'force multiplier effect'. This again is significant as the present debate on the issue dodges some of these issues and makes it seem to be the perfect model where balance sheets are added and with minimal rationalization leads to a superior solution.
- A 'weak bank' should be one whose accumulated losses and net NPAs exceed its net worth or one whose operating profits are negative for three consecutive years. A case by

case examination of the weak banks should be undertaken to identify those which are potentially revivable with a programme of financial and operational restructuring. Such banks could be nurtured into healthy units by slowing down on expansion, eschewing high-cost funds/borrowings, judicious manpower deployment, recovery initiatives, containment of expenditure and so on. The future set-up of such banks should also be given due consideration. Merger could be a solution to the problem of weak banks but only after cleaning up their balance sheets. If there is no voluntary response to a takeover of these banks, it may be desirable to think in terms of a Restructuring Commission for such PSBs for considering other options including restructuring, merger amalgamation or failing these, closure. Such a Commission could have terms of reference which, inter alia, should include suggestion of measures to safeguard the interest of depositors and employees and to deal with possible negative externalities. Weak banks which on a careful examination are not capable of revival over a period of three years should be referred to the Commission.

- The Committee was of the view that there is a need for a reform of the deposit insurance scheme. In India, deposits are insured up to ₹1 lakh. There is no need to increase the amount further. This was finally done in 2020 as it was hardly an issue and was taken for granted until the PMC issue surfaced. There is, however, a need to shift away from the 'flat' rate premiums to 'risk-based' or 'variable rate' premiums. Under risk-based premium system, all banks would not be charged a uniform premium. While there can be a minimum flat rate which will have to be paid by all banks on all their customer deposits, institutions which have riskier portfolios or which have lower ratings should pay higher premium. There would thus be a graded premium. As the Reserve Bank is now awarding CAMELS ratings to banks, these ratings could form the basis for charging deposit insurance premium. This issue too is pertinent today in wake of the PMC crisis. Deposit insurance was never conjectured to be invoked in the 1990s but looks likely today, and hence we do need go beyond just the premium being charged to the amount covered.

- The Committee believes that the objective should be to reduce the average level of net NPAs for all banks to below 5 per cent by the year 2000 and to 3 per cent by 2002. For banks with an international presence, the minimum objective should be to reduce gross NPAs to 5 per cent and 3 per cent by the year 2000 and 2002, respectively, and net NPAs to 3 per cent and 0 per cent by these dates, respectively. These targets cannot be achieved in the absence of measures to tackle the problem of backlog of NPAs on a one-time basis and the implementation of strict prudential norms and management efficiency to prevent the recurrence of this problem.

While these are some major highlights of the recommendations made by the Committee in the two reports, there were several others which went into the details of the operations of the banking system. The important thing to note here is that the outlook provided was quite visionary and almost all such reports on various aspects of the banking system subsequently have largely developed on these issues that were recommended. In a way, it can be said that all reforms in the financial system had their genesis in these reports.

The Narasimham Reports provided the strong foundations for further action on the part of the RBI which was taken up albeit in a calibrated manner to ensure that there were no major shocks for the system. This has worked rather well for a system which was completely closed and credit needs to be given to the RBI to bring in reforms over a period of time. This has ensured that the transition has been smooth since the concepts were new and had to be conveyed to all bankers so that they knew what they were doing. The major learning exercise that had to be conducted was through examinations and classroom sessions and a series of seminars so that bankers were sensitized to the concept of reforms and what banking stood for. In this context, the present Indian Institute of Banking and Finance (IIBF) which was called Indian Institute of Bankers played a major role along with the Indian Banks Association (IBA) as it was realized that to make such a plan work, education was most important because if bankers did not understand what they were doing, there would be a mismatch with what the regulator wanted and the response of the bankers.

2 Advent of New Private Banks

One of the physical changes brought about by financial sector reforms was in the form of issuing licenses to new players in the private banking space. This was a means of opening the doors to more players to foster competition. In a way, the virtual monopolistic position of PSBs was to get challenged over a period of time as the new players embarked on their journey and grew their books. Hence, it was a case of moving away from nationalization where the government owned the system to a more competitive environment where private players satisfying certain conditions were able to apply for such licenses. This was a definite turnaround from the policy of nationalization that was assiduously followed.

The idea was novel as these new private banks while adhering to all the RBI norms relating to regulation had begun to provide an array of services which were presented in a different form. The concept of banking was transformed into an experience with air-conditioned offices and a modern staff well trained to communicate with customers in a friendly manner and backed by technology. The private banks had an advantage of starting new with no legacy issues but had to show they were different from the PSBs as banking is typically a sticky business where customers are loathe to shift to other banks even if the interest rates offered are better for lenders or deposit holders. As they began on a clean slate, there were no issues of the past, and hence the business could be built without legacy challenges. At the same time, it also meant that it had to be done from below which meant that there was a time period involved before they could become sustainable. They had advantage of studying the PSBs and could fine tune their model to ensure that corrections or improvements could be made.

The progress of these new private sector banks is quite revealing because the picture today is quite different from what it was when the initial licenses were issued by the RBI. As Table 2.1 shows, there have been a series of such episodes over the years. The initial applicants came from a motley group—some were driven by FIs including NBFCs, corporate houses or individual entrepreneurs. With the exception of the Centurion Bank in the list of the 1990s, all other banks had to virtually start from the beginning with new structures. Centurion Bank was a NBFC with its genesis being in the 20th Century Finance Company which was able to get converted into a commercial bank.

As can also be seen in Table 2.1, from the set of nine banks which went into operation during the decade, four had closed down or were merged into other banks. The Global Trust Bank ran into serious problems of governance and was finally merged into the Oriental Bank of Commerce. The Centurion Bank and Bank of Punjab merged first and then were taken over by HDFC Bank. Times Bank had been merged with HDFC Bank.

Those that continued operations were the institution-driven banks like ICICI Bank, HDFC Bank, IDBI Bank and Axis Bank (formerly called UTI Bank). IndusInd Bank is probably the only bank driven by a corporate House (Hinduja Group) which has come through these phases and has become a strong contender in the banking space today. The testimony of strength can be gauged by the stock being part of the two benchmark stock indices. A lesson learnt was that a very strong promoter was required to

Table 2.1. Calendar of Establishment of New Private Banks

Bank	Established	Ended
UTI	1995	
Times	1995	2000
IndusInd	1995	
ICICI	1995	
HDFC	1995	
Bank of Punjab	1994	2005
Centurion	1994	2008
IDBI	1998	
Kotak	2002–2003	
Yes Bank	2007–2008	2020[a]
Global Trust	1994	2004
IDFC Bank	2015	
Bandhan Bank	2015	

Source: Annual reports of banks and bank websites.
Note: [a]Under transformation with change in ownership and SBI taking over.

run the business as unlike investment banks which need a smaller infrastructure to scale business, commercial banks are meant for what can be called marathon runners which have to wait for a fairly long period of time before they are able to really make their mark. While growth numbers are manageable given that the bank starts from nil, the challenge is retaining credibility all along and getting the hands dirty. This means meandering through all the regulatory requirements like CRR, SLR, Priority sector lending (involving farm loans) and evolving regulation as reforms were gradually invoked on the system.

The other new banks that have come up in the 21st century have also been significant. Kotak Mahindra Bank had its origin in a NBFC, that is, Kotak Mahindra Finance while Yes Bank has been an independent institution set up after a hiatus of almost a decade and a half. The more recent entrants post the last set of licenses that have been allotted include IDFC Bank, which was a FI called IDFC Limited that got converted into a bank while

Bandhan Bank was a microfinance institution (MFI) which did the same. IDFC Bank has been merged with Capital First to now become IDFC First Bank. Therefore, Yes Bank would be the only bank that started from the beginning and was not a creation of an existing institution being given a license. The story of Yes Bank, though impressive, has run into controversy with a bailout being provided by the State Bank of India (SBI) as management failure came to light in 2020 and a shadow was being cast again on a private bank, which was still promoter driven and which had severe governance issues leading to failure. The progress made by these banks should be looked at from this perspective.

Being an offshoot of an existing venture has the advantage of an existing foundation in terms of physical infrastructure as well as a balance sheet having sources and uses of funds. Also, the existing staff has some knowledge of borrowing and lending as well as basic rules of the game unlike a new bank which has to get everything from the start. This becomes useful to build the future blocks.

However, for a new bank which starts from the grassroots, the advantages are several in so far as that there are no legacy issues and it is able to use the latest technology to build business which is not the case with existing structures. Also, the cost of experimentation will be lower as they would have the experiences of other players to refer to when devising their strategies. But the cost and effort in getting in the physical and human resources is higher and the time taken to build an asset book would also be longer given the competition. The experiences of some of these banks are interesting. ICICI Bank, for example, had started off with hiring mainly public sector bankers while the HDFC Bank model was more inclined towards foreign bankers. AXIS Bank was again tilted to public sector bankers (called UTI Bank) while IDBI Bank surprisingly was again oriented towards foreign bankers. Hence, the models used by new banks would be at variance with their advantages and challenges. Pay scales were different and the approach was different with the foreign bankers tending to be more aggressive and demanding while those with PSB lineage tended to be more gradual but bound thoroughly by convention. These traits stand out even today when one looks at the functioning of these banks, though there have been considerable changes in outlook and cross-fertilization of personnel across all banks. Mergers with parent DFIs also changed the culture of banks significantly over a period of time.

Given the evolution of these banks, it would be interesting to see how they stand today based on some performance parameters. The curious case is of IDBI Bank which started off as a private bank but when the reverse merger took place with the parent, IDBI Limited became a PSB. And more recently with the public sector behemoth, LIC, now the majority shareholder of IDB Bank, gets classified as a private bank. ICICI Bank had also gone in for a reverse merger with the parent ICICI Limited. But the difference was that as the parent dominated the merger, the private bankers from IDBI Bank had chosen to leave the organization as there was harmonization of pay packages with the parent. In case of ICICI Bank, the lead positions came to be occupied by the members of the parent, and the original bankers from ICICI Bank had moved over to other banks/organizations partly also due to overlap of positions.

The RBI officially has a policy which is open to giving licenses on tap. The shadow banking system which comprises the NBFCs is one part which could be looking to get converted into banks and when the door was opened up earlier under Raghuram Rajan's tenure, there were several applications made. However, the decision finally taken was more on the conservative side as the permission was given to IDFC Limited to be converted into a bank while Bandhan Bank which was an MFI was also allowed to do so.

A development in the banking space has been the risk of cooperative banks increasing. This is witnessed in terms of the problem that PMC has run into, which has questioned the idea of cooperative banks. The cooperative banking structure is old and regulation has been less stringent compared to commercial banks. As the RBI has gone in for the introduction of a differential tier banking structure with small banks playing the role of financial inclusion on the side of lending, there has been an argument made for conversion of such banks. This would make a lot of sense though all banks qualifying for the same will have to get their books audited thoroughly before a conversion is made possible. Small banks that should be remembered are those which lend only to the priority sector. For the PACS and SCBs, this may be easy to transform as their lending is based mainly to the farm sector. However, when it comes to urban cooperative banks, lending has not always been to the SMEs and as was the case with PMC, credit was directed to the larger companies too.

Intuitively one can see that there are several advantages in getting converted into a bank since there is access to current and savings bank accounts which come at a very low cost. Presently, there has been a move to link even the savings deposit rate with a benchmark that is variable, which means that there need not be any fixed savings bank rate which can fluctuate over time. However, along with the carrot of access to cheaper deposits come certain responsibilities too which includes priority sector lending along with the regulatory conditions of maintaining a CRR balance and a SLR portfolio. Therefore, for a NBFC converting into a bank, there are stiff trade-offs which are iced with more vigil regulation as the books get to be scrutinized by the RBI in detail which does not hold for the original institution.

What has been the relative performance of banks after a quarter century?

The profitability ratios of banks have been terribly skewed in the last three to four years when the asset quality review (AQR) was introduced as several anomalies came up afflicting both sets of banks. In fact, what appeared to be a problem with PSBs was witnessed in private banks too which cast a shadow on the entire system. Hence, choosing a year as benchmark is difficult. The numbers for FY19 would tend to look distorted for PSBs as their

NPA revelation became more pronounced. The private banks had their spikes in NPA in the previous years. Therefore, the numbers presented here are for FY15 which are prior to the AQR brought in by the RBI. The numbers provided here are only indicative of certain traits which could be clubbed together for private banks as against PSBs. Yes Bank numbers may now be looked at differently but were acceptable at that time on face value.

Table 2.2 clearly shows that there is a significant difference between the performance parameters of PSBs and private banks. Profit indicators like return on advances and return on equity are higher for the private banks which are definitely oriented towards shareholder enhancement which can be evidenced in their annual report where the focus is always on talking of profit-ability. PSBs in contrast are more into revealing how they have served the broader concept of financial inclusion. Therefore, the motivation of these sets of banks is quite different which gets reflected in the financial ratios.

To understand this phenomenon, the cost of deposits and return on advances can be looked at in the next step. PSBs that tend to have lower cost of deposits are more concentrated in a certain range which is reflective of some commonality and in a way an oligopolistic approach where everyone follows the other. In case of private banks, the cost tends to be higher for some of them, but almost for all banks the return on advances is higher—quite sharply which results in better spread for them. In a way, it is also reflective of the higher risk-taking ability of these banks which gets reflected in higher interest paid on advances. An advantage which private banks have here is a lower ratio of salary cost to total operating costs. The relatively larger retinue of service staff adds to the cost pressure of these banks.

Given the episodes of what can be called scams in the banking system at the lower end, a question asked is whether such licenses should be restricted to only institutions or whether it should be open to corporate houses or individuals too. The apprehension that exists when it comes to corporates owning banks is that

Table 2.2. Performance Ratios: FY15

Bank	Ratio of Wage Bills to Intermediation Cost	Return on Assets	Return on Equity	Cost of Deposits	Return on Advances	Return on Investments	Ratio of Net NPA to Net Advances
State Bank of India	58.91	0.02	0.39	4.99	7.85	7.34	3.01
Bank of Baroda	44.64	0.06	0.97	4.49	7.67	7.40	3.33
Bank of India	56.28	-0.84	-14.37	4.41	7.99	7.00	5.61
Canara Bank	54.24	0.06	0.97	5.36	8.48	7.36	5.37
Punjab National Bank	60.35	-1.25	-23.24	4.89	7.87	7.01	6.56
Union Bank of India	43.96	-0.59	-11.43	5.36	8.12	7.21	6.85
United Bank of India	66.31	-1.60	-22.97	4.79	7.82	5.53	8.67
Axis Bank Limited	29.98	0.63	7.19	4.73	8.84	6.90	2.20
HDFC Bank Ltd	29.72	1.90	16.50	4.80	10.50	7.51	0.39
ICICI Bank Limited	37.64	0.39	3.15	4.37	8.72	6.23	2.29
IndusInd Bank Ltd	28.94	1.39	13.07	6.12	11.02	6.73	1.21
Kotak Mahindra Bank Ltd	42.36	1.69	12.11	5.26	9.79	7.18	0.75
Yes Bank Ltd	39.43	0.52	6.53	6.39	10.30	7.66	1.86

Source: www.rbi.org.in.
Note: NPA, non-performing asset.

there could be a fundamental conflict of interest where lending could be directed at interconnected concerns which is not good governance. This is being investigated in case of Yes Bank. Earlier this was also an issue with the Global Trust Bank. This has been a reason for the RBI to be rather cautious when awarding such licenses. As can be seen in Table 2.2, there was a time lag between the first set of licenses issued and the subsequent ones.

However, the other side of the story is that corporates with deep pockets have the wherewithal to actually start a bank which can then be asked to divest to a non-controlling stake so that it becomes widely held over a period of time. This is anyway a rule which has to be adhered to. The point is that merely because the bank is owned by a corporate should not put it at a disadvantage and the field must be open to all. In fact, most of the irregularities in bank lending which have come to the forefront in 2018 and 2019 are in banks which are owned by the government or widely held and yet there has been crony lending. Therefore, ownership is not to blame and the solution is to ensure that there are strong governance practices in place and that regulatory supervision is fool proof. This is the ideal way to look at bank ownership rather than prejudge them based on hunches.

At a broader level, a question is whether or not we need more banks? The curious trait about banking is that after a point, there is less differentiation between banks as the products offered tend to converge and also as will be shown later, business tends to get concentrated in a few regions. And banks tend to flock to areas where there is potential which makes business sense. Hence, having more commercial banks may not widen the canvas. Differentiated banks are probably the way out which have already been introduced with varied degrees of success. But differentiated banks have their problems of being viable as has been the case with small banks and payments banks though it may be too premature to pass a judgement on the same.

Ideally, more banks should lead to more competition but this has not always been the case. There has also been a tendency for banks to operate more likely an oligopoly where scope for differentiation has come down. Customers realize that almost all banks pay almost the same interest rate on deposits and are levied high charges on all services. At one time, PSBs had more reasonable charges but have changed track given that on account of a large deposit base and customers revenue earned from them. The newer banks have tended to give higher interest rate on savings deposits but the interesting thing is that customers too are sticky with their accounts and do not shift easily from one bank to another. Therefore, deposits with banks tend to be fairly stable on account of this inertia.

The direction so far has been in being cautious when giving new approvals and while licenses can be issued on tap, it would be a gradualist approach. An interesting development, however, is that in the wake of the crisis that has been witnessed in the NBFC sector as well as the problem with PMC and other cooperative banks, there is a strong school of thought which believes that these institutions should be converted into commercial banks so that the supervision system becomes applicable and there is more discipline. As institutions have served a specific purpose and getting them to become banks will be a separate exercise that has to be undertaken where these advantages may be lost. For example, they tend to be niche players and cater to the requirements of the local community. However, there would be limitations in terms of their ability to scale up their activity or for that matter also deal with other regulatory requirements like SLR and CRR which involve maintaining a trading desk with sound risk management practices. This will definitely be on the agenda of the government in the next five years as there are attempts made at integration and more coherent supervision.

More banks would also mean stronger supervision from the RBI. With differentiated banking, the challenge is more on the side of the regulator as different aspects need to be supervised as the structures vary. It has already been revealed that the supervisory control over cooperative banks or NBFCs is quite different in scope and rigour compared with commercial banks. This calls for a better trained staff in the RBI who can keep a tab on these banks. The present trend in the RBI is to be economical when it comes to staffing which definitely is not a positive sign from the point of view of regulation considering that there is a pressing need to have more oversight. The recent episodes of irregularities in several institutions clearly indicate that the 'one size fits all' rule does not hold when it comes to regulation, and differentiated banks require differentiated regulation with differentiated skill sets.

In conclusion, it may be stated that having more banks is good for the system. But regulation and supervision have to be robust to ensure that there are few transgressions. Supervision which includes inspection is of paramount importance as the recent experiences of irregularities in banking operations were on account of rather cursory inspection as it is normally assumed that the auditors would have done a good job. This function of the central bank needs more qualified people for sure to ensure that in the quest to do business, banks don't cross the frontiers of prudence.

3

Branches Pop Up Where Business Exists

In India, banking has always been associated with relationships with customers, and hence the branch has been an integral part of the business plan. This is unlike the West where banks have been in the tech mode and customer contact is often through this route rather than the branch. The differentiation is understandable because of the spread of the country and the characteristics of metropolitan, urban, semi-urban and rural areas. The level of financial literacy has been low in the non-metro regions that has access with traditional modes of savings and borrowing being used historically. Therefore, the focus of the government and RBI has been on branch expansion with the overriding goal of financial inclusion being the prime driver. This has meant primacy being given to setting up branches in remote locations to enable deposit collection as well as lending. The branch in a way has become an integral part of the family of the deposit holder and the business of banking has become one which is high on the relationship factor.

Traditionally, banking has been a relationship business. Customers walk in and would like to spend time there talking to others and interacting with the bankers. The branch manager normally knows a large number of customers and this holds for both the deposit and lending side. In fact, this is the first line of checking for a loan before it is processed in the chain depending on the location and the powers bestowed on the manager. A branch, hence, was always an integral part of banking.

With financial sector reforms being ushered, this goal has not really changed and remained important. In fact, with new banks coming in, there was incentive to expand through the country by defining touch points to ensure that few territories were left out. While they could have gone the Western way and brought in internet banking only, there was the realization that customers always want to know what a bank is and how it looks like from inside. Often the reputation of a bank is symbolized by the structure. The logo, colours and décor of the banks can often be the factors attracting customers which are clinched when the interaction with the staff takes place. Therefore, there was acceleration in opening branches post liberalization too.

For the period 1991 to 2019, there has been a 2.35 times increase in the number of bank branches of commercial banks in the country. As can be seen in Table 3.1, the fastest expansion was in case of metro branches by almost 5 times followed by urban branches by 3.2 times. In case of rural branches, the increase was 1.5 times.

In terms of share in total, rural branches came down quite sharply to just a little above a third while that of the metro

Table 3.1. Distribution of Branches of Banks across Population Groups

	1991	Share	2019	Share
Total branches	60,220	100.0	148,137	100.0
Rural	35,206	58.4	51,892	35.0
Semi-urban	11,344	18.8	41,474	28.0
Urban	8,406	14.0	26,780	18.1
Metro	5,624	9.3	27,991	18.8

Source: www.rbi.org.in.

doubled. This trend is indicative of the fact that business in banks in volume terms tends to be concentrated in the metro and semi-urban areas, and beyond a point banks strategize to open more branches where there are deposits to be garnered and credit to be allocated. The rural centres become important more from the point of view of lending to meet the priority sector targets which is a mandatory regulation. Therefore, there is a tendency for all banks to focus on the high footfall centres.

It may be pointed out here that the policy post nationalization in 1969 was to expand branches which were felt to be the starting point of financial inclusion. But post economic reforms, there was more emphasis on quality rather than quantity and as can be seen in Table 3.1, the banks had expanded aggressively where business prospects were better. Hence, there was a tendency to move more to the metro areas where business in terms of credit in particular is better. Therefore, the share of rural branches in total came down as expansion was faster in the other regions. Also, with business beginning to flourish in Tier 2 and Tier 3 towns, banking activity became more popular and demand for such services increased.

It would be interesting to conjecture how this would be moving in future. This is so because with the advent of technology and heavy focus on cashless society, the use of net banking and mobile banking will increase at a faster pace. The pace of activity in this terrain has already increased, and banks are more conscious of using the brick and mortar mode to expand business. The cost of transactions in a branch is much higher than that done using technology like ATMs for cash or deposits and substantially higher than net where the cost is minuscule. Customers too are being discouraged from using branches to the extent that the bank imposes a punishment in the form of charges for extra visits to the branch for any banking activity.

This really means that the expansion of branches will be a thing of the past as banks move to the terrestrial mode. Large value transactions are now through the real-time gross settlement

(RTGS) mode and cheques have become outdated. Banks have been discouraging visits to the branch by charging for transactions. In fact, even cash withdrawals have been limited with a disincentive being provided by charging for excessive transactions. Hence, it will be a matter of years before which physical branches become passé. While there will still be a population of the non-banked ones to join the fold in course of time, they will not be big ticket customers and hence it does not make too much business sense except when there are regulatory orders from above. The main customers which bring in deposits and credit are already part of the system.

Another development which has just started taking place and will gain momentum is the presence of Payments banks which are purely digitally driven by the Internet and mobile phones. This will make commercial banks also work towards rationalizing their operations. Also, the recent talk of bank mergers would mean that there would be rationalization of physical infrastructure which includes bank branches and ATMs. This has already begun because one of the economic justifications of bank mergers is to save on costs by consolidating physical infrastructure. Otherwise a merger of say the Bank of Baroda and Dena Bank will not lead to economies of scale if the same geography defined as one with the similar pin code has two branches of the merged entity. Therefore, with the idea of consolidation of banks catching on, there will be movement to fewer branches and this can mean that the number in metro and urban branches will come down. Also considering that these regions are more likely to be tech-savvy, the use of the e-mode of transactions will also increase leading to reduction in the use of bank branches.

One can really think of a situation where bank branches are more likely to move back to the smaller towns and villages while the rest of the regions are serviced more by technology-driven modes. Hence, the increase in branches which one is witnessing on a modest scale is likely to be curbed in course of time. As most branches are being used more for retail interaction, action is likely to shift more to the corporate branches, which would probably become more important. However, here also with the government pushing forth the 59 minutes loan approval process and the proliferation of fintech companies where online approvals are the way out, the importance of a branch will come down.

Therefore, it will be important to see how long will the concept of a branch really last in India. In Western countries, there are several Internet banks where there is virtually no window open for personal interaction with bankers as both deposits and credits are driven by online practices. While this will still be some time away in India given the diversity in population and propensity to adapt with technology, the ease of making transactions can be the driving factor on both sides which will determine the pace of transition.

BRANCH STRATEGIES AND DISTRIBUTION

A similar picture is also witnessed when the branch count is measured across states. In the period 1991–1992 to 2017–2018, the total number of branches increased from 62,121 to 141,909. Table 3.2 gives the distribution of branches in the major states which have dominated the spread of banking.

Table 3.2. Shares of Top 10 States in Branches

State	Number in 1992	Share	Number in 2019 (December)	Share
All India	62,121	100.0	155,153	100.0
Uttar Pradesh	8,654	13.9	20,408 includes Uttarakhand	13.2
Maharashtra	5,807	9.3	13,909	9.0
Andhra Pradesh	4,745	7.6	12,885 includes Telangana	8.3
Tamil Nadu	4,460	7.2	11,974	7.7
Bihar	4,929	7.9	10,734 includes Jharkhand	6.9

(Continued)

(Continued)

State	Number in 1992	Share	Number in 2019 (December)	Share
Karnataka	4,419	7.1	10,951	7.1
West Bengal	4,329	7.0	9,333	6.0
Madhya Pradesh	4,444	7.2	10,150 includes Chhattisgarh	6.5
Gujarat	3,484	5.6	8,762	5.6
Kerala	2,925	4.7	6,871	4.4

Source: www.rbi.org.in.

For combined states, the author's calculation was based on RBI data from the same website.

These top 10 states had a share of 77.5 per cent in total branches in 1992. This share came down to 74.7 per cent in 2019 which does indicate that the concentration level did reduce to an extent. Within these states too there appears to be a reduction in share of most states. However, where there have been bifurcations as is the case with Andhra Pradesh and Telangana, Bihar and Jharkhand, UP and Uttarakhand and MP and Chhattisgarh, the share of the combined states increased only in the case of Andhra Pradesh.

Ideally with more inclusive banking taking place, the shares of other states should increase as there has been thrust on banks opening new branches in the less-banked areas. However, a countervailing force these days has been the permission given to banks to close branches which are not viable in business terms. Therefore, banks have been lowering their branch networks in areas of less business. Further with the proliferation in technology, there has been the tendency for the branch also to become less relevant as a single branch can serve a larger geography. This is more so because most banks allow one to conduct transactions from any of their offices in the country, and hence has become less branch specific. Also, with ATMs serving the purpose of cash withdrawals from anywhere in the country and cheque deposit boxes being placed in these rooms, the basic requirement of

Table 3.3. Business Per Branch March 2019 (₹ Crore)

	Deposits	Credit
Total branches	86.94	69.82
Rural	27.02	18.03
Semi-urban	52.37	32.46
Urban	100.47	65.46
Metro	225.26	223.35

Source: www.rbi.org.in.

banking has been addressed to a large extent. However, in non-metro areas where physical interface is required by customers, this explanation may not hold as they prefer to deal with bankers for their transactions and may not resort to use of technology for deposits in particular though withdrawals could still be from the ATM instead of the branch.

The business levels in various branches need to be evaluated. Table 3.3 gives the average deposits and credit per branch in different categories of regions.

Table 3.3 shows that the business per branch increases as one moves up the scale from rural to metro regions. Hence from a purely banking perspective, it makes sense to be concentrated in the non-rural areas. The rural areas have lower income and saving power which gets reflected in average deposits per branch. Further, lending here is of a small ticket size mainly for farmers and other lower-income groups, and hence the business potential is limited. On the other hand, business from urban and metro branches is higher as there are higher levels of savings as well as big ticket borrowing.

In conclusion, it can be said that the structure of banks has been driven a lot by ideology with the focus being on inclusion which was a corollary to the socialist model pursued with nationalization. This also included spread across states and habitation and was not linked with a business mindset. This was necessary because of the initial conditions in the country post-independence where a serious attempt was made to move away from the unorganized financial sector framework. But things are changing and we can see branches becoming less important and reducing in number especially with the advent of the concept of merger of PSBs. The foreign banks anyway do not want to move away from the existing model, and hence have limitations on branch expansion. The new forms of banks are technology driven and require less human interaction.

4

Transformation of the Deposits Ecosystem

....

The foundation of banking business is based on the quantum of deposits which account for around 75–80 per cent of the balance sheet of any bank. These savings need to come from across the country and that is why banks use all modes of business to garner deposits. Unlike other businesses which depend on share capital and borrowings to do business, banks are dependent on deposits which is a different kind of borrowings and hence must see this quantum increase if they are to earn an income through the deployment of funds through advances or investments or plain treasury operations. Table 4.1 gives an illustration of the distribution of bank deposits across different regions in 1991 and 2018.

Table 4.1 shows that there has definitely been a sharp increase in growth in deposits for all the segments, and on the whole has been around 60 times. The multiple has been highest for metro region and this poses some interesting points. First, metro regions definitely do have more money than the others and hence the population has tended to deploy their savings in bank deposits. It is also true that in other non-metro regions, people do also tend to convert savings into gold jewellery rather than deposit in the bank. The fact that informal economy has

Table 4.1. Distribution of Bank Deposits by Population Group

	1991 (₹ Crore)	Share	2019 (₹ Lakh Crore)	Share
Total deposits	200,568	100.0	126.39	100.0
Rural	31,009	15.5	13.57	10.7
Semi-urban	41,439	20.7	20.61	16.3
Urban	49,140	24.5	26.97	21.3
Metro	78,979	39.4	65.23	51.5

Source: www.rbi.org.in.
Note: The share of the rural segment in total deposits has come down from 15.5 per cent to 10.7 per cent and those of semi-urban from 20.7 per cent to 16.3 per cent. In case of urban branches too, there has been a decline from 24.5 per cent to 21.3 per cent. The only segment that has witnessed a sharp increase is the metro by 12.1 per cent from 39.4 per cent to 51.5 per cent.

flourished all along does support this argument. In metropolitan regions it is more likely that the money earned by a household is from the formal sector, and hence savings are also kept in a bank account. In fact, even if savings are directed to mutual funds or stock market, the primary touch point would be the bank account from whereon the money would move to other avenues.

Second, if the future of deposits would be primarily in the metro regions, then there would be progressively less incentive to make major inroads into the other segments. This supports the belief put forward in the discussion on bank branches that on an incremental basis having more branches in the rural areas for instance may not be efficiency accretive. As seen, they account for over 35 per cent of branches but get in just 10 to 11 per cent of deposits. In fact, the proliferation of online or other e-forms of banking would only drive home the point that metro regions would be the big driver of funds for banks. The others would be important more from the point of view of the government driving the agenda on inclusive banking where accounts have to be opened in every nook and corner. But they may not be adding very much to the overall funds that can be deployed by banks. Bankers may not like to admit that these accounts are not of economic value but a part of the regulatory cost of doing business in India.

The interesting part of these deposits is that there tends to be concentration in states and are not evenly spread. This is both due to the access to banking facilities and the availability of savings. The more industrialized states tend to have higher deposits. The more literate the population, the higher the probability that households would save in deposits rather than physical assets like gold or land. Financial literacy would, hence, be of importance when it comes to deploying savings across different avenues. Table 4.2 compares the shares of various states in total deposits in 1992 and 2019.

For Andhra Pradesh, it includes Telangana's data from the same source.

Table 4.2 shows that Maharashtra and Delhi account for 30 per cent of the total deposits in the country. Uttar Pradesh (because of size), Karnataka, Andhra Pradesh (includes Telangana),

Table 4.2. Share of Top 10 States in Total Deposits

State	1992 (₹ Crore)	Share %	2019 (₹ Lakh Crore)	Share %
Total outstanding	237,107	100.0	126.39	100.0
Maharashtra	52,770	22.3	26.07	20.6
Punjab	11,341	4.8	3.79	3.0
Delhi	21,660	9.1	12.10	9.6
Bihar	10,161	4.3	5.72	4.5
West Bengal	20,881	8.8	7.79	6.2
Uttar Pradesh	23,088	9.7	11.79	9.3
Gujarat	13,905	5.9	6.74	5.3
Andhra Pradesh	12,462	5.2	7.59	6.0
Karnataka	11,207	4.7	9.34	7.4
Tamil Nadu	15,812	6.6	7.98	6.3
Sum of 10 states	193,287	81.5	98.91	78.3

Source: www.rbi.org.in.

Tamil Nadu and West Bengal follow as these are the states with higher levels of GDP which goes along with industrialization which house metro cities. With 78 per cent being accounted for by 10 states, it is quite clear that the other states and Union Territories do not really feature high on the deposits chart. Madhya Pradesh features in the list of top states in terms of branches as does Kerala but are not in the top list for deposits. Rajasthan, a state which is large in size, does not feature in either of these lists. Hence, there is considerable disparity here.

WHERE DO DEPOSITS COME FROM?

The sources of deposits indicate how much comes from different segments which includes both individuals and institutions. Typically, retail deposits include those of households and foreign accounts which are essentially the NRI deposits. The data provided here is for the year end which has a disadvantage in not being truly representative of what transpires during the year. This is so because in the last week of the year, companies tend to deposit surplus cash with banks which are withdrawn subsequently in the first week of April. Government balances too would come down in April, and hence to this extent there would be an overstatement of their shares through the year. Banks too offer higher rates towards the end of the year to attract corporate deposits (CDs) for short tenures which help them in matching their assets with liabilities (asset liability management [ALM]).

The sourcing of deposits is important for two reasons. The first is that banks would be more certain of the available funds in case it comes from retail as these amounts tend to be steady and rarely move in the downward direction. The second is the pricing of deposits which is different for retail and bulk. Depending on the exigency based on demand for credit and the asset liability mismatches, banks can offer differential interest rates which are permitted by regulation.

Table 4.3. Sources (Ownership) of Deposits

Sector	1995 (₹ Crore)	Share %	2019 (₹ Lakh Crore)	Share %
Government	40,185	9.2	11.86	9.2
Private corporate	15,779	3.6	18.36	14.2
Financial	26,787	6.1	8.01	6.2
Household	303,203	69.2	81.51	63.2
Foreign	52,050	11.9	9.20	7.1
Total	438,004	100.0	100.00	100.0

Source: www.rbi.org.in.

Table 4.3 shows how the structure has changed over time. Retail deposits may be classified as those originating from households as well as NRIs (foreign). Their combined share was 81.1 per cent as of March 1995. The government sector surprisingly has a relatively high share of close to 10 per cent followed by financial entities and private corporate companies.

This structure changed by 2019 where the share of retail has actually come down to 70.1 per cent. The over 10 per cent fall in share is significant as it indicates that this segment is progressively becoming less important for banks which are increasingly drawing more deposits from corporates and the government.

One reason for households to lose their share can be that they are moving away from bank deposits and looking at other avenues like mutual funds to the stock market where the returns are better. This is due to two factors. The first is that the returns on bank deposits have been coming down continuously with monetary policy being always skewed towards lowering of interest rates for borrowers rather than addressing the issue of savers. The second is that households have simultaneously become more market savvy where they have enhanced their risk-taking ability which is manifested through these investments in the capital market.

Second, wholesale deposits have been increasing progressively as companies have been deploying their funds in bank deposits rather than investing them as there are fewer investment opportunities. This has led to an increase in their deposits with banks. Ideally, retaining high reserves in the form of deposits is a safe avenue though not optimal as the returns are low relative to potential income that can be earned through investment in capital in the medium term. Also, as these numbers refer to the end of the year, when there is less activity, there is a tendency for banks to source deposits from companies that want to temporarily park their funds. This helps banks achieve their annual target, and hence appear to be higher.

Third, the government's share in deposits has also increased sharply with the contribution coming from central, states and quasi organizations. Here surpluses of the government are parked with the banks for short tenures which are drawn as the expenditure commitments have to be made. Here too, it can be seen that all levels of government do tend to hold on to these deposits which can be withdrawn at any point of time as useful buffers. Also, towards the end of the year, revenue or debt raised is not used but parked in deposits so that the fiscal numbers are managed. Subsequently, these deposits are withdrawn to make payments for various expenditures including those that are consciously deferred.

The higher volume of government deposits is interesting because normally this entity would tend to spend all the money that was budgeted for the year. It is only when the budgeted amounts are not spent, that they are put as deposits. This includes both central, state and local governments. The government body holds on to the revenue earned and economizes on expenditures to manage the fiscal deficit at the prescribed levels. This often means that certain expenditures are deferred as governments operate on the basis of cash transactions as the accrual mode of accounting is not pursued as is the case for companies. Therefore, the excess revenue earned flows into deposits which get reflected in the accounts of banks. This appears to be higher for state governments relative to the centre.

Clearly, banks prefer to have more of retail deposits as their churn is known and less volatile than the others. In fact, as the data presented here is for the year end, there would be a tendency for banks to both increase their credit and deposits to meet their annual targets. This tends to match deposits with loans of spe- cific maturity, and hence tend to spike the overall savings parked with banks which get reversed subsequently. This is normally achieved by increasing the deposit rates on bulk deposits for shorter tenures so that the balance sheet size is built.

THE CASA FACTOR

While banking is a fairly drab business, it has its set of jargon which has evolved in the last decade or so ever since the private banks brought in the lexicon. Current and savings account deposits (CASA) is one of the often-used acronyms which refer to the current and savings accounts deposits rates. The two are combined when banks talk of their efficiency as these are cheap deposits and fairly steady in terms of rollover. Current account deposits or demand deposits are those of companies which do not earn any interest but offer unlimited cheque facili- ties as the account is used for making all business payments. These are balances used for daily transactions, and hence offer free float to the bank. When companies take loans from banks especially for working capital, the amount is transferred to the current account which is then disbursed by the former for making payments. These accounts offer more free cheques as there is no other cost involved for the bank. In fact, often with online NEFT or RTGS payments being made, the need for use of cheques is also obviated. Banks, hence, like these accounts. Companies typically have a fixed cycle of receipt of payments as well as timings for making payments (including salaries), and over a period of time it is possible for banks to gauge as to how much money would be lying in these accounts. Within banks, there is always this quest to get more company accounts as this 'free float' increases.

Savings accounts are maintained mainly by individuals and other entities that come under the umbrella of retail entities. These deposits are also fairly steady in terms of inflows and outflows as they tend to be linked mainly with salaries which are paid at fixed points of time which can be the end of the month. The withdrawals too would be more or less smooth during the month with the amounts increasing at the beginning of the month and then declining until the next cycle of receipt of money. Even for non-salaried people, this cycle is well known and can be gauged well by banks. Again, the semi-free float of funds is a known quantity for banks. Some opt for automatic swipe of savings deposits to fixed deposits when the balance crosses a threshold level which again is known to the bank.

These deposits have the advantage of carrying a low interest rate for the bank. It was fixed for a very long time to 4 per cent but is now left open with some offering 3.25 per cent and others 6 per cent. As these deposits are fixed, households tend to be irrational and often do migrate some of these funds to fixed deposits and feel secure with high balances. Banks capitalize on the same and treat them as almost fixed long-term funds that can be used. Also given the complexities in processes, banks know fully well that rarely do customers move their funds to banks offering higher savings rate and this quality of 'lethargy' is used to build a strong fixed deposit base.

Table 4.4 reveals some interesting traits about the breakup of deposits into the three main categories. Current deposits share has declined from a high of 15.1 per cent of deposits which is the free float of corporates kept in banks to 9.4 per cent. This decline can be attributed more to the fact that companies tend to move their deposits towards the end of the year to short-term fixed deposits which is a win-win situation for both the parties concerned. Banks are able to get the resources to manage their ALM

Table 4.4. Shares of Deposits by Type

	1991 (₹ crore)	Share (%)	2019 (₹ lakh crore)	Share (%)
Total deposits	200,568	100.0	126.39	100.0
Current	30,285	15.1	11.90	9.4
Savings	56,152	28.0	41.17	32.6
Term	114,082	56.8	73.31	58.0

Source: www.rbi.org.in.

mismatches while companies earn higher interest on the same. Also, it is a reflection of better management of cash as current account is virtual cash for immediate payments and the treasury department makes optimal provisions for the same.

The savings deposits ratio has also been almost stable and moved up only marginally from 28 per cent to 32.6 per cent. The difference is not much in these 27 years post reform. It points to once again a predictable pattern in households where an almost fixed proportion is retained in the savings account which again follows a predictable pattern of inflows which are normally through salaries and outflows in the form of deposits. With banks being given flexibility in the savings interest rate now, they are better able to manage their costs by varying this rate. Given the relative rigidity in these deposits, there would be limited migration to other banks due to the factors mentioned earlier.

With over a third of deposits residing in CASA, two interesting issues come up. The first is that the proportion of cheap deposits is really high as current account comes free of cost and savings around 3.5 per cent. This kind of permanency offers some kind of assurance to banks that these volumes would in general be maintained. However, on the other hand, banks would inherently be running an asset-liability mismatch as with 1/3 of resources being very short term (though rolled over permanently), the equivalent asset tenure cannot be too much out of sync. While working capital loans are rolled over, term loans would be for longer tenures and could be getting financed by these deposits.

This issue becomes important in the current context where a lot of term lending is being done by banks which are being financed by relatively short-term deposits. The genesis of the NBFC crisis of 2018–2019 was the ALM mismatch where short-term commercial papers (CPs) were being rolled over continuously to support long-term lending on the assumption that the market would always be willing to lend to them. A sudden embargo on their CPs has exacerbated the crisis.

On the other side, if these balances are more or less permanent, banks can assume that what is very short term can be used for long-term lending with the premise being that there will always be a rollover of funds such that the ALM mismatch will never arise for this quantum of deposits.

The share of term deposits has gone up, though quite marginally, for two reasons. The first as mentioned earlier is that companies switch funds at the end of the year across these two sets of deposits and the second is that given that households have options of switching over from savings to term or going in for shorter duration term deposits, there is some movement across these kinds of deposits. Households have become savvier for sure and so have banks that have offered more competitive interest rates on deposits while managing their ALM policies appropriately. This was not possible earlier and can be attributed more to the new private banks which came up with such innovative schemes to ensure that account holders never left the bank by offering this switch facility.

It is these advantages that go with commercial banking that there is an incentive for more banks to be set up. Further, even NBFCs are looking to get converted into banks for the same reason. Until the NBFC crisis of 2018 and 2019, most of them tap the CP market for short-term finance and bond market for long-term funds. The activities conducted are almost in line with banks except that most do not accept deposits and rely on market for funding. By getting converted into banks, the cost of funding can be reduced quite substantially.

MATURITY OF TERM DEPOSITS

The maturity pattern of deposits shown in Table 4.5 has witnessed quite a transformation with the lower tenures becoming more attractive. The shortest tenure has become most popular with the share more than double. The same holds for other tenures up to one year. Deposits of less than one year have a share of 21.1 per cent as against 19.4 per cent in 1991. The bucket of one to five years has witnessed some interesting changes. Those between three to five years have come down from 20.6 per cent to 6.7 per cent meaning thereby that shorter durations are preferred as those between one to three years have increased from 41.4 per cent to 58.3 per cent. The deposits of above five years also witnessed a drop-in share from 16.6 per cent to 13.9 per cent.

The longest-term deposits are those normally reckoned by the less savvy customers who would not be looking to maximize their yields but prefer to lock into an interest rate which is acceptable for a longer period of time. This would hold normally for retired gentry and senior citizens who would not like to chance going in for a term deposit of lower tenure and then face a lower interest rate regime at the time of renewal. Banks also tend to keep this rate attractive so that customers would also walk in and park their funds which would help them

Table 4.5. Maturity Pattern of Deposits (% Share in Total)

Tenure	1991	2019
<90 days	8.1	7.8
91 days to 6 months	5.2	4.0
6 months to 1 year	6.1	9.3
1–2 years	14.3	58.3
2–3 years	27.1	
3–5 years	20.6	6.7
>5 years	16.6	13.9
	100.0	100.0

Source: www.rbi.org.in.

match their longer-term lending. The middle range is always whimsical as interest rates are tinkered with by banks depending on their own requirements. This is one reason as to why their share has come down as banks would tend to discourage such deposits. The shorter-term ones normally offer the best rates for customers who would have to consider their options and can roll over these deposits so that they can maximize returns. From the point of view of banks, these deposits are also considered to be more tuned to their tenure requirements.

The future of tenure of bank deposits will hinge a lot on the structure of interest rates. As long as interest rates move in the downward direction, deposit holders would also tend to tune their preference to those buckets that offer the best rates. Short-term views are more likely to be the order as banks would tend to offer the best rates here given that there has been a tendency for the RBI to have multiple interventions in a year once the practice of six policies a year has been implemented. Locking in higher rates for long-term deposits while attractive for savers is not of advantage for banks. Further, with RBI continuously reiterating the need for banks to lower their exposures to large corporates which are being encouraged to borrow from the corporate bond market, there would be a movement away from banks for financing long-term requirements. This will in turn make banks focus more on short-term lending which gets linked to the deposit rates where the shorter maturities would witness more frequent changes while offering the highest rates when there are shortages in the supply of funds. But for sure, those who look at assured returns for a longer time period have to look at other savings avenues, and bank deposits would not be the most favoured option.

5

Credit Matrix

The main source of income for banks is through disbursing credit, and this is not quite an open field as there are regulations concerning lending operations. Banks have to first maintain the two statutory reserves of CRR and SLR on their net demand and time liabilities (NDTL). After making these provisions, they can use the funds for lending. However, while deciding on their loan portfolio they have to first adhere to the priority sector norm of lending 40 per cent of total credit to specified sectors before making further allocations. The scope of the priority sector is defined by the RBI through various notifications over time. Again, within commercial lending, there are caps as to how much can be lent to individual companies and groups to ensure there is no concentration. Therefore, lending activity will tend to be influenced by all these factors.

WHERE DOES CREDIT GO?

The mirror image of the distribution of bank deposits is the spread of credit. The disbursement of credit tends to follow business prospects which intuitively are in the more developed areas especially the metro centres.

Here too it can be seen that there has been an increase in the share of credit to the metro regions by around 15 per cent while those of other segments have come down. Bank credit flow can also be classified according to the economic segment involved such as agriculture, industry, services and personal. The farm loans given are purely rural based and the priority sector norm mandates a stipulation of 18 per cent of total credit.

Non-large manufacturing credit would be for the SMEs and micro enterprises that would be spread across all regions while large companies that borrow, which would be the big tickets, are concentrated in the metro regions. Even if the factories are located across the country, the head office or corporate office which handles finances would tend to be located in urban or metro regions. In fact, often for large value loans the sanctioning authority would be in the metro location even if the loan origi-nated elsewhere and would get so classified.

Table 5.1 shows that there has been a major shift in the pattern of lending where there is a movement to the metro centres away from the rural and semi-urban regions. In fact, even in case of urban India there has been a decline in share. Close to 60 per cent of credit is now concentrated in the metro regions which is expected in a way because most corporates would be having their head offices in these cities from where the loan would originate. The interesting aspect of the share of rural

Table 5.1. Distribution of Credit by Population Group

Region	1991 (₹ Crore)	Share (%)	2019 (₹ Lakh Crore)	Share (%)
Total credit	124,203	100.0	98.97	100.0
Rural	18,599	15.0	9.02	9.1
Semi-urban	20,307	16.3	12.68	12.8
Urban	27,772	22.4	16.69	16.9
Metro	57,523	46.3	60.57	61.2

Source: www.rbi.org.in.

segment coming down can be attributed to the spread of farming to semi-urban areas and more importantly the inclusion of several other activities like SME lending, affordable housing, economically weaker sections and so on, residing in other segments.

While the distribution per se for credit may not be very relevant, the important point is that from the point of view of banks, it makes sense to have more touch points with customers in metro areas as well as urban centres as around 20 per cent of total branches account for 52 per cent of deposits and 61 per cent of credit. Therefore, having branches in other areas is more out of compulsion than motivated by business. A similar picture is obtained where urban centres contribute also more efficiently to sources and uses of funds relative to the other regions.

DIRECTION OF CREDIT

The direction of credit is interesting because changes over time reflect both the business angle of banks as well as regulatory changes that have taken place. When the financial sector was opened up, there was also a tendency to put fewer curbs on bank lending even though the priority sector commitments remained unchanged with 40 per cent being the limit. Within the 40 per cent level, there have been some changes that have come in over a period of time as noticeable, one being affordable housing which is now a part of such regulated lending. At the same time, banks have been looking at alternative business opportunities too when it comes to lending, and looking at different segments that could be tapped for the same. As prudential regulation came into play with the definition of NPAs also changing regularly over time, it was but natural that the banks had to weigh the pros and cons of lending to various segments.

Retail lending typically has a lower probability of default while corporate lending, especially to large manufacturing, would have a higher probability of default. On the other side, retail loans tend to be very small, and building a sizeable volume of business takes a lot of time and effort with the cost of client acquisition being higher. Even monitoring such loans occupies a lot of business space which involves more employees to monitor these loans and track servicing payments. In case of corporates, the amounts that are borrowed are of higher values which make it easier for banks to meet their business targets. This is one reason as to why banks have been tempted to stick to corporate lending in good times but move over to the retail segment when the quality of assets is under pressure.

Table 5.2 shows some interesting trends in terms of flow of credit over the last 29 years. Agriculture had a share of 15 per cent in 1991 which has come down to 12.6 per cent by the end of March 2020. Banks have been making use of all the provisions that are available for lending to agriculture in terms of direct and indirect to meet the target of priority sector lending.

Industry is the surprise factor where the share has come down from close to half (47.6%) to 31.5 per cent in 2020. This sharp fall is due to four factors. The first is that this was the period when the NPA levels had peaked and banks had diverted their

Table 5.2. Distribution of Credit by Occupation

Segment	1991 (₹ Crore)	Share (%)	2020 (₹ Lakh Crore)	Share (%)
Total	124,203	100.0	92.11	100.0
Agriculture	18,573	15.0	11.58	12.6
Industry	59,093	47.6	29.05	31.5
Services	36,996	29.8	25.94	28.2
Transport	3,639	2.9	1.44	1.6
Professional	3,667	3.0	1.77	1.9
Trade	18,296	14.7	5.52	6.0
FIs	2,866	2.3	8.07	8.8
Miscellaneous	8,528	6.9	9.14	9.9
Personal	9,598	7.7	25.53	27.7

Source: www.rbi.org.in.

lending to other segments as the stress level was high in these segments. In fact, a large part of the NPAs that was stuck with the IBC resided in this segment. Second, manufacturing companies have been also accessing other sources of funds like bond market, external commercial borrowings (ECBs) and NBFCs for finance. NBFCs in fact have grown to become a very important source of finance and have a loan book which is equivalent to almost 20 per cent that of the banking system.

Third, the overall pace of investment in the country has also slowed down post 2015 with several companies cutting back on expansion plans. This has lowered the demand for credit by manufacturing companies. The capacity utilization rates of Indian industry has been in the range of 70 per cent while ideally a mark of 78–80 per cent is required before fresh investment takes place. With demand conditions being soft, there was tendency for utilization levels to be low which came in the way of generating demand for investment.

Lastly, there has been the tendency for some large companies in the manufacturing and infra space to deleverage as the overall economic growth in the country had slowed down and companies did not want to carry high cost debt on their books.

The share of services has tended to decline albeit marginally over the years though within this category there have been some changes. The share of FIs, that is, NBFCs has gone up while that of trade has come down. NBFCs became progressively important in stature as they have better last mile connectivity at the ground level and have appetite for higher risk. While the better-rated NBFCs prefer to use the market route, the lower-rated ones access banks for funds which then in turn are lent to industry and individuals. Given that they add their margins to the cost of borrowing before lending, it means that there are borrowers who do not get access to banks but are able to source the same from these institutions.

The main winner has been retail where the share in total credit has gone up from 7.7 per cent to 27.7 per cent. This has been associated also with a boom in mortgages as banks have caught on to the bandwagon of financing homes as the country has progressed. Hence, what was once the preserve of housing finance companies has now been successfully picked up by banks which have made fairly good inroads in this field. This shift to housing is also important from the point of view of maintaining a cleaner balance sheet which is quite insulated from market-related developments which can impact quality especially when linked to manufacturing and services too to an extent. The second category to dominate here is auto loans where increasing incomes especially at the younger age groups has meant preference for better lifestyle where the starting point is a vehicle loan. While NBFCs also are aggressive in this space, banks have also widened their exposure here. With a margin of 20–30 per cent being maintained on such loans, the probability of losing money in case of default is low with the hypothecation of the vehicle to the bank unit the loan is repaid.

Also, with the focus on digital banking, cards have become progressively important and while their share in total credit is still very small at 1.2 per cent, they have been increasing. But this component has been rising as banks have been aggressive in selling this product to customers. There is another category called 'other loans' which has a share of 7.9 per cent in total outstanding retail credit as of March 2020. This comprises loans

Table 5.3. Distribution of Credit by Type of Loan

Type of Credit	1991 (₹ Crore)	Share (%)	2019 (₹ Lakh Crore)	Share (%)
Total credit	96,880	100.0	96.14	100.0
Term	29,616	30.6	56.65	58.9
Cash credit	34,554	35.7	16.88	17.6
Overdraft	7,505	7.7	7.35	7.6
Demand loan	3,364	3.5	13.75	14.3
Others (bills)	21,841	22.5	1.51	1.6

Source: www.rbi.org.in.

given by banks to their employees and general public for purposes such as marriages and other functions.

The level of outstanding credit can be viewed in terms of the type of loan which is favoured by the system (Table 5.3). The share of term loans has gone up quite sharply from 30.6 per cent to 58.9 per cent. There are two reasons for this change in focus. First, banks have started taking on the role of term lender ever since we went in for universal banking where DFIs were converted to universal banks which in turn meant that commercial banks were the major source of term funding. Hence, funds moved from DFIs to banks which also focused on infra lending and built up a good portfolio of such assets. This has not been an unmixed blessing because term loans appraisal requires a different set of skill sets which banks had to acquire along the way. The second is that as mortgages caught on, the proportion of term loans continued to increase as these loans were typically for period of above 10 years. The same holds for vehicle loans where funds are sanctioned for period between five and seven years.

The share of overdraft has remained unchanged while that of cash credit has come down from 35.7 per cent to 17.6 per cent. Here too, banks have been trying to get corporates to convert these limits to term loans so that there is more certainty in terms of the tenure as well as return in the form of interest for the bank. The share of bills has come down while that of demand loans has gone up once again indicating the shift that has taken place in type of lending.

SIZE OF CUSTOMER

Another aspect of bank credit to be looked at is the size of the customers based on the credit limit range. It is true that most of the credit comes from a smaller set of accounts rather than the smaller ones which are well dispersed. Table 5.4 gives the shares of various credit limit sizes in total portfolio of banks as per

Table 5.4. Distribution of Credit by Size of Loan

Range of Credit	% Share in Number of Accounts 1991	Share in o/s Credit	% Share in Number of Accounts 2019	% Share in o/s Credit
Less than 5 lakhs	98.3	41.5	90	16.2
5–10 Lakhs	1.4	4.1	5.6	6.9
10–25 Lakhs	0.1	6.0	2.9	8.5
25–50 Lakhs	0.1	6.3	1.0	6.3
50 lakhs–1 crore	–	6.8	0.3	4.1
1–10 crore	–	24.3	0.2	11.3
›10 crore	–	10.8	–	46.6
Total	619 lakh	₹1.24 lakh crore	2323 lakh	₹98.98 lakh crore

Source: www.rbi.org.in.

number of accounts as well as outstanding credit. The results are definitely quite revealing.

Table 5.4 shows that the number of credit accounts has increased more than threefold in the last three decades or so. The outstanding loans have, however, increased by around 80 times. As can be seen over the years, there has not been much change in terms of the number of accounts in the smaller loan brackets. The share of accounts with limit of less than ₹5 lakhs had come down from 98.3 per cent to 90 per cent but is still dominant. This means that the very small accounts dominate the structure of credit in the country in terms of number of accounts or borrowers (there could be multiplicity with borrowers being on the records of multiple banks). However, in terms of their contribution to overall credit, these small accounts are not that important today. In fact, their share was quite high at 41.5 per cent in 1991 but with liberalization and greater freedom to banks to cherry pick their customers, there has been a decline in share to 16.2 per cent.

At the other end, the large accounts of above ₹10 crore had a share of 10.8 per cent with just 577 accounts in 1991. The number of accounts in this category rose to 87,444 in 2019 in a total of 2,323 lakh accounts and while the share was insignificant in the total accounted for nearly half the credit outstanding. In fact, in 2019, there were 12,580 accounts which accounted for 31.6 per cent of total outstanding credit.

Therefore, there is major asymmetry in terms of the size of the accounts and their contribution to total credit. While banks have to be universal in reach and cater to all the demands that come in the form of regulation as well as work towards widening their retail outreach, the big tickets are the ones which actually get in the business.

The trade-off is quite clear. Banks can go for the big tickets loans which will help to grow the business book with ease but can run the risk of default as a single customer not servicing the debt will mean a larger amount of money deployed. On the other hand, small ticket disbursals are not really economical as it takes more time and involves higher cost in terms of scrutiny and due diligence. But it has very low probability of default and even if there is one, it would be very small in magnitude and will not affect the bank unless all borrowers are under default which is very unlikely. Even in case of agriculture where a drought can affect farmers of a region, the aggregate amount involved could be well dispersed across several banks which would lower the intensity of the bad loan hit for an individual bank. A single infra project on the other hand that is unable to service debt could affect the books of the bank quite sharply which can be seen in the data that was presented initially by the IBC where the 12 identified companies in 2017 accounted for around 15 per cent of the outstanding loans of around ₹9.5 lakh crore.

This is the asymmetry matrix that banks have to work with and accordingly plan their strategies. If a bank is going retail and looking at small tickets, the machinery has to be revamped to look for a larger universe and the use of DSAs has been popular in the past. Now with the focus on SMEs where the latest focus is on sanctioning loans in less than an hour—the famous 59 minutes scheme—the use of technology has caught on to handle such volumes. Here banks have to necessarily hone their skills for such small ticket loans. In fact it can be argued that banks have perforce been operating at the micro level to disburse such loans and in the absence of regulation would probably prefer to lend to only the bigger clients.

To sum up, it can be said that in terms of credit dispersion:

1. There has been a shift from rural to metro centres.
2. The form of lending is now tilted towards term loans.
3. The importance of industry has come down and the shares of retail and services have gone up over this period of time.
4. While most of the loans tickets are of small size, the big business comes from a small set of large clients.

How the Structure of Income of Banks Changed?

The composition of income of banks is important because it tells one whether or not banks have been able to diversify their activity in a manner such that different income streams are generated with less dependency on conventional lending. Table 6.1 provides this information about interest income and other incomes.

Over the last 24 years or so, there appears to be not much of a change in the composition of the total income for banks as shown in Table 6.1. Interest income continues to be the prime driver with

Table 6.1. Structure of Income of Banks

	1995 (₹ Crore)	% Share	2019 (₹ Lakh Crore)	% Share
Interest earned	45,239	87.4	11.40	86.1
Other income	6,496	12.6	1.84	13.9
Commission	4,303	8.3	0.97	6.6
Sale of investment	54	0.1	0.14	1.1
Exchange	1,376	2.7	0.22	1.7
Others	763	1.5	0.51	3.9
	51,735	100.0	13.24	100.0

Source: www.rbi.org.in.

a share of 86 per cent in total income and has come down from 87.4 per cent which is not very significant. This, hence, continues to be the main source of income notwithstanding the changes that have taken place in the direction of banking with focus on fee income and trading.

Interest income also includes income earned on the portfolio of investments which is primarily in government paper and other eligible securities. The returns are directly linked to the regulatory pre-emption levels as well as the prevailing rate of interest in the market. The former is a regulatory requirement and comes under what is called the SLR which has to be adhered to by banks. This means that lending is the mainstay of banks and there is less diversification in terms of income. It is true that banks are not allowed to do other businesses like mutual funds, insurance, securities trading and so on, which have often been hived off to different entities.

The other two sources of income are fees which are related to banking where the charge is for services rendered to clients and treasury income which is income earned from dealing with essentially securities and forex. The slight decline in the share of fee income is significant because banks have all been trying to move away from vanilla, lending and earning a fee on other value-based activities. This gets linked to the contingent liabilities where a fee is earned on a non-fund-based activity.

CONTINGENT LIABILITIES

Contingent liabilities of banks are an integral part of the business and bring value in the sense of not being related to funding, and hence get classified as off-balance sheet items. These include three major components: forex transactions, guarantees and acceptances. Within this group, the forex-related transactions which involve booking forward contracts on behalf of clients account for the largest component followed by guarantees and acceptances.

As all foreign trade involves movement of foreign currency where the rates vary on a daily basis, customers normally get into forward contracts to protect against volatility. This is a good source of revenue for banks as there is a fee income earned from such services. Guarantees are again given mainly when the counter-party is a foreign entity where a letter of comfort has to be provided by the bank so that there is an assurance of payment. Therefore, contingent liabilities become a critical part of the trade ecosystem and do not involve deployment of capital and are hence beneficial for banks. However, in case of any default, the bank would have to indemnify the concerned parties.

Contingent liabilities become critical for banks when there is a breakdown across the globe which is the time when losses have to be booked. It happened during the financial crisis when companies which were involved in the securitization operations in the USA faced the backlash which then had to be booked as losses by the banks. Normally when banks have a high level of global operations, they would also tend to take on these operations and would have high contingent liabilities. Intuitively, it can be seen that foreign banks would have an edge here as they would be dealing with the parent company overseas and be well networked.

There has been a very sharp jump in these liabilities over the two-decade period and is reflective of the maturity of the system. Contingent liabilities, as seen in Table 6.2, increased from

Table 6.2. Structure of Contingent Liabilities of Banks

	1996–1997	Share	2018–2019	Share
Forex	2.09	65.7	183.09	89.9
Guarantees	0.52	16.4	11.42	5.6
Acceptances/Endorsements	0.26	8.2	6.03	3.0
Others			3.22	1.6
Total	3.18	100.0	203.77	100.0

Source: www.rbi.org.in.

₹3.18 lakh crore in 1996–97 to ₹203.77 lakh crore in 2018–19. Forex and guarantees continued to dominate with shares of 82.1 per cent and 95.1 per cent, respectively. These activities generate fee and are a useful source of income.

Foreign banks have an advantage here and nearly 52 per cent of the total liabilities reside on their books while around 18 per cent was from PSBs in 2018–2019, and the balance 30 per cent from private banks. In 1996–1997, the picture was not very different where the foreign banks had a share of 47 per cent, while private banks had just about entered the fray and had a share of just 7.3 per cent.

An interesting aspect of contingent liabilities is that the dynamism of banks can be ascertained from the multiple times their balance sheet size. For the system as whole in 2018–2019, contingent liabilities were a multiple of 1.22. This is where the sharp difference stands out. In case of foreign banks, contingent liabilities were a multiple of 10.6 while for private banks it was 1.1. For PSBs, it was low at just about 0.36.

The problem with contingent liabilities is that they become serious threats only when there are defaults on any score. The allusion is more to guarantees where there can be a default. This is done normally as part of its project financing and commercial banking activities. Also while forward contracts are booked on behalf of clients and a fee income is earned, any problem with the servicing ability of the company can have serious consequences for the banking system and hence need to be monitored.

Treasury income has been a very important activity for banks as they are an integral part of the money market which involves dealing with securities of all kinds. The GSec market, for example, is typified by their action as they hold on to such paper for a variety of reasons. The portfolio of banks is divided into different headings—held for trading, available for sale and held to maturity. As the names suggest, securities thus defined at the beginning of the year would be used for specific purposes of which trading is important. Banks do buy and sell securities on a daily basis and accordingly are able to book treasury income. The same happens when they deal with trading in currencies, which are carried out with the necessary caveats in place as laid down by the RBI. In general, not all banks have very active treasury departments and while some are very active in terms of making money, others do so to manage the liquidity situation in banks.

The way things work is that when interest rates are falling, the prices of securities increase and banks tend to sell their stock to make an income. In case of rising interest rates, prices come down and this usually is associated with higher purchases. As this is a zero-sum game where there are buyers for every sale, individual banks work out their trading strategies based on the securities they hold and the maturity and liquidity profile of the same. In fact, at times banks may like to hold on to securities when prices come down as the yields are higher which get accounted for in interest income. At the end of the day, it is a treasury strategy that is adopted which matters.

An interesting aspect of the structure of income across banks is that non-interest income through fees, trading and so on, account for a higher proportion of total income for foreign banks compared with others. In 2018–2019, the share was 21 per cent for foreign banks, 16 per cent for private banks and just 12 per cent for PSBs. Quite clearly the foreign banks are more aggressive here and are able to de-risk their portfolio by looking more on contingent liabilities to earn a fee income.

7

Chipping of the PSB Market Share

The entry of private banks was always going to dislodge the hegemony of the PSBs. This would hold in any business as has been witnessed in the insurance industry as well. In fact, for the mutual funds industry, the so-called public sector UTI has been reduced to being just another player. Mathematically, it is bound to happen as any business garnered by a new player will lower the shares of other players, which is also the ethos of competition when more players are encouraged. In case of banks too, this has happened at a fairly rapid pace.

The size of the market can be denoted by the overall size of the aggregate balance sheet of all commercial banks put together. It can also be looked at in terms of aggregate deposits or aggregate credit or the sum of both. However, given that banking assets, though predominantly bank credit, have other important components like investments that are mandatory and hence quite sizable, it is necessary to include them also when sizing the system.

Prior to the introduction of financial sector reforms which had at its core the entry of new private banks, PSBs ruled the system with a share of nearly 85 per cent in 1995. They comprised the SBI and its associates as well as the nationalized banks. Foreign banks and the private banks (also called the old private sector banks) held on to shares of 6.5 per cent each and the RRBs had a share of 2.8 per cent. The last was virtually PSBs as the ownership was in the hands of the government indirectly.

Almost 25 years post the arrival of the new private banks, the structure of the banking system has changed quite drastically. The share of private banks has increased to 28.2 per cent which is a little above the quarter figure mark. The interesting part is that they have continued to maintain momentum in terms of growth which is probably the important factor here. They have grown at an annual compound growth rate of 23.4 per cent over this period. In contrast, the PSBs have grown at 14.6 per cent per annum. Foreign banks grew by 15.1 per cent per annum during the same period of 23 years. The overall system grew by 15.8 per cent which was mainly due to the higher growth registered by the private banks.

The pace of growth of PSBs has definitely not been unimpressive as a CAGR of almost 15 per cent is very competitive. The private banks do have the advantage of starting on a smaller base which becomes easier to scale up with time as they grew by using different channels of delivery with a lot of focus on technology. Therefore, the PSBs can take heart at this growth

Table 7.1. Market Shares in Total Liabilities

All Banks	1995 (₹ Lakh Crore)	Share (%)	2019 (₹ Lakh Crore)	Share (%)
	521,537	100.0	166.01	100.0
State Bank of India	156,325	30.0	101.62	61.2
Nationalized banks	282,535	54.2		
Other private banks	33,955	6.5	52.98	31.9
Foreign	33,977	6.5	10.57	6.4
RRB/others	14,745	2.8	0.83	0.4

Source: www.rbi.org.in.

rate even though their share in the business has come down quite sharply from 84.2 per cent to 65.7 per cent (Table 7.1).

Can these growth rates be sustained? The entire financial market has undergone a metamorphosis albeit gradually with several other pockets growing in importance from the point of view of both savers and borrowers. This means that banks will have to compete with the equity market, bonds, NBFCs, mutual funds, small savings for a larger share of the economy's savings. In addition to the existing structure, the entry of new kinds of internet banks like Payments banks and small finance banks open interesting possibilities in terms of providing alternatives for customers and potential competition for commercial banks. It is still not certain as to how these structures would evolve and whether they would be able to build meaningful volumes to add another dimension to the existing banks. Therefore, sustaining a growth rate of 15 per cent on a continuous basis will be tough going for banks as the size of the cake may not increase at the same rate.

The two main regulators, SEBI and RBI, have been working hard to move borrowers from banks to the bond market, which though open today have some inherent constraints which restrict access at the practical level. The RBI too wants long-term borrowing to move away from the banking system to the markets. Therefore, there is a push factor involved that will be hard to dodge. Intuitively, it can be seen that the market route is more efficient from the point of view of cost of raising debt relative to banks as the intermediation cost is avoided. Intuitively, there is an incentive for companies to use this route, though there are rules laid down by SEBI which makes transparency critical. Also, there are unwritten rules in the bond market based on history that it is only the highly rated companies that are in a position to raise funds from this market while the others prefer banks which are willing to lend against collateral and other considerations and not go by purely the credit rating. But as the bond market evolves and credit enhancements become popular, especially with credit default swaps (CDSs) becoming active, there is scope for even the lower-rated entities to fancy their chances in this market.

On the liabilities side too, banks could see some erosion in the flows of funds in the form of deposits. Banks have been more effervescent when it comes to lowering interest rates on deposits which make it progressively difficult to retain deposit holders. While temporary problems will be present periodically with mutual funds, they have grown to become an important source of deployment of funds for households who are able to get better returns by combining debt and equity investments depending on their appetite. This will continue to be the norm in the coming years. While banks seem to be fairly happy with the situation of deposits not growing, there would be challenges in case credit picks up and there is a paucity of funds as was the case in FY19 when deposit growth lagged credit.

This is the likely scenario for banks where the process of intermediation will be questioned periodically. The implication is that linear growth will not be possible under these conditions. In this kind of a situation, banks will have to innovate on the process of deployment of funds over time. While narrow banking where banks invest only in government paper is not a feasible option, they would need to look harder at the smaller-size tickets which would be retail as well as the SME sector to grow their businesses. This would mean changing the present strategy of concentrating on the larger ticket sizes which bring in bulk business with lower costs as these companies are well established with track records.

Banks may also have to move over to the off-balance sheet business lines which fall under the category of contingent liabilities to add value to other markets in the form of providing guarantees and enhancements to support growth. Credit cards offer potential to banks and those that are able to move ahead can reap the benefits. Diversification will hold the clue and the private banks have shown how this can work. It will be necessary for PSBs to also grow their business for which the government will have to provide independence so that they are able to think differently.

This will be a challenge for PSBs which are on one hand still controlled by the government and are less aggressive when it comes to both assets and liabilities. For example, the strategy of giving higher savings deposits rate was an innovation of private banks which actually makes the customer lock in funds forever given that this amount is rolled over. The rate is somewhere between a term deposit and a conventional savings bank account rate which thus has given an edge to the private banks. Similarly, when it comes to personal loans, private banks have been more advanced and innovative and reached out to customers which is not really done by PSBs. The constant phone calls and messages to make use of the loan facility is always from a private bank or foreign banks and rarely from a PSB. With competition increasing, there would be a tendency for PSBs to lose market share unless they are able to change gear and become more market oriented.

8

The Human Factor

Banking has traditionally been a relationship business on both sides. The branch staff would normally know the deposit holders personally as the branch would become a meeting place for households where bankers would develop a rapport with the customers. Lending is always based on relations as borrowers have been nurturing this relation historically and this is one of the reasons as to why corporates still prefer to borrow from banks rather than the market which is impersonal. Hence, it is just not loans to individuals but also to corporates which are based on such relations. Deals can be customized so that the transaction is not just based on an objective criterion.

Nationalization was meant to socialize the business and the banks had to open offices across the country. This also meant that the headcount had to increase commensurately as more people were required to run the offices. Often recruitment would be regional based, though the common examination taken was at the national level. Those selected would be given option to work in the region of their choice and often the staff would like to work in their region of residence. This helped as it was easy to connect with customers as while languages can be learnt, knowing cultures of people also makes a difference.

Also, this framework had given emphasis to employment generation which was the ethic of all public sector enterprises. Hence, along with banking business the headcount had to increase. Staff tended to be classified into different categories with the officer class being on top and service gentry including peons and clerks at the step-down levels. There were unions which were created to ensure that labour got a good deal and the IBA even today negotiates the salaries and wages for the entire set of staff of PSBs. Along with this multi-tiered system came the different capabilities of the staff. The officers do the high-level work which involves credit appraisal and other activities like those in treasury or risk management which requires a higher level of skill sets. The routine jobs like accepting deposits and disbursing cash could be done by the clerical staff while the more menial jobs of moving files would be done within the purview of the category of peons.

From the point of view of broad classification, the staff could be divided into officers and support staff. It was felt that given the hierarchical structure in any organization that is associated with the government, there would be a biased ratio in favour of the support staff. Table 8.1 shows the structure of staff in various categories of banks and the share of officers in total headcount. In 1991–1992, the share of officers was just around 27 per cent for the entire system, with foreign banks doing better than the average with 35.2 per cent. Even the private banks had a ratio of less than the sample average which means that in general the hierarchy was fairly well ingrained here.

Things did change after the new private banks came in where there was a sea change in the way in which banking was conducted. To begin with, these new banks had started off without much of the support staff concept and were leaner in terms of staff strength. The culture of banking changed as staff was generally in the officer cadre and worked longer hours than traditional bankers did. This went with higher-pay packages with added incentives like bonus of variable pay and the gap between what PSB staff and private banks earned changed significantly.

Table 8.1. Share of Officers in Labour Force: 1991–1992 and 2018–2019

	Total (Number)	Officers (Number)	Share (%)	Total Number	Officers (Number)	Share (%)
SBI Group	284,910	69,540	24.4	806,893	389,956	48.3
Nationalized	562,502	148,314	26.4			
Others	66,121	27,711	41.9	55,781	43,226	77.4
Foreign	13,081	4,598	35.2	23,249	22,046	94.8
Private	50,317	12,119	24.1	477,495	443,554	92.9
All	976,931	262,282	26.8	1,363,508	898,782	65.9

Source: www.rbi.org.in.

Simultaneously, there was a lot of focus on getting in technology which started from the time they started business. Hence unlike PSBs which had to convert their manual activity to a networked database (also called core banking solutions which took a long time for linking all branches), the private banks were at an advantage by doing it from inception. This did help to make them more efficient. Also, the concept of ATMs which was restricted more to the foreign banks at that time became common for the new private banks which worked on different ways of keeping customers out of the branches. Using the ATM for withdrawals as well as depositing money meant that customers need not enter the branch and to that extent fewer manual transactions took place. In fact, from using ATMs belonging to the branch in which a person had an account, the same could be done through any ATM of the branch for both deposits and withdrawals. And now with portability of ATMs coming in, one can withdraw cash from any ATM of any bank anywhere in the country. The evolution is hence complete.

At the next step, net banking took over which was even cheaper than the ATM as it did not require any brick and mortar structure. The cost per transaction for net-based transactions was minimal while that of ATM came somewhere in between that of the Internet and the branch. Today the e-wallet is catching on and has been adapted by all kinds of banks and has in a way been a leveller.

As can be seen from Table 8.1 over the period of around 25 years, the share of officers has gone up across all the bank groups with even PSBs having shares which are in the range of almost 50 per cent. As the private sector norm of layoffs is not possible in the government sector, the banks have been able to achieve a change in this ratio by hiring more officers and not replacing support staff when they retire from service. And this has been supplemented with VRSs so as to rationalize the headcount.

Another interesting development is that there has been a substantial shift to the outsourcing mode where certain menial

jobs are hired from other agencies. This increases other operating expenses but keeps the headcount in check. Hence security guards, for example, for all branches and ATMs tend to be
outsourced and are on the payrolls of agencies which hire them
and deploy their services in these banks. This is a smart way of
keeping the headcount under check as this echelon is not union-
ized and does not have any rights as employees. Yet they perform
the function at a lower cost as their salaries are not aligned
with the general banking staff. In a way, it does disguise the
real headcount as there is still space being occupied by this category of workers who are still doing a certain kind of job. But
while such information is not available, visits to banks and their
branches does definitely reveal that with mechanization there
is also a visible reduction in the need of manpower.

A fundamental question raised is that by removing the category of clerks which includes also typists and secretaries, some
of the functions are being handled by the officers such as taking
appointments and typing out reports and letters which was earlier
done by these gentry. A point of view put here is that while part of
the work has been taken over by technology, some of the manual
functions are being performed by the officer category which is
paid more and hence the cost of the service has increased. This
holds more so for the private banks and foreign banks where there
is a very small retinue of support staff. The flipside is that they end
up working longer hours which in a way justifies the cost of the
employee. Hence, there are arguments on both sides.

It would be of interest to see as to how do the mergers of
PSBs which would be hopefully consummated in 2020–2021 get
reflected in this staff matric and whether there would be scope to
reduce headcount. It has been stated upfront that no jobs would
be lost but the possibility of having a VRS cannot be ruled out
where staff which overlaps functions or locations may be given
an opportunity to exit.

This leads to an interesting issue relating to the cost of
human resources as it is generally felt that non PSBs pay a very

high compensation to their staff relative to their peers. The PSB complaint is that their staff is not motivated because of low pay packages which are fixed by statute and is homogenous across banks. How far is this true and has this really changed over the years?

9 Managing Employee Pay Scales

The common argument when it comes to comparing PSBs with private banks is that the staff is not paid well which is a disincentive when attracting talent as the brighter ones prefer to work with private banks or their foreign counterparts. This is definitely true to an extent as most private banks do campus recruitment while PSBs have to follow the due processes and have their hands tied as they cannot offer differential salaries as the structures are laid down and is common to all. The common entrance exam is a must for PSBs and the compensation packages offered are the same across all grades, and hence there is little to distinguish the pay packages with the differences probably being in terms of perquisites offered like housing and other home allowances at the officer level.

A counterargument which is put forward is that the perquisites that PSB officials get in terms of housing and other allowances which may not come under the cost to company (CTC) concept for such officials actually help to narrow down the pay gap, and hence the difference may not be very significant. Private banks normally tend to provide what is called a CTC approach to remuneration which is a CTC offer including imputations for discounted loans that one can get, gratuity, company contribution to the provident fund and so on, which public sector does not count as it comes as an additional benefit. Hence, if home loans or vehicle loans are offered at a concession rate of say 5.5 per cent, then the difference between the market rate of say 9 per cent and 5.5 per cent, that is, 3.5 per cent is computed on a loan of, say, ₹10 lakhs for a vehicle and hence a sum of ₹35,000 is added to the CTC. The same is done for an assumed home loan. Various banks in the private sector have a different way of computing the CTC whereas for the public sector which includes the RBI, the salary is what one gets on the salary slip while the other benefits are considered to be additional ones.

Hence when salaries are calculated for the two sectors, this needs to be kept in mind. Table 9.1 compares the average employee cost for various sets of banks between the time period 1994–1995 and 2017–2018. The salary cost which is taken here is the total staff compensation expenses which may not be necessarily received by an individual as even certain canteen expenses or picnics that go under staff welfare would be added for the PSBs which could go as administrative and miscellaneous expenses for their private counterparts.

On the whole, there has been a tenfold increase in average compensation over the 24-year period which is a CAGR of almost 10 per cent per annum. This growth rate has been maintained also by the private banks (which includes both the new and old banks) while foreign banks have increased at closer to 15 per cent per annum. Therefore, there has been a fairly even growth in the salaries to bankers over the years. Interestingly, during this period the consumer price index (CPI) for industrial workers increased by a CAGR of around 7.5 per cent per annum which means that for the sector as a whole, the real compensation increased by just around 2.5–3 per cent per annum.

The increase in salaries of private banks may come as a surprise but it should be noted that post the regulator nudging banks to use their own staff for business, there are several staff employed which are on a different pay scale which are typically

Table 9.1. Salary Bill: 1994–1995 and 2018–2019

Bank Group	Total (₹ Crore)	Employees (Number)	Average Salary (₹ Lakhs)	Total (₹ Crore)	Employee (Number)	Average Salary (₹ Lakhs)
SBI Group	3,340	310,607	1.07	100,940	806,983	12.51
Nationalized	5,237	569,816	0.92			
Private	487	57,967	0.84	39,201	477,495	8.20
Foreign	3,144	12,870	2.44	6,720	23,249	28.90
All	9,882	1,019,025	0.97	148,988	1,363,508	10.92

Source: www.rbi.org.in.

lower than those of the so-called professional staff. This will become stark when the pay scales at the higher levels are compared. For example, a public sector banker as a chairman and managing director (CMD) could have a pay which is not more than ₹30 lakhs per annum with the other benefits that flow to the position. The same CTC for a private banker could be upwards of ₹5 crore with other benefits like stock options being part of the deal. Further the old private banks are still on lower pay scales relative to new private banks which bring down the average. Also, within private banks, there is a high degree of skewness in pay packages where the higher echelons tend to get higher pay packages compared with those below.

PART 2

CONTROVERSIES

10

The NPA Conundrum

One of the most controversial issues in Indian banking since economic reforms has been the NPA issue which came to the fore in 2016 when the RBI passed an order saying that banks need to follow a new set of norms which were termed as Asset Quality Recognition. This became important because it has led to a lot of reforms in the resolution process of NPAs. But this has also raised a rather acrimonious debate on the merits of the entire process.

How did it all start? NPAs in the banking system have been fairly orderly as the RBI has over time brought in the global norm of 90 days. Basically, this means that if a loan is past overdue in terms of servicing for 90 days, then it is considered to be non-performing. The consequence of such a classification is that the bank has to make a provision for a permanent default or a write-off which means that the profits of a bank gets affected. Once the profit gets affected, it affects the valuation in the stock market which gets suspicious of such banks. Also, there is a reputation issue for banks which would not like to show that they have built up such an adverse portfolio. Therefore, it has become a very touchy subject for banks, which would rather not reveal the true picture.

Also, as lending has not been a very transparent activity for both public sector and private (as seen recently) banks, there is always the fear of the investigative agencies getting behind the CEOs for such NPAs. Hence, it is not surprising that in case of PSBs new CMDs/CEOs tend to reveal all before they commence their tenure while these numbers taper towards the end of their tenure that again increases when a new head takes over.

Interestingly, when the NPA issue became acute, the system found a way out of not recognizing the same. The RBI had created a system called CDR wherein bankers got together and then decided that based on the merits of the case they would restructure the loan. Restructuring meant that the tenure of the loan would be elongated so as to make it easier for the borrower to perform given the time space. Also, the rate of interest would be lowered substantially so as to ease the pressure on the company. This was a joint decision taken by the lenders and hence was collective in nature. The regulatory structure allowed this to be called a restructured loan.

Year 2015–16 was a cut-off year (Table 10.1) as this was the time when the restructured assets were revisited and their classification changed into NPAs, while the former was redefined again and added another percentage point to the NPAs.

Table 10.1. NPA Ratios across Bank Categories

NPAs	PSBs	Private	Foreign	All
2012–2013	4.42 (3.24)	1.77	3.04	3.23
2013–2014	4.96 (4.09)	1.78	3.86	3.83
2014–2015	4.30 (5.30)	2.10	3.20	4.27
2015–2016	9.30	2.80	4.20	7.50
2016–2017	11.70	4.10	4.00	9.30
2017–2018	14.60	4.70	3.80	11.20
2018–2019	11.60	5.30	3.00	9.10
2019 September	12.70	3.90	2.90	9.30

Source: www.rbi.org.in.

Would all loans qualify for this tag? The answer is 'no' because there had to be a strong justification for the same. It was argued that these assets were not NPAs because they were unable to keep pace with debt servicing commitments on account of extraneous conditions and hence required special attention. This was the time when there were several scams in the country relating to telecom, coal, iron ore and other structures relating to the power sector. In particular, the power sector had a very adverse ecosystem. The generating company had set up capacity given the forecasts drawn up on the Indian economy growing at 10 per cent which no one countered. Once the capacity was set up, the company had problem in getting coal as there was a scam, which led to access being limited to the raw material. To top it all, the power produced was sold to DISCOMs that were loaded heavily in the public sector. These units were running high losses by selling power at a low price or free to the public for political reasons. This being the case, they were unable to pay for the power and the generating company came to a situation where receivables had increased. Further the power purchasing agreements (PPAs) signed with government authorities were not honoured which meant that the business model collapsed. In such a situation, money borrowed could not be repaid and led to an NPA. Thus, it was argued not really to be an NPA and could qualify as restructured assets.

Similarly, several steel companies had built capacities and did not get access to coal and iron ore, which led again to projects being stalled and later abandoned. Once this happened, the banks bore the brunt in the form of loans not being repaid. Such forbearance was accepted by banks, RBI and the government. Given the political equations in the country, there is always a tendency to blame the earlier regimes for these ills and the corollary was that these loans were treated differently.

The advantage was that banks were able to kick the can and take cover when it came to provisioning. The RBI had asked for provisioning norms to come into effect for restructured assets in 2013 but the rate was much lower than that for NPAs. While critics argued that this was plain evergreening under the auspices of the regulator, the defenders of banks highlighted the unfortunate circumstances under which banks came to this position that was well beyond their control. The ideological question was that in the absence of mala fide intent, all NPAs are due to business cycles or failure which can be linked with an external cause. Where does one then draw the line?

In fact, the situation was quite ironic because the CDR cell set up consisted of bankers who had given the loans and then decided that they should not be classified as NPAs when they were not serviced due to these extraneous reasons and instead put them in the category of restructured assets. While a due diligence process was followed, there was a tendency to move most of these assets to this category on account of the special dispensation meted out.

But things changed when the RBI decided in 2015 that there should be a fair recognition of NPAs and this was called the AQR. In this set up, banks were asked to do a due diligence and report their NPAs. The concept of NPA suddenly came to the front as attention was focused on them and the actual processes were reviewed. It was highlighted that when there was a syndicated loan given which had say five banks, if four banks were being serviced but the fifth wasn't, then the four banks called it a good asset and only the fifth treated it as a NPA. This anomaly had to change and all the banks had to treat it so.

Suddenly the NPA numbers started spiralling and this went for both the private and PSBs. The concept of stressed assets came in which was reported which included both NPAs and restructured assets and crossed the 12 per cent mark. As banks classified restructured assets as NPAs, the balance shifted to the latter and this was the goal of the RBI. The manufacturing sector recorded the highest levels of NPAs followed by services and retail. Within manufacturing, steel (metals), power (infra), auto, textiles and so on, led the bad pack and the entire system look fragile with some of these sectors registering stressed assets ratios of above 20 per cent. The RBI inspection and audit started revealing the incorrect allocation of assets related with quality and several banks were questioned and fined for not revealing the true picture.

There were two consequences of this recognition process. First, banks had to make accelerated provisions for these assets which led to net profit getting converted into losses with net worth getting dented for some banks. This has second-round effects on the slippage in capital requirements as erosion of net worth meant that banks needed more capital to continue business and as most of those which witnessed such erosion were PSBs, the onus was on the government to provide the same.

Second, banks became wary of lending, especially for long-term purposes and migrated to the retail end where the delinquency rates were typically lower. This did not escalate into a macro economic problem because it was a time when the economy just about maintained growth in the 7 per cent region and with different policy shocks like demonetization and goods and services tax (GST), companies too were sceptical of going in for fresh investment. In a way, it was a comfortable equilibrium where demand for funds came down as supply dried up. The issue would have become problematic in case the economy was booming and there was continued demand for funds as banks would not have been in a position to lend due to absence of the required capital.

This phase of 2016–2019 was also one where the RBI came down heavily on the banks for misstating their NPA levels which made the headlines mainly due to the involvement of some of the high-profile private sector banks. Meanwhile some of the high profile NPA cases involved the investigating agencies getting after the CMDs of PSBs which made things messy. A fear psychosis spread with bankers being driven on the back foot as they became averse to taking decisions. This is not the first time that such a scenario has played out when NPAs have increased and bankers have borne the burden of the investigation which can haunt them post retirement.

Has the situation improved? The answer is yes, as this was a much-needed measure to clean up the operations of banks. The two main takeaways have been that first banks have to play according to the rules and must recognize with alacrity the quality of asset. Here too the regulator has a role to play because the NPA resolution process had several schemes adopted such as sale to asset reconstruction companies (ARCs), strategic debt restructuring (SDR), scheme for sustainable structuring of stressed assets (S4A) and so on.

Second, with the hand of discipline being stern, banks would have to hone their credit appraisal skills to ensure that there is no repetition of this episode of NPAs.

It is still not certain whether we can say with a fair degree of confidence that the entire process of recognition is over and that the future numbers on an incremental basis will be low and linked more to the generation of new NPAs rather than an admission of past impaired assets. The Yes Bank controversy has delayed the reassurance process just at the time it was felt that the level of NPAs have stabilized. The RBI has surely done a remarkable job in this cleansing operation and in a way had to take a tough decision to do what it did. Prolonging the process of recognition under various umbrellas was certainly a mistake which if addressed earlier may have saved the nation from a lot of pain. It can be now said with a modicum of confidence that such a situation will not be allowed to spring again.

It would nonetheless be interesting to see as to how the NPA issue pans out post the COVID lockdown being removed. There is a high probability of the moratoriums being provided for borrowers to at some time get recognized as NPAs depending on how various industries and companies are able to get back to normal. This, however, will be known only in the next couple of years.

In a way, it can be said that we have come a full circle from the time we went in for reforms in the early-1990s. Before the Narasimham Committee recommendations were implemented, banks had their own version of income recognition and showed much higher income than that was actually earned. As the NPA concept did not exist, profits tended to be very high as they did not have to make provisions. To top it all, evergreening was the norm where loans were repaid by giving new loans, which held for the DFIs too which camouflaged the state of banking. As RBI brought in these norms, it did appear that banks had been transformed and while the system was never really tested as it had almost sailed through the Lehman moment with ease, the scam-ridden economy had sown the seeds of this new crisis which has led to a fresh look at what can be termed as the second generation of reforms which now look to be stronger and more effective. The process of creative destruction so as to call it has been in progress with institutions remaining firm through practices being transformed that will serve the economy well.

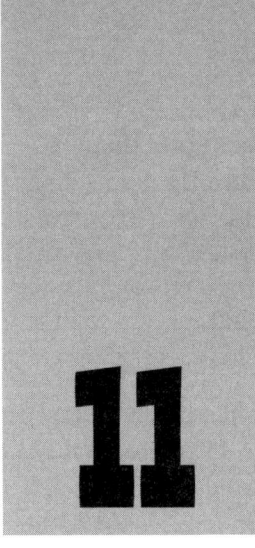

The IBC

Are We Serious?

One of the major challenges posed to the RBI is to have a system of resolution of NPAs. The IBC is probably one of the biggest moves taken to control the growth of NPAs by having a time-bound framework for resolution. Lending targets are easier to meet than recovery and the systems to enforce the same are still weak. The borrower appears to have the upper hand and the banker too is normally reluctant to enforce recovery and prefers to stretch the terms of engagement so that it is not classified as a NPA. Further once an asset turns bad, provisions are made by the bank which is one part of the story. But the tale does not end as there have to be efforts made to recover a larger part of the loan which is always a challenge. Therefore, the recovery rate has been quite low in our context and the World Bank Doping Business study for 2020 puts the time taken to resolve a case as 1.6 years and the recovery rate at 71.6 per cent. In 2015, it was 4.3 years and 25.7 per cent, respectively.

There have been different routes chosen for recovery starting with the concept of the Debt Recovery Tribunal, ARCs, SARFESI, CDR, S4A and so on. The success has been quite limited and something big was required. This next big thing was the IBC which was introduced in Parliament 2015 and became a law subsequently.

The problem with NPA resolution has been that there has always been a perverse incentive not to resolve the issue. The borrower never wants to repay the loan and as long as it was possible to roll over, the loan through a restructuring process was able to keep things moving. The system allowed borrowers to procrastinate and the CDR scheme was just what they required to keep the ball rolling.

The bankers too had reason to keep the asset called 'good' as this would help them in a number of ways. First, the quality of the asset would be standard. Second, they would have to make less provision for the same. Third, the profit line would look good. Fourth, the bank chief would also look good by carrying along a smaller load of NPAs. This was hence a win-win situation where everyone gained. The view taken was always short term when it came to PSBs as they never thought beyond their tenure. It was not surprising that all new CMSs/MDs started off their tenure by cleaning their books which showed that there were some bad assets that were not recognized by the previous head. Interestingly, no one thought of investigating what had become a habit across all PSBs.

The RBI had various schemes to resolve the NPA which meant getting the bank and the borrower to sit across and resolve the asset by taking a haircut and then working out a plan for repayment. This was also acceptable to the borrower who never wanted to repay in the first place. The ARC would come in and buy the asset at a lower rate and then hope to recover the balance from the borrower where the proceeds would be evenly shared. But, banks were not too happy with this arrangement because they would tend to sell the asset at say 15 per cent of the value to the ARC. If at some stage it was found that the asset could have been sold at a higher rate, then the investigative agencies could hunt down the banker who would probably have retired by then. Therefore, it was much safer not to settle the case. There were other schemes introduced like the SDR, S4A, JLF (Joint Lenders Forum) where part of the loan could be converted into equity and part would be drawn down and restructured at a lower rate. As long as there was a committee of bankers who took decisions, it was agreeable for all but on a bilateral basis was associated with personal risk. Therefore, it was not surprising that the resolution of NPAs was insignificant and the recovery given default rates were low at 10–25 per cent compared with the global norm of 70 per cent plus.

The IBC was novel in the sense that it had a timeline which had to be adhered to. When there was a default, there was a time period of 180 days given for the two parties to come to an amicable understanding on restructuring the debt. If this could not be done, an extension of 90 days was permitted, and after 270 days, the case would be presented to the IBC where a different set of professionals would take over and resolve through sale. This meant that the asset would be evaluated and then auctioned to the best bidder. Here, there was a definite threat of the company losing its asset or the promoter losing the company. Hence, if a steel company was in default and could not come to an understanding with the bankers, then the company would be sold to the highest bidder. This fear was strong enough to deter wilful defaulters.

The system worked well to begin with but had run into anomalies where the defaulters also wanted to bid for their own assets as well as others in their industry. This had revealed the complex web of corporates where the most audacious bids were put by defaulting companies to buy other defaulting companies. Game theory was in action where A, who was a defaulter and had the asset under the process, could bid for another insolvency case B. The system had to be refined to ensure that this did not happen.

The RBI had gone one step further with the now famous 12 February 2018 notification where it was clearly stated that for all loans above ₹2,000 crore, a one-day default—not the normal 90-day NPA criteria—would evoke a period of 180 days for resolution failing which it would go to the IBC. There were other add-on in terms of resolution plans (RPs) being evaluated by 2-rating agencies which would be presented to the committee of creditors failing which the sale would take place. Also, the RBI abolished all the other resuscitation schemes such as CDR, SDR, S4A and so on with the coin having only two sides—resolve and pay or get ready for sale. The success rate according to IBBI is around 40–50 per cent in terms of recovery which is a substantial improvement over the rather very low numbers prior to this process.

There were two fallouts here. The first is that incremental NPAs came down as companies were afraid of defaulting as they fully knew that once the asset went to the IBC, it was curtains down for them. Second, certain sectors like power took umbrage at this notification and took recourse to the courts. The argument was that power companies had a problem which was historical. Their default was more due to failure of the government on the buy-and-sell sides. They were not able to repay because they were not able to collect their revenue as the companies to whom they sold power were the state-owned discoms which were not in a position to pay as they made losses due to inefficiency and defective pricing policies. If their assets were sold, then that would be the end of the industry as no fresh investment would come in if the conditions were so stringent. There was merit in this argument.

The counterargument was that this held for all industries and if an exception was made for power, the same can be argued for by steel and textiles and so on. Therefore, the ideological battle remained. The government wanted the RBI to relent which the latter was not willing to which stoked a controversy. Both sides had valid points. The RBI's stance was backed by the moral hazard argument. Besides diluting, the policy would make it less potent and hence it made sense for the central bank to take a firm stance.

However, in April 2019, the Supreme Court had passed an order that quashed the RBI circular. The verdict simply put says that the RBI cannot have a blanket order which says that all those who default on Day 1 have to be in the pipeline of 180 days before IBC. It can be only on a case-by-case basis. Therefore, companies were free once again to deal only with their banks and the RBI could not make it an automatic route.

Leaving it to the banks actually takes the game back to what it was before the IBC came in. The IBC and the threat of force which was invoked were engendered by the fact that the two parties were reluctant on their own to resolve the issue. If the ball is back into their court, then it would be interesting to see as to how the cases proceed as the same incentives that existed earlier come back to play and there is little reason for one to expect that things will be very different from now on. As the February circular held for companies with NPA of above ₹2,000 crore, the amounts involved are evidently high and create an incentive to prolong the repayment process.

The RBI has come out with new guidelines on addressing the issue of NPAs on 7 June 2019 where the onus has been put on the banks to do the needful. It now says that all lenders must put in place board-approved policies for resolution of stressed assets which also covers the necessary timelines. As default is a lagging indicator of financial stress faced by borrowers, lenders have to initiate the process of implementing such a RP before a default. Once a borrower is reported to be in default, the lenders are to review the borrower's account within 30 days and decide on the resolution strategy. For such RPs, all lenders must enter into an inter-creditor agreement (ICA) to provide for ground rules for finalization and implementation of the RP. The ICA shall provide that any decision taken by lenders representing 75 per cent by value of total outstanding credit facilities (fund-based as well as non-fund-based) and 60 per cent by number shall be binding upon all the lenders.

The catch now is that when a viable RP in respect of a borrower is not implemented within the timelines, all lenders shall make additional provisions of 20 per cent up to 180 days and another 15 per cent, that is, 35 per cent for 365 days of commencement of review. This is pragmatic as it throws the ball in the court of banks which have to act fast or else make these provisions.

The jury is still out on this issue. The latest data from IBBI shows that the recovery rate now is around 43 per cent as of December 2019 and below what the World Bank reported which captured the initial cases where the recovery rate was higher. The problem is that this is the first time that such stringent actions are being taken against recalcitrant borrowers. The issue really is with legacy NPAs, as the amounts involved, are large and it is hard to also sell the asset. Putting it simplistically, it can be seen that if a steel plant is to be sold which has stopped operations, the value of the asset would automatically come down and the realization value would fall as time goes by. This is one reason why valuation is always a challenge in such cases.

It can be argued that having such a framework in place is a good start. The important thing is to ensure that it works well because this will be a prerequisite for also developing a corporate bond market which is what the regulators are aiming to do. The idea is to have a robust resolution mechanism in place so that one can be sure that in a period of say one year, the asset is sold and the creditors compensated. This is the medium-term goal for the RBI and SEBI. Presently, an NPA is a problem of the bank which has to sort out the issue with the borrower. In case of a bond which is widely held, there is no single entity which can take up the case with the issuer of debt. Hence, a strong IBC framework is essential to ensure that resolution is quick and time-bound with the ground rules firmly in place which can be enforced. The next year will be critical to get a fair sense on how resolutions are taking place and whether the framework is effective.

PCA Banks

That Hurts Now!

One of the measures taken by the RBI to control the NPAs was to put a check on the asset creation activities of those that were distressed. This was called the PCA framework. The basic idea is that if a bank falls in this category of PCA, then its activities would be restricted to the extent that it would only do basic banking and maintain the existing clients without going in for any expansionary policy. These restrictions would hold until such time the banks were able to improve on their performance and get back to normal.

The framework was actually an old one from 2002 but was operationalized in April 2017. The PCA framework was not intended to constrain normal operations of the banks for the general public. The PCA framework involves monitoring of certain performance indicators of the banks as an early warning exercise and is initiated once such thresholds like those relating to capital, asset quality and so on, are breached. Its objective is to facilitate the banks to take corrective measures including those prescribed by the central bank in a timely manner in order to restore their financial health. The framework also provides an opportunity to the RBI to pay focused attention on such banks by engaging with the management more closely in those areas.

The PCA framework is, thus, intended to encourage banks to eschew certain riskier activities and focus on conserving capital so that their balance sheets can become stronger.

Capital, asset quality and profitability continue to be the key areas for monitoring in the revised framework. Indicators to be tracked for Capital, asset quality and profitability would be CRAR/Common Equity Tier I ratio, Net NPA ratio and Return on Assets, respectively. Leverage would be monitored additionally as part of the PCA framework. Breach of any risk thresholds (as broadly given below) would result in the invocation of the PCA. Different responses of the banks and actions of the RBI would be invoked at each of these stages. There are thresholds that have to be adhered to or else the bank would risk falling into this mode. Some of them are:

1. CAR up to 250 bps below the minimum with further gradations.
2. NPA ratio ranging from 6 to above 12 per cent.
3. ROA negative for last two years and onwards.
4. Tier 1 leverage ratio specified at different ranges for action to be taken.

Is this right or wrong? Everyone cheered when the PCA framework was announced and progressively 11 banks came under this net which meant that banking business was held up when it came to these banks. They could take deposits and continue providing working capital to existing clients. But they could not lend afresh and had to maintain tight vigil over all their indicators.

The defenders of the PCA framework argued that this was the only way to revive these banks because as long as there was no check, they would continue to do business as usual and this would exacerbate the situation as things would get worse. By restricting what could be and could not be done, they were given time to do their housekeeping.

Just like how the NPA resolution through the IBC was greeted with cheer, the same went for the PCA action of the RBI. But along the way there were some nagging issues that came up.

With 11 banks out of the regular business of banking, the onus of lending fell on the other banks. This created a challenging situation because all banks were inundated with NPAs and were keen on cherry picking their new loans. This meant that those that were in vulnerable sectors or did not have a good internal credit score were excluded as there was limited capital in existence which had to take care of all requirements. In a way, it was argued that credit flow was choked. A collateral effect was that the cost of funds went up as there were fewer funds to lend. Also banks not in the net preferred to lend to the retail segment where the probability of delinquency was lower. Hence, there was a tendency for some borrowers being crowded out.

The NBFC crisis in late-2018 had borne the brunt because some of them had a problem in raising funds while the banking system was also handicapped with limited funds to lend with a preference for non-corporate loans. Hence, there has been a debate on whether this is the best way out as there are few alternatives in the system. In fact, the NBFCs are large borrowers from banks and compete with them when they lend in the same sectors, the transport sector in particular.

Bank lending is still the most preferred channel of delivery of funds to the borrowers as relations have been built over time. While disintermediation has caught on in the form of the bond market and the CP segment evolving, given the flexibility shown by banks there was a tendency for them to prefer this channel. Putting banks under PCA can be problematic for borrowers who have little access to other modes of finance. This will hold for companies which are in the SME segment or have a low credit rating. They would not be able to borrow in the bond market and with fewer banks willing to lend to them can confront a situation of facing a paucity of finance which can affect their economic activity.

A curious factor that needs to be highlighted here is that most borrowers from banks would be in the sub-investment grade and would not be able to access the capital market. Banks still lend to them because of the collateral provided to them.

But from the point of view of the RBI, this is a direct way to discipline banks which are getting into a tangle of low performance driven by the quality of assets. Banks do not fall into PCA immediately and have to underperform for at least two years in succession. Hence, there is always a warning signal before which the banks have these checks coming in. They need to be cognizant of how they are compliant with these norms so as to take remedial steps before the position becomes one where a barrier is erected. In the absence of such constraints, there is no incentive to improve and given the protection that such banks get from their promoters especially if it is the government, they would carry on business as usual.

The RBI norms on PCA act as checks at various levels and force improvement on banks as they would not be allowed to return to normalcy unless certain corrective action is taken. The central bank is finally responsible for the stability of the system and cannot relax such norms when the integrity of the realm is in question. It has been an extreme action taken by the central bank when conditions ran out of hand. Hence, it cannot be really faulted for taking a stringent stance.

The ideological question is whether we want a strong banking system or not? One must remember that banks are a different set of companies which do not operate on shareholder's capital but deposits. This is the difference. In case of a non-banking company, it can be argued that failure first erodes the net worth which is the shareholder and then trickles down to the lenders. But when it comes to banks, they work on deposit holders' money which has a certain understanding that it will always be repaid. If this is the deal, then the deposit holders have to be protected and it is hence necessary to rein in the banks whose NPAs are increasing continuously. Some action has to be taken to control the proliferation of NPAs and the PCA framework, which is actually an old one and suited for the purpose. It only lays down a roadmap that has to be followed so as to get the erring banks back on track. It is anyway not intended to be a permanent operation, and while the first set of banks which has been classified thus has been challenged, it sounds a future warning for others who now know how to run their business as the contours have been set by the RBI. Banks can hence rework their plans internally as they come close to any of these parameters.

In fact, banks can and should set up special cells within which they continuously monitor these parameters and signal to the management in case any of the thresholds are likely to be breached. Ideally, they should be reporting directly to the Chairman/MD/CEO office and flag any danger signal that may have to be heeded. This would be pragmatic and make banks more cognizant of the risk that is being carried on their books which can be addressed through appropriate action. In this context, it should be pointed out that the concept of narrow banking was espoused by the RBI in the 1990s which addressed this issue by ensuring that banks lent less money and invested more in government securities. It is the same now with the PCA framework.

It may hence be said that the PCA framework is an excellent step taken to control banks which could be slipping down on critical viability indicators. The criteria are objective and well known. As these indicators are tracked over a period of time, there is plenty of scope for remedial action. While the sudden implementation surely did cause disruption, it can be assumed that in future there will not be too much bunching of such cases as banks would be closely monitoring the progress and take corrective action. The important thing is that there should be no compromise along the way, which unfortunately is a revealed habit in our context.

13 Going beyond PCA and the Collapse of Governance

Banking governance has been an issue of debate as the fall of any bank has been traced to breakdown in governance standards. There have been several such cases in commercial banking history where various banks have been involved that have required strong intervention from the regulator like in the case of the Global Trust Bank or more recently the Yes Bank. There have been some issues in other banks too like PNB, ICICI Bank among others which caused considerable controversy and government/ RBI intervention. While most of these cases are under investigation, the fact that they dominated media headlines for quite some time is significant. Banks run on trust and ideally there should be no element of doubt in their operations.

In almost all cases which involved some dilution of governance standards at the time of lending, which could be due to either pressure from outside or personal fulfilment, a crisis-like situation had emerged. While a post-mortem invariably looks at turning the responsibility to some entity which normally is the regulator, the reaction has been to keep passing the pillow. The final word is in terms of a solution being found where management is changed or a bank is taken over or merged with another entity, it does not stop the recurrence of another episode.

It must be understood that there are limits to which the inspection process can reveal the gaps in governance. An ideo-logical conundrum is when the inspection team finds something amiss in the portfolio with a PSB which is laden with assets that have been given loans due to political compulsions. Can one really expect a red flag to be raised practically? The answer is probably no. Can any inspection team really find out that when Bank A has given loans to customer B, the latter is investing heavily in compa-nies X, Y and Z which could belong to the owner or CEO of Bank A? This can never come out from an audit of the bank. In fact, even if company B is partly owned by the owner of Bank A, it may be difficult to point the same and will never be out in the open. This is because while the best principle of corporate governance calls for declaration of such a relationship, it need not be followed in case it is not easy to discover. Such have been the storylines of allegations made when it came to banks like Yes Bank and ICICI Bank though nothing has been proved as yet, while the heads of the organiza-tions had to step down. Admittedly, it may not be possible for the inspection team to assess whether a loan given to a firm which is not doing well will actually be serviced or not.

The way out is to learn from such blunders and create a system of early warning signals which provides clues on what could be going wrong in the system. Can we really think of what structures should be built in the system? The most impor-tant part here would be transparency in such revelations. The suggested model that needs to be followed is in two parts, one which is objective and the other is still subjective as it can be influenced by the CEO.

The objective model would involve the revelation of the following on a continuous basis, probably in the quarterly results so that there is complete transparency and would also guide the regulator as well as investors.

First, the growth in credit has to be monitored carefully which should be further broken down in the sectors where credit is growing at a fast rate. A complete schedule of the structure of credit and growth thereof would put in perspective the routing of credit. Presently while the growth in credit is known, the way it is disbursed is selectively revealed. Ideally, a detailed sector-wise breakup of credit will be indicative of the risk being taken by the bank. In case exposure to sectors which are in trouble increases, it would be known that the risk of NPAs increases. Often government policy can create turmoil in prospects for industry like telecom which needs to be highlighted by the bank.

Second, the growth in NPAs is a good indicator that has to be monitored. Here it is not just the headline number but also in incremental terms. This will give a good idea of how the assets are being managed. Often we tend to look at the NPA ratio which can be managed by increasing the denominator, which has been a standard practice followed by banks.

Third, while there is quarterly reporting of NPAs, a sectoral exposition in a stylized format should be revealed. This would again give an idea to investors on the state of the bank. Banks tend to be very selective here too and often reveal only the better part of the story. Presentations often will talk only of the sectors where the NPAs have come down and not where they have gone up. Here the RBI needs to specify the format in which information has to be given so that there is little flexibility afforded to the bank to change the format of presentation.

Fourth, all banks need to get their portfolio rated by external rating agencies. Here, it should be mandatory to state what proportion of the portfolio falls in various categories so that the investors are able to judge the quality of portfolio that is being carried. Today the decision is made on how growth takes place in business and the profit numbers. Those which take higher risk tend to settle for lower-rated companies where the returns are higher. There is nothing amiss in such a strategy, but the revelation of the same will add to transparency. In the west, the junk bond market is quite vibrant where institution invest in low-rated but high-yield bonds as part of strategy. As all listed banks work to enhance shareholder value, the investor can actually put a greater watch on bank policies than the regulator provided there which has enough transparency.

At the level of governance, the challenges are more acute because while the RBI can compel banks to be more transparent in sharing information, getting people to behave well is always tough. The issue of interconnected lending has to be dealt with more severity. Written statements need to be taken from the top management (which may be defined by the RBI) so that the lending decisions do not involve any such relationship. Taking a written declaration would make a difference in the way in which bankers behave. In fact, if there is interconnected lending, it should be stated upfront that there is an interest along with a justification that the project is a viable one. This would throw the onus on the top management to justify such loans.

The process of giving loans has to be through committees that are defined in a manner such that the top person does not have any say in the decisions. This is hard to crack because even when the CEO steps out of the Committee, the very fact that there is an inclination to garner business would mean that the others down the line would support such decisions. To bring in some discipline out here, the RBI should release a list of top 100 large companies that are facing high risk where the size of the company or loan can be stated as a threshold for which credit committees would have to provide a detailed explanation for disbursing the loan. This would be referred to in case of any enquiry in future if things go wrong.

The basic idea is not to stop such interconnected or risky loans from being given but to ensure that the concerned committees have debated the same and noted down their reservations when sanctioning such loans.

It can still be debated that this may not be adequate to thwart such decisions but would certainly put in some more checks. In fact, the transparency which has been advocated in providing certain numbers would be a market-oriented solution as investors would move out of a company if it sees decisions being taken that are not good for the bank.

14 Corporate Governance in Indian Banks

Corporate governance is an issue which pervades all discussions today when it comes to management of companies. For several years, corporate governance was more of an ideal that banks were to follow and those which did supposedly got good valuations in the market. When banking leaders spoke a global language and were ruthless in terms of how business grew which could also have meant dispensing with the old guard on grounds of being with the times, the markets applauded and investments just poured in.

The concept of corporate governance lays down the basic principles of how boards are structured and how they govern companies given that there is a principal-agency relationship between owners and management of any company. Owners of public limited companies are scattered and the management which runs the affairs of such an entity needs to be controlled in some way as they could tend to run their firms in their interest as distinct from the owners. This is where boards play a role as the directors who are appointed serve the interest of owners and hence bridge the asymmetrical relationship that is there.

Governance as an issue that came to the fore at the time of the financial crisis or the Lehman episode where it was realized that bank managements tended to take abnormal risks which brought in short-term gains for the company that in turn went with sharp rise in compensation. When the crisis set in and financial firms went down under, there was nothing that could be done and the owners and lenders took the hit. The management went free as there was no clause in their contracts which held them responsible. In fact, they got huge bonuses when the business expanded as did profits. In fact, being given stocks created a perverse incentive to take higher risk, make higher profits which led to higher valuation and hence increased their net worth.

As most members of senior management were given stock options, they were able to monetize the same when their firms did well. But as enterprise collapsed, their past gains remained intact. While reputation suffered for some, others have managed to come back into the corporate world. Such episodes have highlighted the importance of corporate governance in banks because this is one sector which thrives on other people's money. There are no tangible goods produced which support profits and accounting practices which involve complex systems and are accrual based which tends to cast a shadow on real performance. While the idea of stock options was to ensure that the management had skin in the game, there was a perverse incentive structure built which made boards award obscene stocks to the top management that had further incentive to take a high quantum of risk to prop up profits in the short run.

With this background, the concept of corporate governance in the Indian banking system can be analysed. There are two sets of banks which are of importance—public sector and private. Foreign banks are governed more on the overseas office rules and hence are out of purview of the discussion.

Some of the cases involving breach of governance are well known. The alleged nexus between Vijay Mallya and the banking system is still being investigated as is the case of Nirav Modi and the PNB. In both the cases, there were allegations made of connivance of the senior management with the business entrepreneur.

Similar allegations have been made about connected lending in case of the ICICI and Yes banks which are still being investigated. The truth will be known only after the investigations are completed. Also, in banking, such allegations are going to be a regular story because it is hard to maintain complete transparency when it comes to lending especially if the management has other business dealings indirectly. What is really required is transparency where lending decisions are put on the table and it is clearly noted that there is a connected interest. This would clear the way for the management personnel involved.

Let us look at PSBs first. They are owned by the government and will probably continue to be presently structured as there is an inherent incentive to keep them this way for reasons explained in other chapters of this book. The board members are selected by the government and hence would be bureaucrats, retired bankers, academicians, industry experts and so on. While they follow the processes of independent directors and executive and non-executive directors on the board, they are still appointed by the government. Next, the top management is again selected by the government and there is a Banking Board Bureau (BBB) in place which appoints senior management of PSBs. But the members of the Bureau are again selected by the government. Hence the structures are such that the owner has control over both the board and management. It is but natural that there would be a tendency for congruence between the two with the owners having the upper hand, which in this case is the government. All departments of the government work in a set up where the top man is always right and as political superiors have the power, their word becomes binding informally on everyone. Hence there tends to be a spirit of over-obedient behaviour rather than one of equals which makes such governance structures fragile.

The problem of NPAs in India in the PSBs came up mainly due to the process of lending which was dictated by the politicians. The various scams associated with different industries which finally led to creation of bad assets were due to what came to be called phone banking where an instruction given by a minister to a bank chairman that was never recorded became a practice. This is how several industrialists got favours as the nexus with politicians was stark especially when the industry was over regulated and involved natural resources. The management had no choice but to lend and the boards allowed all this to happen because of the conflict of interest. While at the end of the day it was logical to blame the collapse of governance for such developments, the fact is that the structures were such where the bankers could not be blamed for action because instructions came from the top. Hence, while there were incorrect decisions taken as there was no proof of written orders, there has been a tendency to chastise these bankers for incompetence or complicity, both of which are not necessarily true. Hence, it was the politicians and corporates which benefited from such loans while the bankers bore the brunt of investigation, loss of reputation and chastisement when things went wrong.

The onus is now on the government to really change the way in which governance is addressed as it is the owner of these banks. It is necessary to provide more independence to the directors as well as management to operate and achieve higher standards of governance. If appointments to boards or management are linked with patronage, governance can never be attained in a proper manner.

Therefore, corporate governance is elusive when it comes to PSBs. Even when phone banking has stopped bankers, it still has challenges as several so-called recommendations made by the government are orders to banks to execute them. Let us see how this plays out. The government calls all heads of PSBs to Delhi and they are told to lower interest rates. While owners have such a right, it is not in the spirit of corporate governance as commercial judgments should be left to the entity. Second, orders are given to lend to SMEs with threat of increments being held up. This does not give a choice to bankers who become slave to the fancies of the owners. Third, bankers are told to open 'Jan Dhan' accounts which do not hold for private banks. These are examples where governance norms are violated.

It is also revealed behind doors that appointments to boards of PSBs are based on the unwritten rule that awkward questions should not be raised especially if it comes to following dictates from above. Is this right? At one level it can be argued that as these banks are owned by the government, they have a right as owners to pass such instructions and whether right or not is representative of the owners' wishes. Directors are supposed to represent the owner which in the case of PSBs is the government. This cannot be contested but is not within the realm of true corporate governance.

If one scans the names of all directors on PSBs or heads (CMDs or MDs) one can trace whether or not they have been compliant with the wishes of the authority, and the way to go about is to see if they have gotten any postings in government-driven organizations post retirement. This will be indicative enough of the way things function in the public sector.

How about private banks? For a long time, it was believed that private banks were very different and that corporate governance was high on the scoring points of these entities. In fact, the heads of private banks always took a condescending tone on the issue of governance in PSBs to the extent of being more than sympathetic. Most of the private banks have a very esteemed Board of Directors and the composition of the top management, including the MD and CEO, are very good names with excellent credentials which include qualification that can be from the top-rated management institutes and iced with foreign degrees. This structure was not questioned ever except a couple of years back when the NPA issue surfaced. In fact, most of these heads were recognized for their brilliance, dynamism and ethics by various outfits which bestowed awards. They also tended to be involved in all the decisions and policy-making committees of the government and RBI, and had far greater representation than the PSBs due to the reverence which went with the term 'new private bank'.

They had ushered in technology and efficiency and changed the way banking was conducted by making everyone pay for all services which was unheard of in the past.

Some of the issues that have come to the fore are the following. First, the recognition of NPAs was an issue with these banks too which gradually came out in the open. Interestingly, what was initially felt to be a PSB issue, where NPAs were supposedly not fully revealed and came out once AQR was introduced, spread to these banks too. The under-reporting of NPAs was pandemic to the system as RBI inspection showed which led to penalties being imposed on these banks. They however agued it was only a case of interpretation by the regulator and that they had done nothing wrong. Second, the so-called reckless lending for which the PSBs were chastised held very much for these banks too as was evident in the last couple of years when the big cases revealed that they too had a good share. In fact, with the NPAs being taken to the IBC, the names of all lenders came out into the open. Third, some of the practices of the top management of some of the banks have come under enhanced scrutiny which has tarnished the image of the bankers and banks. Lending did not always seem to be based on an unbiased effort and decision taken could be linked with vested interests of those in power. Hence, while for PSBs it was a case of owner interference, for the private banks it was more of the CEO interference. While this is not widespread across banks, there have been instances which have been highlighted which sort of exposed their functioning.

Fourth, the selection process for the top management too has been on the discussion board as the concept of coteries which got created along the way is deep-rooted. It has become more of a revolving door where the top management remains the same and shares not just the top positions in critical areas like risk, credit, retail and treasury but also the spoils with the highest levels of compensation. Fifth, while PSBs often complained that the CEOs did not get a good enough tenure to make a difference to the bank, in case of private banks, critics argue that the issue is that the tenures appear to get extended for decades which are not good governance practices. Therefore, the governance practices in private banks have not been above board and questioned by critics on these grounds.

The RBI notification on the pay structures in private banks is in a way tough as it has been discussed elsewhere in the book; such interference does have a counterargument on the independence of such companies. The problem here is like this. Bank managements have awarded themselves very high salaries and stock options besides perquisites which as discussed elsewhere make the packages multiple times that of their counterparts in PSBs. Most of these packages were justified on grounds of superior performance as these banks posted accelerated growth in assets and profits when the times were good. However, aggressive lending in the early part of the decade was responsible for the pile of NPAs for which the senior management took no responsibility. Hence, while the PSB heads had to face the three Cs (Central Bureau of Investigation [CBI], Comptroller and Auditor General [CAG] and Central Vigilance Commission [CVC]), the private counterparts had their pay intact with no accompanying worries. This is the basis of the RBI coming down on the private bankers and bringing in the rule of the claw back of pay in case of failure of the bank.

Another issue which came up with private banks and governance is the structure of boards. While the RBI has brought in new structures for compensation of key management personnel especially those associated with credit and risk besides the executive directors, the board cannot be above it as it has in a way ratified all such packages. The observation made by critics is that even in the private sector, there is a symbiotic relation between the CEO and the board where the former appoints the latter who in turn decides on the compensation and tenure of the former. While this can never be proved, critics argue that the fact that what the RBI has found amiss has been missed by the Boards of the concerned banks which does testify to there being possibly some truth in some of these cases.

One of the questions that has been posed in this context is that the difference between the pay packets of PSB heads and private banks started deviating significantly in the last 15 years or so though to be fair to the latter, approval was given by the RBI. During the high growth phase of banking which also coincided with the regime that generated the high pile of NPAs, the private banks too were involved. Expansion of balance sheets had the downside of taking on higher risk which got exposed during the same time that the PSBs first came under the scanner. However, the management which was associated with this implosion did not quite face the flak like their PSB counterparts. This is a point that would set one thinking hard on the subject.

Also, the fact that most of these boards were overweight with very respectable names gives the feeling that the members were either indifferent to what went on or did not take action due to the symbiotic relationship that was built. This is a serious issue which came to the fore in the light of some irregularities that were highlighted in some cases.

Therefore, the problem of governance is prevalent for both the kinds of banks and is not specific just to the PSBs. A solution that can be put forward is the following. For PSBs, the appointment of Directors should be distanced from the government, which ostensibly does it through the BBB which is considered to be an independent body. The problem is that when appointments to the independent board are by the government, there would be a tendency to become compliant as it is possible that those appointments are based not completely on merit but also on the extent of human flexibility. In case of the private banks, the appointment should not be left to the management, which is what it all comes to. Normally the management would scout for good names and get it ratified by the regulator which in turn would agree with the same.

A way out is to have a repository of all persons who are either eligible to be directors or are already serving on other boards to be the ones to be tapped for this purpose. There can be a drop-down menu where there are certain qualifications that would be required with respect to having prior experience in banking with years of experience as a director on some other company. This would narrow down the list which can then be allocated by the RBI independently based on the size of the bank. In fact, given the talk of Artificial Intelligence in almost all business, the allocation can be made by an algorithm that will be independent of any interference. This would be even better than having RBI take the decision as there can always be the case of the central bank being influenced by the government when it comes to PSBs. This would be a transparent way in which the directors can be selected with a fixed term so that they would be free to give their view without the shadow of the government or the private sector management lurking.

Progressively, it has been realized that governance has become a major challenge in the corporate sector in every field. There is always a tendency for management personnel to pay themselves higher amounts irrespective of the performance with a cozy relationship with the Board. Often this gets stretched to tenure too which can roll over for several terms. This is something which can be checked when there are independent boards. While for non-deposit taking institutions, there can still be a case made of the management having such prerogative given that they could be majority owners of the company, in case of banking this is not the case. Therefore, to truly have independent boards, there needs to be such algorithms used. In fact, it is often felt that even the so-called independent directors or public interest directors may not be really immune to pressures from the owners (for PSBs) or management (private banks).

Also, such independent boards would ensure that a very important stakeholder, that is, employees get a fair deal. In some private banks, it has been seen at times that the management go in for VRSs where staff are forced to leave and the board ignores the same on grounds of it being an internal issue. The justification is always that costs have to be cut but invariably post such measures; the top management takes a very sharp hike in compensation packages.

It will be agreed that there is definitely a pressing require-ment to change the structure of these boards and use a different approach as the existing ones have not quite worked all the time and in all the cases. Also, this will help to bring in fresh ideas which are required for bringing about better governance prac-tices in a system which requires overhauling as it does appear that the time has come for the same.

15 Bank Mergers
Do They Make Sense?

Bank mergers are the flavour of the day. And the main reason is that everyone says that we need to have fewer banks especially if they are owned by the government. There are historical presentations made by management consultants which argue for having a three-tier structure, where the top layer consists of large banks which can get global. The middle tiers are meant for the urban areas while the smallest are niche entities that cater to specific segments. How is one to look at this issue?

The genesis of PSBs can be traced essentially to the era of nationalization where all banks which were in the private sector were nationalized in two stages in 1969 and 1980. The motivation was that these banks were to fulfil the socialist dream of inclusive banking (which is ironically still being spoken of for all banking). That is how several banks came up as the private banks were owned by the government. The number had grown to 29 including SBI and its 6 associate banks and 21 nationalized banks.

The purpose of nationalization was to first ensure that banking was available to all as were loans. This meant opening more branches irrespective of the business potential which also meant that more staff had to be hired. Hence, the employment

objective got embedded in this framework. There was less attention paid to how banks performed as the owner was the government and the prudential norms which exist today were not in
fashion even in the world.

While the purpose of nationalization was to bring the
entire structure of finance under the government, it led to
banks looking similar. While each bank tended to be strong in
a particular state, they were told to open branches and employ
more people so that banking becomes universal (this is again
being spoken of today when we look at new forms of banks like
payments banks and small banks). Therefore, there was scant
attention paid to quality or productivity and scale was most
important. It was not surprising that branches were opened across
the country and several echelons of staff employed as it became
an employment-generating business with a retinue of clerks,
peons and support staff. There were also important positions
to be given to those who worked well in the form of Chairman
or CEOs or Managing Directors depending on the stature of
the bank. There were second-level executives which could be
Executive Directors or General Managers or Deputy Managing
Directors who oversaw regions and could aspire to head the
bank. Therefore, there were plenty of jobs to be had and there
was in a way a race for the same as the spots were limited. While
these jobs were based on tenure and merit, the latter always was
flexible and was not free of political influences. The deal which
was informal was that once they became heads of, they had to be
more amenable to the requests from above which meant taking
a soft stance when it came to disbursing loans to their interests. The infamous phone banking phenomenon became the rule
where the bank head could not say no to the bosses in Delhi.

This structure was actually very firm and while the idea
of privatization was spoken of, there were few chances of this
fabric changing. While the normal reason given is that the trade
unions would not permit such change in ownership, which is
a fact, the absence of political will is palpable given the strong

expectations from the bankers. PSBs have traditionally been an important tool for the government to dispense of favours or implement a political agenda.

It has been almost two decades since the big management consultants have espoused the idea of merger of PSBs to create size and usher in efficiency. While this has been more of theory for a very long time, it is now a reality with three phases of such mergers being witnessed in the last few years. The first was the merger of SBI with its associates in 2017. The second was Bank of Baroda with Dena Bank and Vijaya Bank in 2018 and the third is a set of four mergers of various PSBs announced in 2019.

But the question to be asked is whether this will serve any purpose in case the basic ethos of PSBs does not change. This can be argued both ways.

Let us look at the arguments for such a merger. First, by merging banks which are strong in different regions like is the case of Bank of Baroda, Dena Bank and Vijaya Bank, there is useful consolidation as the strengths are leveraged. Second, the bank attains a size and can compete globally as well as internally for larger loans as the exposure norms are linked with the size of capital. Third, such a merged bank will command a better value in the market that will benefit the shareholders, which in this case is the government. Fourth, the strengths in human resources can be combined to enhance efficiency. Fifth, physical resources like ATMs, branches, technology can be shared and made seamless. In case of any such assets being superfluous, they can be dispensed with. Sixth, the culture can be changed to be more competitive as employees get out of the comfort zone. Finally, by also getting in a weak bank in the package, the merger in a way, addresses the issue of reviving the same as it now gets merged in a larger combined entity.

Now let us play the devil's advocate. First, if a private and PSB are merging, one can understand that there is value to be created. When it is two PSBs, the governance structure remains the same and hence does not make a difference. If the appointments are still being made indirectly by the government and the boards have limited power to guide the bank, then the same set of structures remains. As has been seen in the last five years, the government continuously urges banks to take decisions on interest rates and ensures compliance. Bank chiefs are summoned to Delhi and given instructions on what has to be done which holds irrespective of which government is in power. Strictly speaking, when the government is the owner, this can be done though it may not be proper from the point of view of corporate governance. There will be no change in this reporting structure and hence the merger will not change things in terms of governance.

Second is the quantum of staff. Whenever there is a merger, there will always be redundancy of staff as there are duplicate roles in the merging entities. When there are three banks concerned, there are three treasury heads, traders, credit appraising staff, risk management, HR and so on. What can one do with such multiple staff for each function? While in the private sector, rationalization is the order where normally the weaker bank sees wide-scale retrenchment, the same cannot be done here as the unions will not allow the same. The government has also assured the staff that there will be no rationalization and that all jobs would be safe. Adjusting staff becomes even more challenging when branches are closed down as often the two banks have branches in the same vicinity. Therefore, overstaffing cannot be ruled out. At times a VRS can be offered and the cost is amortized or capitalized over a time period. When such schemes are offered, they are fair and could also be attractive which adds to cost which can be amortized but subsequently has a leaner look.

In private banks, the policy followed is quite different and straightforward. A VRS is floated which is actually a mandatory order in practice. The staff that is not required is told to take the handshake and leave or else face retribution in terms of postings to a remote area or a transfer to a less relevant department. If there is an RBI order restricting lowering of staff for a time period, the senior members of the bank which is taken-over have to deal with smaller portfolios and loss of seniority as they end up reporting to juniors in the bank which is taking over their bank. The signal is that they have to move on as conditions become distinctly uncomfortable.

Third, while there is talk of the merged entity becoming bigger and stronger, it should be remembered that we are adding two balance sheets. If one bank is undercapitalized and the other is over capitalized, the merged entity will have the sum of both, which is similar to how the total capital of all PSBs is reckoned. Similarly, if one is profit-making and the other is loss-making, the new entity has a net profit of the sum and does not really improve the overall position of PSBs in general and only camouflages the same. We are not getting in new money as everything belongs to the government anyway.

Fourth, while there is always talk of taking larger exposures in case the bank is big, there is a contradiction. The RBI is trying its best to move banks away from large exposures as it is rightly argued that such borrowing has to come from the bond market. This being the case, there is not much reason for us to have larger banks on the grounds of taking larger exposures. With effect from 1 April 2019, the RBI has fixed the large exposure limit of a bank to any company at ₹10,000 crore which means that additional borrowing has to be from the corporate bond market (the rule says 50% of incremental borrowing). Not adhering to this norm would attract penalties in terms of additional capital charge on banks for the incremental amounts. The objective was twofold. The first was to develop the corporate bond market and the second was to de-risk the portfolio of banks in terms of concentration to large companies.

Now, if the idea here is to lower the concentration risk of banks by lowering the overall exposure norms on large companies, then the argument of having bank mergers to foster such exposures does not fall in place.

Fifth, merger of PSBs will mean substantial disruption in hierarchies which have been earned over time. This is a real issue when they have to be reworked with a substantial number of overlapping senior professionals getting a deal which is less rewarding than the existing portfolios.

In the past, bank mergers have been between private banks for various reasons like the Centurion Bank with the Bank of Punjab, which later were merged with the HDFC Bank. There has been a takeover of other banks like the ING Vysya Bank by Kotak Mahindra Bank. In other cases where PSBs were involved, it was more a case of failed private bank like the Global Trust Bank being revived through merger with the Oriental Bank of Commerce. In the past, it had bought up Bank of Credit and Commerce International (BCCI), which was again a failed bank. SBI had taken over the associate banks, and the jury is still out on whether or not this has added value. The same will hold for the Bank of Baroda–Dena Bank–Vijaya Bank merger.

But the important point here is whether or not merging PSBs really makes sense at the ideological level of theoretically leveraging on synergies which is what is normally posited. The other point is whether the act is one of the governance structures changing or not and in this case will definitely be retained. Therefore, the main benefits from a bank merger involving PSBs will be a horizontal summation of balance sheets in the accounting sense. There would be some rationalization of costs in terms of human and physical infrastructure that may not be very evident in the first few years. But beyond these potential benefits, the functioning of these banks may not quite change.

The decision taken in 2019 was to bring about mergers of PSBs within specified timelines. The first amalgamation done was Bank of Baroda with Vijaya Bank and Dena Bank which has become the benchmark for the future. The ones to be brought about now are PNB with OBC and the United Bank of India, Canara Bank with Syndicate Bank, Union Bank with Andhra Bank and Corporation Bank, and Indian Bank with Allahabad Bank. While there has been a strong rationale provided for merging these banks based on synergies to be had, they are still not too convincing as the governance structures are not to change.

The puzzle here is that PSBs have been an instrument of politics irrespective of the government in power. A number of policies which score high on the political agenda can be implemented only through PSBs. Hence, when it comes to directed lending to say the small-scale sector or implementation of Jan Dhan, there is need to have control over the implementation of the same. Hence, irrespective of whether there are 20 PSBs or 10 merged PSBs, the directive would still hold with no flexibility being provided to deviate from the norm. This means that as long as these banks are owned by the government, the operations will not really change. To make a merger successful in the context of PSBs, getting in private ownership can make a difference though as has been seen in case of any such action in any other field, the terms of engagement are cast in stone to get the staff along, which is a challenge though not impossible. Presently, mergers of PSBs may not really make too much difference and the timing of the same would divert a lot of attention from the business of banking as all concerned banks start reworking their models.

The merger of PSBs analogy can be carried to the kind of disinvestment that we are pursuing where the government retains 51 per cent ownership. The fabric of the company does not change and it is only the shareholding pattern which can be diversified. The working principles are the same and there is hardly any distinction from the earlier structures.

Therefore, there is not a very convincing argument for the merger of PSBs with one another. To the extent, there will be less time spent in supervising a dozen banks compared with twenty, the regulator may be better off. But this was never the point anyway. The mergers seen so far are still a bit too early to judge with the present environment casting a shadow on all banks.

16

Privatizing PSBs

One Step Forward, Two Behind

The idea of disinvestment of the government in the banking space is open for debate. It is often felt that the government needs to move out of commercial activity, which includes banking so that the private sector ethic comes in and banks are able to function on market principles. In this context, there is talk on the government reducing its stake in the PSBs to less than 50 per cent and letting private investors hold at least 51 per cent. But this has not been acceptable and so far the working of the disinvestment process has been to keep it above the majority threshold so that the ownership remains with the state. Let us see what are the issues involved.

To begin with, it can be posited whether at all private banks are better than PSBs? While the general performance has been better in statistical terms, the recent episodes of slippages in governance in some private banks and controversies raised in others has made it even more debatable whether a private setting is better than a public setting. In fact globally too when one looks at the financial crisis, some of the biggest failures were in the private space which means that while overtly government ownership makes the structures clumsy, private players could be worse in terms of governance which was at the heart of the matter a decade back. The argument was that shareholders decide on governance in private banks and hence the government is out of it. But since any banking failure normally means rescue by the government through the PSBs using public money, this defence is not sustainable.

The *raison d'etre* (reason for being) of privatizing banks in India is to just free them of interference. PSBs become breeding grounds for dispensing favours and while bankers are supposedly free, often there are instructions that come on phone which cannot be disobeyed. The favours granted to several large business houses have their genesis in these structures where decisions are taken in the political houses and passed on to the bankers. This is one reason as to why the NPA levels have been higher in the PSBs compared with the private banks as there was indirect coercion to lend especially when it came to infra projects or large steel-and-power projects. If the private banks also were impacted by similar consortium lending, they could be blamed for bad judgment or cronyism but the finger of doubt cannot be directed at the government. Therefore, another set of regulation is required to ensure that the best practices are followed.

Once it is agreed that private ownership is better than public ownership, then the case of moving the government out can be taken up. In fact, the government is almost always in agreement that it should move out of commercial activity as this is not what it is good at doing. Yet, there is a level of hesitation which is close to reluctance to do so because some enterprises are very useful sources of revenue for the government especially those in the oil and energy sectors. The same holds for banks where the government is not willing to dispense with the socialist ideology even though this has been done in all other areas.

Presently, the government holds a substantially large share in all PSBs as given in Table 16.1 for 2017.

The government's predicament is quite understandable. Moving below 50 per cent would also mean that the private investors would have a say in the running of these banks. The unions

Table 16.1. Share of Government in PSBs in Percentage

Bank	Share	Bank	Share
United Bank of India	85.2	Vijaya Bank	70.3
Indian Bank	82.1	Dena Bank	68.6
Bank of Maharashtra	81.6	Canara Bank	66.3
Central Bank of India	81.3	Allahabad Bank	65.9
Punjab and Sind Bank	79.6	Punjab National Bank	65.0
Indian Overseas Bank	79.6	Union Bank of India	63.4
UCO Bank	76.7	Andhra Bank	61.3
IDBI Bank Limited	74.0	State Bank of India	61.2
Bank of India	73.7	Bank of Baroda	59.2
Syndicate Bank	72.9	Oriental Bank of Commerce	58.4
Corporation Bank	70.8		

Source: www.rbi.org.in.

would never support such a move as it would put a large number of jobs in jeopardy. Second, there would be umbrage from the opposition parties and hence it would be a political issue. Third, when they were performing well, there was a regular flow of dividend from the banks to the government. Banking is a very profitable business as the spreads in India are much higher than that in other markets and hence in the absence of NPAs and provisioning, can earn high profits which are returned to the government in the form of dividend. Therefore, it is profitable to keep them under the fold just like the oil companies, which continuously churn dividends for the government. Fourth, continuing majority ownership of banks is always useful for the government as several programmes can be pushed forth through these banks. There can be a long list of these motivations:

- Loan melas of the 1970s. These were very popular as the central and state government went overboard giving loans to farmers in general as well as corporates where strict targets were put. Controlling the channels of finance is a strategic tool used by all governments. More recently, banks were asked to lend to SMEs with new innovative schemes being brought in with bankers being warned of retribution in case of not meeting targets. This was for only PSBs.

- Jan Dhan accounts had to be opened by banks which ran the risk of not having an economical size of balance to justify such accounts. But a choice was not given and PSBs had to open 305 million accounts of a total of 383 million as of March 2020 with another 65 million coming from RRBs. Interestingly, the contribution of non PSB-RRB was very much limited as these accounts by nature were not net income accruing as there were to be no charges on these balances. Also, the per ticket size was too low to justify them on commercial grounds.

- SME lending is a fad at times when banks are told to aggressively lend to this sector under the MUDRA scheme. While non-PSBs also meet their targets, this can be pushed more aggressively beyond the target by the government when it is a PSB.

- Infra lending was the big push given in the post-financial crisis period where the PSBs had to lend aggressively to these projects while the RBI was accommodative in terms of lowering the interest rates.

- Affordable housing is one of the more recent fads of the government where a push is being given here to ensure that the poor have access to low-cost housing which is financed by banks. Small ticket mortgages are typically less lucrative for banks and private banks steer clear of them while PSBs have little choice here.

Therefore, pushing forth any development agenda which could have political undertones is possible when banks are owned by the government. Once they are out of the fold, it would be challenging to have these programmes fulfilled. This is so as orders concerning banking come from the RBI as the regulator which cannot impose measures which are not prudent. But as owners of PSBs, the government can order the chiefs to have certain targets achieved.

Lastly, selling off banks to the private investors is always a dicey issue as the timing of the market is always challenging. There is always a fear that if a major sale takes place at a lower price, then there would be ruckus in the Parliament in case prices go up subsequently. The opposition, which holds for any parties out of power, would make a charge that the financial heights have been sold at a very low price. Hence, there is an inherent incentive not to take any hasty action and status quo appears to be very much in order.

Quite interestingly, just when the idea of privatizing PSBs gained favour in the discussion circles, the RBI came up with the AQR process where there was a change in the way in which assets were classified. This had exposed the fault lines in several PSBs which raised questions on their practices as the NPA revelations increased which in turn impacted their profitability as provisions increased commensurately leading to an erosion of capital.

The curious case here is that the government had got in the BBB to address issues of governance when the INDRADHANUSH scheme (a scheme launched by the NDA government in August 2015 on assuming power to reform the entire structure of PSBs) was launched. The basic idea was that all appointments at the higher level of Chairman and Board members would be appointed by this Board. However, after taking in a couple of private bankers as Board members and one as head of a bank, it was back to the normal route of appointments. The reasons were also that there were not too many private bankers who were willing to risk coming to the PSB circle where there would be more constraints in operation besides the compensation. Also, with the number of cases being slapped against PSB heads due to the NPA crisis, being in this segment was unattractive for anyone who had not faced the CBI, CIC and CVC.

Therefore, the issue of privatizing PSBs will continue to be debated but it would be very unusual if it actually does happen. It would require a lot of will to go in for such a step given the myriad issues which have been discussed. Also, the present state of disruption even in private banks can make the government ask the bigger question: Are Private banks really very different from PSBs? While the temptation to garner funds to support budgets will always be there for the government, as a first step it needs to be seen if there is at least a part stake sale closer to the 51 per cent level when the banks are back to normal and valuation is attractive in the market. The market will finally take a call also on whether the merger of PSBs which hopefully should be consummated in a year or so strikes the right chord.

17

Capitalizing PSBs
Whose Baby Is It?

PSBs are owned by the government and for all practical purposes it looks like that the latter is not willing to give up control of these entities. The reasons, as argued elsewhere, can range from social-istic tendencies to controlling the flow of credit decisions and can be taken as given. Against this background, what should be the role of the government when it comes to capitalizing banks?

Capital adequacy is probably the most critical regulatory norm for banks which has been designed by the BIS framework that has been evolving over time and has been implemented in stages. The rule says that banks have the backing of what is called own capital which is broadly speaking the sum of share capital and reserves which is defined as a ratio to risk-weighted assets. A ratio of 9 per cent says that if risk-weighted assets have to be created of ₹100, then ₹9 should be the bank's own capital. Within this classification, there can be two tiers with more detailed classifications. The entire purpose of this exercise is that if the bank is going down, then there is enough of own capital which can take in the shock. There is also the Basel III version which brings in liquidity ratios and capital conservation buffers, and hence the ratio can be defined the way the individual central bank wants over a period of time.

The assets too are given risk weights depending on the quality of the asset. Hence if it is a government security, there is virtual zero risk and if the loan is non-standard then there can be higher risk based on the rating assigned by external rating agencies. This is a practice followed in India under what has been called the standardized approach of Basel II where every asset or rather loan has to be rated independently. Depending on the rating given, the risk weight assigned would vary. In some countries which have followed the advanced approach, banks are allowed to rate their portfolio. But then there can always be an incentive to overstate the quality of the assets so that less provision is made for capital as all banks want to save on the same. Therefore, the approach taken by the RBI makes sense. It is not surprising that as banks become reckless in lending, the risk-weighted assets increase in value and put pressure on them to get in more capital.

The situation that developed post the AQR was that as banks increased their NPA levels, provisions had to be made which led to losses being incurred which were made up by drawing down on the net worth. This meant that the capital adequacy ratio slipped as one component of the capital, that is, reserves turned negative. The remedy was to get in more capital. How could this be done?

There are two options here. The first is to go in for disinvestment of the capital so as to get private players to also participate. But this was not acceptable as the idea of privatizing these banks is a big 'no'.

The second was that even if one went to the market given the state of these banks, there would not be any taker for such shares and the exercise would have been futile. Here, there would be a fresh issue of capital that would be placed in the market which could get in some equity. Therefore, the finger pointed back at the government which had to capitalize them.

Logically the government should be capitalizing these banks as they own them. Just like how the promoter is called upon to capitalize firms which could be going down under, the same holds for the PSBs. This is where the conundrum lies. The government has limited ability to capitalize the banks as there is not much fiscal space. With the budget being tight, the government has not been able to allocate more than ₹20,000 crore to 25,000 crore on an annual basis in this regard. Further, there has also been the tricky question of which banks have to be capitalized? Should it be the well-run banks which can grow and contribute to the credit requirement and hence growth, or should it be used for resuscitating banks in trouble? To begin with, the government preferred to say that capital would be looked at as 'growth capital', that is, which will help the better-run banks to expand. This did not answer the question of what would happen to those which were making losses? Subsequently, it was decided to provide for both sets of banks so that growth and sustenance objectives were met.

This is where the concept of floating recapitalization bonds was mooted. It is one of the more innovative methods used for providing capital to the banks without really taking on any fiscal strain. The process followed in 2018 was that the government would raise recapitalization bonds of ₹65,000 crore. These bonds would be subscribed to by the banks which required capital. However, they would not pay any money for these bonds which carry a fixed coupon rate, as the same money would be given back to them in the form of the capital that is required to stay afloat.

Therefore, by a simple accounting entry the problem has been addressed. The only cost for the government would be the interest that has to be paid on these bonds to the banks. The banks would be happy as they get capital as well as interest on these bonds. This is a marvel in financial engineering. The disinvestment process in India has been quite warped as this has involved a roundabout method of a company's stake being sold to other public sector companies so that ownership remains with the government. The same could have been done here too where the SBI instead of, say, the LIC buys stake of other PSBs. The recap approach has been singular in that it becomes a direct transaction between the government and the banks with little pain except the interest which will be a recurring expense.

This is similar to the concept of oil bonds that used to be floated earlier when fuel was heavily subsidized wherein the OMCs (oil marketing companies) would subscribe to these bonds in lieu of payments that were due. This was a compromise solution so that the subsidy bill did not increase any further. In both cases, liability of the government increases and interest is the recurring cost but there is no transfer of money from one entity to the other.

Ideally, capital infusion should be through additional funds rather than such accounting entries which merely transfer funds from one account to another and make the bank viable. This cannot be done on a regular basis for sure and it is essential for banks to actually enter the market and raise funds or have the government disinvest and get other buyers to infuse capital. The practice of issuing bonds should be the last resort and never the first option. This would also be analogous to one PSB issuing bonds and having other PSBs subscribe to the same. But the same has been justified on grounds that the IMF also allows such transactions and hence there is nothing amiss.

The view here is that while such practices are legitimate in terms of being acceptable by global standards, it still smacks of our approach of 'jugaad' where we look at ways to move around the system rather than play within the same. Playing within the system would mean funding the same through the budget which is what parent companies do when subsidiaries need to be rescued for any reason. We have now set a precedent which can serve as a justification for further such action.

18

How Free Are Banks?

....

How free are our banks in the decisions taken by them? There are two sets of banks which dominate the banking horizon—public and private banks. Prima facie it appears that private banks are relatively freer than their counterparts in the public sector. Foreign banks too exist but are fairly niche in nature and for all purposes fall outside the ambit of this discussion. This can be examined in detail.

PSBs are owned by the government and hence by their very nature are subservient to the owners. This does not hold for private banks where the owners tend to be anonymous and hence do not really exert any pressure on the management by virtue of being owners. This was not the case earlier for DFIs and FIs which had established commercial banks where there was scope for the owner to drive the bank by virtue of dominating the board of the bank and having the prerogative to appoint the managing director and CEO.

The control starts from the organizational setup. The staffing pattern and process for recruitment is decided by the government and the Banking Services Board takes a call on these aspects. Hence, banks have limited flexibility in recruitment as well as compensation. In the last decade, lateral recruitment has been permitted for specialized functions where the compensation structure is different as these are contract-based. Therefore, there is dualism in some structures like economists, legal, communication experts who could come in as consultants and have a pay scale that is different from the rest of the staff. This has been a challenge as it is hard to get the right talent at times as there is preference for private banks where the pay packages are substantially higher. Also, the perception is that private banks offer more vibrancy in terms of work culture with little red tape and hierarchies. Working with PSBs gives a *sarkari* (official) feeling where everything is top-down and the rules are intractable. The presence of unions ensures that for normal banking activity the hierarchy holds and there is limited scope for lateral movement, though this can happen across PSBs which will not distort the pay structures. Banks have been trying to push the case for recruitment from management institutes which is difficult given that the normal process involves a competitive examination which is open to all persons with the requisite qualification. The regular staff has to take competitive exams which are followed by an interview process.

Is this right or wrong? Based on performance across banks, there is no strong reason to believe that private bankers with higher pay packages deliver better results even though this is the preconceived notion.

Second, PSBs have limited flexibility in terms of dealing with staff numbers. While voluntary retirement is a scheme that exists, it is often used by personnel who have served tenure and move over to a private bank and take this advantage. But staff rationalization through the 'hire and fire policy' is not possible where a plus is for the employees but a negative when the bank which wants to cut on costs when it is believed that the workforce is less productive. This is the main reason why it has been argued elsewhere in the book on PSB mergers that cost rationalization is not easy to accomplish. The same holds for other expenses like travel or perquisites which go with public office that cannot be reduced irrespective of the state of the finances of the bank. Hence while basic salaries are much lower than private banks, these benefits add considerably which cannot be rationalized.

Third, the physical infrastructure like banks has been tough to touch. Nationalization meant opening branches everywhere and while banks have been allowed to close down branches if they are not viable, it does become difficult to take such a decision given the varied interest groups. One of the challenges is relocating the staff as well as accounts as deposit holders cannot be told that their balances are now in a different branch in another town or village. This holds especially for the rural and semi-urban branches when business levels are not high. In urban or metro cities, it is still possible to do so.

Fourth, political programmes have to be pursued to the hilt by these banks. For example, Jan Dhan was forced on PSBs and often branch managers faced the repercussions of transfers and increments being affected in case a certain number of accounts were not opened. The same holds for other initiatives taken by the government in the sphere of inclusive banking. At times, the Minister makes a threat of holding back of increments in case branch managers are not meeting their SME lending targets. This cannot be done for private banks and hence the freedom to lend is often masked in these pressures.

Fifth, the basic act of lending is also opaque and the big lending is normally ordered on the phone line where the CMD has no choice but to obey the political leader. Non-compliance can lead to a transfer or withdrawal of patronage post retirement. One can savour the importance of this patronage when the post-retirement assignments of retired bankers and central bankers are tracked over the years. Some of them would always be on committees or be directors on boards of public institutions. Often it is not possible to separate the true value of these personnel as against being compensation for being compliant when in service.

Sixth, the appointment of heads of PSBs and the other board-level members, which can be both as executives as well as independent directors is far from being transparent. The BBB was established to bring in such transparency but here too there could be strong preferences based on recommendations made from above. Ideally, a UPSC-like system must prevail where the applications are scrutinized independently and the shortlisted candidates are called for interviews for selection. When it works for the entire bureaucracy, it should hold for these senior positions too as it reduces the scope for interference.

Seventh, we do hear of PSB heads being summoned to Delhi often where there are instructions passed on how to deal with interest rates. This normally happens when the government is not too happy with the interest rate transmission in the system that it almost orders the bankers to lower interest rates. This is not done for private banks which have autonomy. This can however be justified by the supporters on grounds that the government is the owner of these banks and has the prerogative to have these changes made. But freedom to make commercial decisions definitely impinges under these conditions.

Therefore, the entire retinue of selection of personnel is structured and tends to get opaque as one moves up the echelon. The compulsions to fulfil political agenda are more on PSBs and hence flexibility is limited. While compensation in monetary terms is low, there is a large variety of perquisites which could exceed what those in the private sector get. But at the time of retirement, the CMDs could feel the sudden fall in income which can affect their lifestyle which provides an incentive to move away from ethical standards when in office. This has been one of the reasons given for some bankers to get tangled with the investigative agencies on this score.

How about private sector banks? Here the picture is different where there is no ordering from the top. While the names of the CEOs have to be agreed upon by the RBI, the shadow of the government stops here. The CEO is answerable to the Board which is supposed to represent the interests of the shareholders. These shareholders are generally anonymous and do not really get to know how the bank works and often only look at the dividend paid or the share value. Actual operations remain out of the range of interest for these bank boards.

These banks have full freedom in staffing pattern as well as compensation. There are no fixed structures when it comes to promotions and often there are strong biases in promotions which can be seen in banks that have projected the prodigies that tend to be very young compared with the PSBs—the very senior level could be in their late-30s or early-40s compared with their counterparts who would tend to be in their mid-50s. The lending processes are also opaque but of a different variety as was witnessed in the case of some banks in the recent past. This can be retained because the buck stops at the Board and if this structure is subservient to the CEO, then everything falls in place. Therefore, this kind of freedom can breed different kinds of challenges for these banks.

What is the right structure then? The private sector framework is definitely more robust and would attract talent because there is more freedom to work within the rules laid down and no interference from outside. This is a big advantage in any FI and should ideally be brought into the PSB architecture. It is not necessary to privatize to get in the private sector ethic but is more a case of owners changing their mindset to ensure that freedom is given to bankers in running the business. If this can be achieved, we need not really have to talk of privatizing PSBs which can reach the same efficiency levels as their private counterparts.

19

Loan Waivers
Making Merry When the Going Is Good

Loan waivers are probably the most populist policy of successive governments at both the state and central levels. Giving waivers is always a standard elections promise which is followed up with fairly grandiose announcements once the party comes to power. It is a way to directly impact the lives of farmers and help them out of their stress levels. This has become very important of late as the monsoons have been erratic in various pockets which invariably cause distress to farmers who do not have access to irrigation. Normally, farmers in the more arid and rain-dependent areas are vulnerable which includes Maharashtra, Madhya Pradesh, Chhattisgarh, Telangana, Andhra Pradesh, Rajasthan and Karnataka. In the last few years it was also noticed that even when there were good supplies, farmers did not get the requisite price and distress sale was the result which in turn impacted their incomes and ability to service their debt.

The idea of loan waiver is the following. The government announces that all loans of a value of up to a certain amount would be forgiven by banks which would be compensated for by the concerned government. The waiver amount can be shared by the centre and state or could be done unilaterally. Farmers are identified on the basis of the recorded size and it could refer to those owning a certain size of the land who qualify for the same. The scheme could be 100 per cent waiver or part waiver. At times, for those who service a certain proportion of their debt, the balance could be written off with the compensation coming from the government to the bank. The amount that is waived is to be provided for in the Budget as at the end of the day it has to be paid by the government. The farmer is better off because the loan does not have to be repaid and the bank is glad that the NPA is off its books now. Therefore, it is a win-win situation where the government gains the favour of the farmer who is now debt-free.

How does this really work? This is interesting because there is a difference between making an announcement and invoking the same. Often it is felt that the amount cannot be borne by the government because of the fiscal deficit going out of hand. The point here is that while the government makes such announcements, it never specifies the time period when this will be spread. It can be over a period of time or may not be the specified amount for various reasons.

Let us look at some of these cases of loan waivers. Table 19.1 is drawn from RBI's publication: State Finances: Study of Budgets 2019–2020. During the last five years, some states have made an impact by making rather grandiose announcements on the waivers to be made. Andhra Pradesh in 2014–2015 announced ₹24,000 crore but so far has just about made allocations of a little over 50 per cent, with FY20 giving a skip.

Both Maharashtra and Uttar Pradesh made announcements which had economists cringing as the numbers were significant in terms of potential increase in the fiscal deficit. But as can be seen in Table 19.1, after the first year, the allocations for the same came down sharply. More recently, three states—Rajasthan, Madhya Pradesh and Chhattisgarh—made announcements post a new government being formed, but the allocations made in the budget were quite insignificant as it has been done keeping in mind the fiscal space permitted.

Table 19.1. Fiscal Impact of States' Farm Loan Waiver Programs (₹ Crore)

State	Year of Announcement	Amount Announced	Amount Provided in the Budget						
1	2	3	2014–2015	2015–2016	2016–2017	2017–2018	2018–2019 RE	2019–20 BE	
			4	5	6	7	8	9	
1. Andhra Pradesh	2014–2015	24,000	4,000	742	3,512	3,602	875		
2. Telangana	2014–2015	17,000	4,250	4,250	2,957	4,016		6,000	
3. Tamil Nadu	2016–2017	5,280			1,682	1,870	884	807	
4. Maharashtra	2017–2018	34,020				15,020	6,500	405	
5. Uttar Pradesh	2017–2018	36,360				21,102	5,500	600	
6. Punjab	2017–2018	10,000				348	5,500	3,000	
7. Karnataka	2018–2019	44,000				3,917	11,965	12,650	
8. Rajasthan	2018–2019	18,000					3,000	3,240	
9. Madhya Pradesh	2018–2019	36,500					5,000	8,000	
10. Chhattisgarh	2018–2019	6,100					4,223	5,000	
Total		231,260	8,250	4,992	8,151	49,875	43,447	39,703	

Source: www.rbi.org.in.

Arguably, these announcements are made more as political statements which are not backed up with action as there are fiscal constraints along the way. But they have an impact in terms of being populist as they hold out hope for the farmers who think they could qualify for such waivers. Human memory is short and one may never recollect the amount announced and actually given.

This is the factual position of loan waivers which can be kept in mind when theoretical arguments are given in support of against such acts.

When it comes to discussing loan waivers, there are different groups involved with each having their perspective. First is the farmer constituency which would always welcome such measures as it actually means that they do not have to repay loans. This is a welcome step at any time as it means a monetary gain. Normally the waiver schemes have conditions attached where it could be cherry-picking the farmers to be covered which would normally be from the marginal and small categories. Also, at times there is an added condition that the loans of a smaller limit would qualify to ensure that the larger farmers do not get included in the scheme. It can also be linked with the crop concerned as drought, for example, can affect the cotton crop in which case the sugarcane farmer should not be covered and hence the loan scheme would target this particular farmer category. And last, there is also a condition put where the chosen farmers would get a percentage written off in case they repay a larger part. Hence, if the farmer repays 80 per cent of the loan, the balance will be forgiven. Therefore, the farmers' position is always at an advantage and in the worst-case scenario can get excluded.

But interesting fallout is the moral hazard concern which is there in all such schemes. Farmers will have an incentive not to repay even if they had the ability because there is a forgiveness plan which has been announced, or could be announced. This holds especially if there is a prospective date and therefore the government has to be careful in making the announcement. Often it is based on a past date where it is easier to identify the beneficiaries. Here too there is a perverse incentive created not to repay loans because once farmers get to know that there are adverse weather conditions which can lead to crop failure for other farmers, they could drag their feet when it comes to repaying their debt with the hope that a waiver scheme will be announced at some point of time. This is a credible assumption to make when the elections are around the corner and hence the game options are opened for them.

Bankers are the second set of concerned persons when these waiver schemes are announced. Normally such schemes would apply to only PSBs in which the private bankers get excluded. But if they are comprehensive, they would cover all banks. The idea of a waiver is that the banks do not keep the loan which is not being serviced by the farmer on its books but write it off as the government will be paying for the same. This is useful insofar as that capital gets released as the NPA level comes down. Practically speaking, bankers are not too comfortable because of two reasons. When the government has to pay for it, the money will not come in immediately and there is a time lag which can get extended as the former may choose to roll over such payments in case there are financial constraints which are almost always the case. Bankers however are ultra-cautious when commenting on loan waivers and normally prefer not to make any statement especially if they belong to the public sector. While the compensation has to come from the government, even if there are delays they prefer not to talk about the same and invite the wrath of their owners.

The second is that the credit culture gets vitiated. Farmers would deliberately choose not to repay knowing that the government will step in and until the picture is clear on whether or not support will be provided, the banker has to keep the account alive. Also, bankers may be more liberal while giving loans and lower their due diligence once this kind of culture comes in. Therefore, ideally, bankers are not too comfortable with such waivers as it disrupts the core principles of banking.

The third party involved is the regulator, RBI. The central bank is the regulator which oversees credit and is keen on the system being strong with few slippages. Regulation is being framed continuously to ensure that loans given follow certain principles and are also adhered to completely be in spirit. There are regular audits and inspection to ensure that the rule of the book is being followed. Therefore, a central bank would be against such waivers as it creates leakages and, in a way, tarnishes the culture of lending and borrowing. Hence while the RBI is never too vocal about criticizing loan waivers, the view taken is that this should not ideally be there as it can become a nasty habit in future.

The last party involved is the government, which can be either the central or concerned state government or a combination of both in case the amount is shared. Here, there is a direct gain for the government as it first helps the farmers in distress and based on the latter's memory can be useful at the time of elections. However, such outflows have to continuously match in the budget numbers and this is where the challenge lies. As shown earlier, the initial announcement made is always lofty and of a high magnitude. But accommodating the same in the Budget has its limitations as funding can be a problem especially so if it is not made during the budget formulation. Therefore, while the announcement is for a certain number, in practice it could be much lower as and when it is implemented and could also be spread across the years to accommodate the amount. But strategically, it is a very effective move to show that it cares for the farmers and to the extent that it is provided will help farmers.

At the ideological level, the question to be answered is whether this is sustainable or not. Indian agriculture, especially kharif crops, is always susceptible to the monsoons as not more than 60 per cent is covered by irrigation. Therefore, there will be crop failures on account of inadequate monsoon which will lead to the farmers' distress as they will not be able to repay their loans. Does this mean that governments will pitch in every year in various states at the time of elections to write-off loans of farmers? Further, if this is what governments believe, then it should be an ongoing scheme every year where these waivers are announced and implemented. This is clearly not sustainable. Also given that there are a lot of cash transactions taking place between the government and farmer, adding this additional scheme can be financially onerous. Also, it penalizes farmers who pay on time as they would not be getting any benefit for being regular with such payments.

Is there a solution away from waiving loans which is more feasible? One can actually think of having insurance for farmers which becomes mandatory when a loan is taken. This should be automatic so that the premium is added to the cost of the loan. Hence if a farmer is getting a loan at 7 per cent, the one-time insurance fee can be 0.5 per cent of the amount which can be charged with the amount. The premium that is charged can then be subsidized by the state and central government so that the farmer pays only a part of the insurance fee. This way every loan has an insurance cover which can be overseen by the bank.

Alternatively, crop insurance can be made mandatory so that a crop failure will make the insurance company pay for the loss so that the loan can also be repaid. A combination of the two should be implemented with the government chipping in with the subsidy on premium so that the right mix is obtained and a solution is found. This will be equitable and spread across all farmers so that there is no exclusion. This is a better way of addressing farmer distress, which has turned out to have more political overtones that have marred the operations and not addressed the core issue of protecting farmer income. Here too insurance companies are not too keen on providing such coverage because of the risk involved.

At a different level, it is argued that there can be nothing amiss in a system of waivers especially so if one looks at the amount of money lost by the banking system when they write off debts of corporates or restructure the same which involves lower interest rates (which is a loss of income for banks) and haircuts on principal payments at times. If corporate loans, which are the bulk of big-ticket NPAs, can be written off or compromised, what is wrong is merely waiving off loans of farmers where there is actually no loss for the bank.

The last argument is compelling as it is based on the ability of the government to provide for the same through the budget. Ideally, waivers should not be there either for farmers or corporates. It cannot be right for one set and wrong for another. A developing country like ours is in a tricky situation where NPAs arise for reasons which are specific to our environment. Sudden change in regulation can affect a sector that goes down under and an under-insured farming sector runs the risk of crop failure and bad debts every year as it is heavily dependent on the rainfall. Waivers hence should be selective and can be given for farmers as this is a vulnerable section which requires support the most. As agricultural reforms have never really taken off in a big way in the country, support-like waivers can be justified even though the credit culture is affected. This can be the cost of maintaining farmers' viability.

20

It's Business After All

Banking is serious business as it deals with other peoples' money. In this case, the other people consist of deposit holders who are primarily from the household sector. This is why the most important thing in banking is prudence as it has to be staid organizations which look after the money that has been given to them by savers. The idea is to lend in a judicious manner so that money is returned on time and in the process banks earn a net income which is the cost of intermediation. Savers can always go directly to the market and invest in the debt of companies. But this does not happen frequently at the individual level because there is information asymmetry which though bridged to an extent by the prevalence of credit ratings is still quite open-ended when it comes to decision-making. The reason why a household is willing to put money in a deposit and earn 6 per cent interest knowing very well that the bank can charge anything between 8 and 15 per cent on the same money is that it has the expertise to lend to the right customers and is in a position to do due diligence. Therefore an interest rate spread is acceptable, though the level is open to debate.

Banks are supposed to do a good job and normally would do so but for the fact that there are always compulsions that force them to be aggressive when lending. Let us look at the factors that drive banking business these days which make banks aggressive when lending which often is associated with laxity in credit appraisal.

First pertains to the issue of banks being listed. This is what all banks do when they are in the public domain where a listing ensures that the owner which can be an institution/s in case of a private bank or the government in case of the PSBs is able to raise money. This goes into the reserves of the bank and hence their ability to lend also increases as their capital increases. But once a bank is listed, it falls into the 'quarter syndrome' where they have to report higher growth in profit every time which cannot be done unless there is top-line growth. Every bank has become profit-motivated and targets are set for all the employees to meet which can get onerous. In conditions when the economy is growing at say 7 per cent and the banking sector at say 10 per cent, targets of 15–20 per cent could be set for growth in credit. If one is in a private bank, there is pressure to meet the target or else forego a variable pay which can be 20–40 per cent of the remuneration. In the case of PSBs, promotions are linked with targets being met and this is when the due diligence process comes under pressure.

To get these high targets, banks prefer to go in for big-ticket credit as it takes them closer to the goal. Lending ₹50 lakhs per borrower for a home would need the effort of getting in 200 such customers to reach a target of ₹100 crore. The same target when given to a corporate which is planning an expansion makes the job simpler. Therefore, banks tend to latch on to these larger ticket sizes so as to meet their targets. This has been shown in an earlier chapter where the concentration of credit is at the highest ticket size. Also, the incentive to charge a higher rate of interest on lower-rated companies is compelling as it helps to meet the targets set for every branch manager. Therefore, under the force of performance, banks could overstretch themselves in terms of lending. This happens in the normal business course.

Second, the pressure exerted by the government is quite high, especially the PSBs. This becomes more acute when it is time for elections when banks are forced to lend to specific segments. While priority sector targets are well specified, the pressure comes to bankers to lend to say the SMEs with numbers being specified. At times, the political leaders occupying positions in the ministry can threaten the managers that failure to meet such targets can result in increments being held back. In such cases, bankers perforce push aggressively without paying much attention to the quality of loans. Often it is hoped that they do not turn all at the same time. Or when they do turn bad, the assigning manager would be in some other branch and it would be difficult to put the blame on specific personnel. In the 1970s and 1980s, the concept of loan melas was commonplace where even state chief ministers would announce the same and get banks to lend to all and sundry, especially those which came with recommendations from the political classes.

Third, at times the loans given by the large bank in a consortium can have the smaller banks join the fray without due diligence. The smaller banks which have lower levels of credit assessment experience would prefer to go along with the herd. This has negative implications when the asset turns toxic and the backlash is felt more on these banks which have a smaller balance sheet size. This is the conundrum when it comes to consortium lending where there can be upwards of 10 banks pitching in to lend to a large client. This is an efficient manner of lending where risk is diversified but practically has the problem of the lead bank actually doing the appraisal and the others simply following.

Fourth, the phenomenon of loan waivers also has a negative impact on bankers as often they are confused on the lending front. The entire credit culture gets vitiated as bankers tend to be more liberal when giving loans. While farm loans may get such protection at times, the same laxity percolates to the other commercial loans. This is a result of the culture in the bank being changed where the absence of responsibility sets in.

Fifth, political interference in the disbursal of loans has been a part of the PSB culture from the time of nationalization. While public ownership was to foster inclusive banking, they became vehicles for political patronage and the stories of how a phone call was adequate to get a loan disbursed are plentiful. The problem here is that when such orders are given the head of the bank, they have no choice but to facilitate the same as non-compliance can lead to a transfer to another bank or extensions can be held back. Such practices work down the line too where the phone call moves downwards from the head of the bank to the other echelons which finally end up with the credit analyst who has to justify the same. While serious attempts have been made to distance the government officials from the PSB CEOs, interference is still common.

Sixth, as seen in some of the recent cases involving non-PSBs, there could be close links between India Inc and the bankers which extend the symbiotic relationship to another level whereby funds are provided without the necessary level of due diligence. Here too the compromise is over the quality of asset as the loan is linked to the name of the promoter. For several decades it is just assumed that some really large corporates are just too big to fail and hence will always manage their way through the banking system. Evergreening was accepted in the 1990s which then became a habit in the restructuring of loans. These corporate celebrities often got propped up by the media and the various awards given for being the best businessmen that such lending activity looked to be in place. But when these enterprises failed, it was then that the deck crumbled which is what has been witnessed in some really high-profile defaults that have gone to the IBC.

Seventh is the case of a combination of competence and negligence where the bank does not have the expertise to deal with certain categories of loans. Often a bank is well versed with say retail loans and if they diversify into infra loans, they may not be in a position to evaluate the same as different standards and benchmarks come in. This is one reason why some banks would be weak in a certain category of loans and may also prefer to tag along with bigger banks where it is assumed that the requisite work has been done. This was the problem with universal banking when the onus of infra lending fell on them which otherwise was the persevere of the DFIs.

Hence, the case of banking is fraught with the risk of compromise and while models are supposed to be used when evaluating every proposal which could go through a series of checks in the form of committees that do a deep dive analysis of the viability of the project, corners tend to get cut for various reasons. This is why at the end of the day things turnaround when the economic cycle gets reversed.

The entire culture in banking needs to change where decisions should be taken responsibly and not just keeping in mind targets and profits. A fundamental question remains on the listing of banks as this drives banks to work for very high profits and hence valuation. Shareholders enter and leave to make money which should not be the case for banks as they are a different kind of institutions. Wider discussion is required for not just banks being listed but also financial infrastructure companies.

21

Freeing Banks from Term Lending

It is now agreed that the banking system is not the right mode for providing finance for long-term investment. Banks inherently run an asset–liability mismatch as the funds they take in are normally for three to five years in case of deposits while loans extend to a long term which can be 5–10 years depending on the class of loans. Infra loans can run for above 10 years while those for homes can extend to 20. Corporate loans for funding machinery can be for a shorter duration. However, banks normally are able to manage this matching because there are funds in the form of current and savings deposits which are almost perennial in nature and the ratio is in the region of 32–35 per cent for most banks. While time deposits have shorter maturities, there is a tendency for them to be rolled over continuously thereby balancing the asset tenure.

But banks have often run into such mismatches which result in their accessing various markets like the CDs to shore up their liabilities to match the tenures of their assets. This is a concern because as long as it is localized to some banks, there is no major issue. But if this is pervasive then there could be a problem which is what can lead to a crisis. Therefore, there is an argument for trying to wean banks away from such mismatches and one way is to shift long-term borrowing to the corporate bond market.

Also, the fact that banks find an easy way out to meet business targets through long-term, lending means that they tend to take on more concentrated risk than would be normal. This is one of the reasons that the NPA issue has become prominent as banks have ended up having large exposures here. Interestingly when the concept of universal banking was mooted, it was expected that certain innovative means of financing would evolve over time when it came to financing infrastructure. This involved schemes like taking out finance where a bank takes exposure for 15 years with the understanding that after a tenure of say four to five years, it would be passed on to the books of another bank which would then pass on to another so that no bank actually took 15 years exposure. However, this has not quite worked out and banks have been carrying such assets on their books. This has led the RBI to come up with 'large exposure norms' in a graduated manner, with the cut-off now being ₹10,000 crore from 1 April 2019.

In short, the central banks says that banks can have exposure of not more than ₹10,000 crore to a company and if there is any incremental borrowing, it has to be done in the bond market to the extent of 50 per cent. If this is not adhered to, then banks have to take on higher risk weights on such exposures when reckoning their capital adequacy ratios. How can this be evaluated?

The RBI's concern on concentration is justified as the system cannot be exposed to such bunching of exposures. Banks will now have to take more effort to grow their business or else make higher capital provisioning. Hence they will have to work this one out. The level of working capital requirement tends to be more granular compared to term loans and hence would take more effort. Also, there would be better matching of assets and liabilities and to this extent, their cost of funds would be regulated and be more predictable.

How about borrowers? Companies have been borrowing traditionally from banks as this is a good source of finance. The relation between the banker and client is historical and there is a lot of comfort as banking is based on relationships. And this has worked well for them. Some of these companies may have not accessed the bond market because this space is reserved for better-rated companies as there are not too many takers for lower-rated paper. This is where there is an anomaly. Banks lend to lower rated clients because there is the comfort of collateral. But when companies go to the bond market this is not reckoned by the credit rating agencies and normally if the rating is not AA or better, it could be difficult to get investors and when there are willing lenders, the cost goes up. This at times vitiates the so-called advantage of disintermediation. Besides once a company goes to the bond market, there are a number of compliances which can push up the cost of issuance. Borrowing from a bank is much simpler.

Against this background, companies could be in a spot theoretically in case they want to increase their borrowing from banks once they cross the ₹10,000 crore threshold and now have to get the funds partly from the bond market. As long as they have a good rating, it is fine but once they are down the pecking order then there can be challenges. What if they are not able to raise funds from the market? Will the projects have to be abandoned? While banks can still continue to lend to them, they would increase the rate of interest to make up for the higher capital provisioning that has to be made. Hence borrowers can be at a disadvantage. For term loans extending to 15 years, the interest cost can be high and affect the viability of the project.

Curiously, the problem is more acute when this is juxtaposed with the new regulation in force in the debt market mandated by SEBI where all AA and above rated companies have to borrow 25 per cent of incremental requirements from this market when long-term borrowing (defined with some exclusions) exceeds ₹100 crore. Here it has been mandatory and while for the first two years it would be tracked by the regulator, the same would invite a penalty subsequently. The question raised by critics is whether this is fair? Can the regulator dictate where the borrower should borrow from? This comes from an announcement made in the Union Budget and hence is a dictate from the top. The difference between the RBI and SEBI norms is that while RBI does not forbid the same but puts in a capital charge for banks which is more agreeable which can lead to higher interest being charged to the client, the SEBI norm actually works on the borrowing choices of the company.

Therefore, this is a rather singular situation where the bond market has to develop and to ensure it does, the regulators are forcing the companies to change their borrowing pattern and move away from banks to the market arena. This must probably be the most direct push being given for this purpose. Looking ahead the regulators also must work towards developing a junk bond market because we need investors for lower-rated bonds. In developed markets like the USA, the junk bond market is vibrant where lower-rated companies raise funds albeit at a higher cost and there is a class of investors which is willing to take a risk. The default rates are comparable to the normal NPA levels in the banking system and are at around 4–6 per cent. The existence of such a market would make the SEBI rule more feasible at the practical level.

The positive thing so far is that presently most of the companies, if not all, which get covered here under these new regulations are already in the AA bracket and may not really face major problems in borrowing more from this segment. Therefore, any criticism would be more at the theoretical level. However, those companies that would be falling in this bracket will have to work with these strong assumptions on future borrowing that can cause distortion in their cost matrix. It may be assumed that SEBI is introducing this reform in a calibrated manner to see how the response is before making any extensions. This could be a practical way of looking at the issue. But the concept of migrating companies to the bond market is realistic and makes sense as this is how it works in other developed economies.

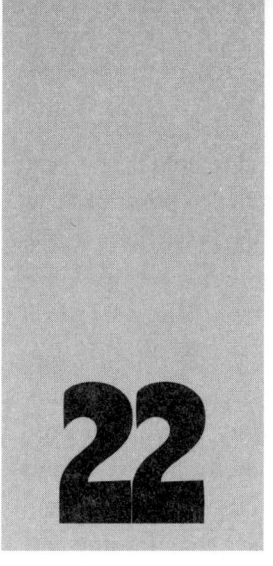

De-risking Banking
RBI's Large Exposure Framework

One of the steps that the RBI has taken to lower the overall risk of banks to individual borrowers is to introduce the concept of large exposures which is now fully operational. As of April 2019, any exposure of banks to a company of above ₹10,000 crore would trigger the clause that 50 per cent of additional borrowing would have to be from the market in the form of debt or equity. Non-compliance would mean that there would be an additional capital charge on the bank which in effect would force banks to raise the interest rate charged to the customer. While there are several qualifications, the main objective is to move borrowers from banks to markets.

This is a sound move on the face of it. Banks typically borrow for tenures of less than three years from customers in the form of deposits and lend for various purposes. While there will fundamentally be a mismatch of tenures of assets and liabilities, it gets accentuated when the loans are for long tenures of say 10 years as they get bulky in size which also means that the risk is carried for a longer period of time. Further, if the loan is for infrastructure the risk could be higher as any regulatory change in this period can have a bearing on the performance of the company. Banks also have the comfort of CASA deposits which are even more permanent in nature and can be assumed to hold in the long term too as this ratio rarely changes. Yet from the point of view of de-risking the business of banking, the RBI has set these limits which started with a large exposure being defined as ₹25,000 crore to begin with which has come down now to ₹10,000 crore.

For banks, this is definitely a change in the playbook. Large customers with large borrowings made banking easier for banks as they could build an asset base with less effort. These large borrowers are well known to the banks with a credit history which made taking decisions easier. Servicing a customer with outstanding loans of ₹25,000 crore is much easier than finding and maintaining 2,500 accounts of ₹10 crore each or 250 customers with an average loan size of ₹100 crore. Hence in terms of growing business, such a measure would pose a challenge as the effort to be put in growing business will increase. It puts pressure on building a diversified asset portfolio which will increase in terms of the number of accounts and maintenance of the same.

However, on the other side the quantum of risk to be carried on their books would come down as these large customers are more prone to risk. This will be hard to judge as banks normally feel they have taken informed decisions when lending to such large customers. Besides the possibility of default prima facie tends to be low though admittedly post the AQR process implemented by the RBI, several companies in the power, steel, engineering, textiles, mining sectors came under this umbrella. Often banks lend when they are in a consortium and assume that the bigger lenders have done the due diligence when deciding to lend to such a large company.

From the point of view of the customer, the impact is dualistic. If the company was already borrowing in the market, this would not make a difference as incrementally going for bonds would be a path that they were following. In fact, market borrowings could cost less than bank loans and hence companies would normally like to diversify their borrowing programme across different avenues of borrowing.

However, for companies which are not borrowing in the market, this would pose a conundrum. While the bond market is open to every entity, in effect only the better-rated companies can raise funds here. This is so because investors are discerning and would not normally invest in lower-rated paper. Often investors like provident funds, insurance companies or even mutual funds have a policy of investing in only AA or AAA rated bonds. If the company does not have such a rating then it will be hard to find buyers for their paper. Now the Indian market consists of mainly sub-investment grade companies which go to banks because access is open. While the cost of borrowing is high due to the intermediation cost, it is nonetheless available which makes it the preferred option. Further, there is a cost of issuance of a bond and more importantly, there are regulatory compliances to be adhered to when borrowing from the public which is not required when it comes to banks where it is more straightforward. Banking is more a relationship business which has been cultivated over the years and trust built between the two parties.

While from a regulatory standpoint such a classification sounds appropriate, customers can argue that their freedom gets affected when such a rule is applied. But here it can be counter argued that companies can still borrow 100 per cent from banks but will end up paying a higher price in terms of interest. Besides, there are already exposure norms for banks concerning companies and group companies to ensure that there is no concentration or connected lending which is always an ethical issue that comes up when dealing with deposit money.

In fact, the reason why banks are to be widely held is to ensure that there is no interconnected lending which is one of the biggest moral hazards involved when giving licenses to private parties. This is also one reason why the RBI has been careful in awarding such licenses so that there is no corporate capture of the financial system. Even when a license is issued, there are caveats put that the promoter has to divest stake within a time frame so that the bank becomes widely held. This ensures proper governance.

Therefore, all the three interested parties, RBI as the regulator, banks as the lenders and customers as borrowers, would have their perspectives on this new regulation. There are some points however to consider here.

First, while companies would perforce to diversify their funding options, the question is one of feasibility. This becomes pertinent if one juxtaposes the SEBI guidelines of long-term exposures of above ₹100 crore requiring companies to do incremental 25 per cent borrowing from the bond market. If a company does not have a good rating and is unable to get investors, then it can lead to stalled projects at the limit. The regulators need to ensure that there is an effective credit enhancement scheme in place which can provide this cover to companies in the form of a guarantee so that the credit rating is enhanced to an acceptable level. Presently the schemes which exist only talk of moving the rating from investment grade to two notches upwards and do not cover less than investment grade. If these companies want to borrow in the market, they could automatically get excluded. In such an eventuality, the road map has to be worked out. While RBI rules don't preclude lending as it can be done at a higher cost, in case of SEBI there is a time frame where companies will have to provide an explanation on the same. The non-adherence can have punitive action, which so far has been specified.

Second, there is also the need to develop a junk bond market where there should be potential investors for less than investment-grade paper. This is prevalent in developed countries but has only traces in our context. Junk bonds are high-risk bonds with low ratings but have proved to have a low incidence of default and hence there can be potential buyers. Such an appetite has to be built for sure over time because when the market has only long-term risk-averse investors, there is little scope for the development of a secondary market which in turn limits overall growth. Hence, even from the perspective of the bond market, a new class of investors has to be created who can then take positions and create a market. With a majority of investors being in the 'buy and hold' category, the scope for active trading or even portfolio diversification reduces significantly.

Third, this can also lead to re-routing of funds through NBFCs where the shadow banks borrow from the market and banks and then on-lend to these companies. This is a possibility as these institutions are already dominant in the bond market accounting for anywhere between 70 and 80 per cent of the issuances and have the wherewithal to borrow from both the sources. Therefore, we can visualize a system where the case of double intermediation becomes pronounced. In fact, this could be a big opportunity for companies to access NBFCs which have less stringent terms presently while lending though may not be in a position to take such large exposures. It is more likely to be partial diversification for the borrowers. However, as business shifts to NBFCs the overall cost increases for the borrower as the NBFCs are active borrowers from banks and the bond market and average the cost before adding their spread when lending. Therefore, the economics of pricing becomes important here.

Fourth, companies may attempt to access the ECB market within the limits prescribed by the RBI for additional funding. This has an advantage of lower interest cost globally which is unlikely to change significantly with the interest rate differential being favourable for Indian borrowers. From a regulatory standpoint, this can be problematic as such loans would be vulnerable to adverse exchange rate movements. With forward cover cost being high, unhedged positions can pose a risk for the company. Further, if the same is summed over all borrowers, this can be a potential risk for the balance of payments of the country in the extreme case. Therefore, this avenue though attractive has to be monitored continuously by the RBI so that the quantum of risk carried is tolerable. But this will be the fallout of limiting access to bank finance.

It needs to be seen as to how this plays out. Presently the demand for funds is low especially for large projects. This is because of low demand conditions as well as the NPA issue which has also witnessed several companies being put in the IBC bracket. As there are ambitions of having investments of above ₹100 lakh crore for the period 2020–2025, there would evidently be a very high demand for funding. This is when there would be pressure on funding.

To conclude, it can be said that while from the regulatory point of view the large exposure framework looks prudent as the RBI does not prohibit, such lending the SEBI rule comes in the way of the company which seeks to source funds for investment purposes. Ideally, companies should not be barred from any market because of size though the charge for the same can be higher as is the case with the RBI norm.

Universal Banking

Should We Go Back?

Post-independence in India, there was a requirement to finance investment for faster growth. It started with the Second Five-year plan, which had the famous Mahalanobis model which focused heavily on industry to bring about growth with the focus on heavy industry. In this context, it was decided to create a unique kind of FI called DFI to exclusively finance long-term investment. This led to the thrust on the expansion of business of specialized DFIs–2, of which were already in existence while the third was established later as an institution hived off by the RBI. These were IFCI (1948), IDBI (set up in 1964) and ICICI (1955). The first two were in the public sector while the last was in the private sector.

The ethos behind FIs was that they borrowed long-term and lent long-term and hence ran equivalent maturities on their assets and liabilities. This was a good model. There were other FIs besides DFIs like insurance companies, state finance corporations, specialized institutions like HDFC for housing, SCICI for shipping and so on. The model worked well as long as they got their finances in an efficient manner. Typically, they would get loans from multilateral institutions like the World Bank or the Asian Development Bank or concessional loans from the government. As funds came in at reasonable costs, they were able to lend at the same rate as banks and hence the benchmark lending rate of IDBI and SBI were on par. This made sense as they would otherwise not have been able to lend at rates that would make large investments feasible.

Such finance had enabled the creation of infrastructure in the country as they were able to finance projects for industrial expansion as well as infrastructure in the private sector. With the cost of borrowing kept low, it was also possible to under-take such investments in a profitable manner. This was the time when there was foreign exchange scarcity and it was not possible to borrow from overseas markets. The debt market did not exist and hence the DFIs provided the funding for these enterprises.

Things changed after 1991–1992 when the nation went in for economic reforms. The government decided to withdraw the channel of concessional finance for these DFIs and they had to source funds from the market. This intuitively meant that they had to rework their models which also meant lending to projects at higher rates. The period from 1992 onwards was also the time when licenses were issued to new private banks which were starting afresh and were driven by technology and hence did not have the legacy issues which were challenges for the PSBs. Two of the DFIs, ICICI and IDBI had set up private commercial banks which conducted regular commercial banking business under the aegis of the RBI while the DFIs ran independently.

To support the refinancing of projects in infrastructure, IDFC was established with the shareholder being other public sector institutions as well as HDFC which was supporting such activity.

The DFIs had to fend for themselves and while IDBI and IFCI were backed by the government and could support their structures, ICICI had to look outside India and leveraged the liber-alization laws on FDI and FFI (Foreign Institutional Investment) and got listed outside the country through GDRs and ADRs. It was at this stage that there was serious talk of getting into a reverse merger with the commercial banking outfit to create a universal bank. The idea was that once the reverse merger took place, ICICI Bank would continue to do commercial banking but with the advantage of cheap funds in the form of current and savings deposits could actually lower the overall cost of funds and support infra lending. While the RBI debated this issue for some time, it was finally decided to give permission to ICICI Limited to get converted and thus was born the first universal bank in 2002. The conditions attached were that they were to meet the priority lending norms as well as adhere to the CRR and SLR requirements.

At that time, it was argued that Indian PSBs were already universal in nature as they lent money for infra projects. This was the final justification for this reverse merger which had an addition many years later with IDBI merging with IDBI Bank in 2005.

The creation of universal banking as a concept was flawed, to begin with, and would not be sustainable. Typically, an infra project required funding for a long-term period of 10 years after which it would be in a position to service the debt adequately. Banks typically take deposits up to three years (the share of above three years is just about 20%). Taking in deposits and lending for 10 years or more is an asset-liability mismatch that cannot be sustained unless all deposits roll on forever in the same proportion. Otherwise banks will run into maturity matching.

The other factor which makes such lending problematic is pricing. How does one price a loan for 10–15 years when there are no liabilities of an equivalent maturity? When an insurance company buys a bond of 15 years, it can match its policies of such maturity with this term. For a bank to take a call, it has to also conjecture how interest rates move over this period which is virtually impossible. At best, it can relate a deposit of five years with the 10- or 15-year maturity. While using G-sec yields is a way out, these securities are sovereign and cannot be mapped easily to commercial loans, though this is the best option.

Another issue which came up was the expertise in evaluation for such projects. While ICICI and IDBI banks had legacy expertise in this field to some extent, the same was not the case with other commercial banks which also followed suit. Often when a big bank was involved in such finance, smaller ones followed by rote assuming that the due diligence was done by the lead bank. This is the challenge in consortium lending where several banks are involved in a large sanction of loan.

This was the reason why DFIs were created. Globally, all long-term funding comes from the bond market so that there are investors like insurance companies, mutual funds, pension funds which have long-term investment goals and find these bonds attractive. While banks do buy these bonds, a liquid secondary market means that they are able to sell them whenever required. This is not possible in India as the secondary market is narrow.

The system now looks more fragile than ever before as long as such long-term lending is conducted by commercial banks. The genesis of the NPA problem can hence be traced to high levels of lending to sectors like power, telecom, metals which require long-term funds. Banks preferred to lend to them because it helped to increase their balance sheet size and they were able to meet their business targets in an assured manner as a single loan gave a big business mass. The repercussion has hence been severe because failure of loans in such projects has led to severe problems for the banks. Counterintuitively, it can be argued that banks were still the best bet because if these projects had used the bond market and were successful it would have been chaos in the financial system as banks, as institutions are able to tackle such NPAs better than individual investors if that was the case.

An interesting development while this was on, came the decision taken by IDFC to convert to a commercial bank. This was an admission again that the business model of the DFI was not viable and that a move to a commercial bank was the right choice. This means that the onus of infra funding falls once again on commercial banks. There is IIFCL which was also set up for term financing of infrastructure which is done in the form of refinance. However, the volumes of lending have been limited and the main suppliers of credit continue to be banks and markets.

A decision really needs to be taken on how to fund long-term investment. Bank finance can be a medium-term solution as other options are limited. ECBs are open for companies but, practically speaking, are not accessible to all firms as the servicing of debt is mandatory and cannot be skipped as happens when dealing with banks. This requires companies raising money from this route to have CDS (which is a kind of insurance taken) written which pushes up the final cost. The only way to go is the bond market and while such companies will not be able to raise funds directly, there is need to bring in enhancements to improve the credit rating so that the investors get interested.

There is some talk of bringing back the concept of DFIs which are dedicated to only investment and not any other form of short-term lending. It will be a tough call given that the model has not been tenable for an institution like IDFC and at the same time there is pressure on banks to lend less for such projects as it interferes with their ALM mismatches besides them not having the expertise to fund such projects. It does look like that the market will be the place to go for such funding and the institutional set up will not be able to take on this job.

It may be pointed out that the RBI has also brought in the large exposures framework which restricts bank lending to less than ₹10,000 crore for a company or group which really means that the move is to lower their risk levels. This being the case, banks may not be expected to fund large infra projects. NBFCs were supplementing the efforts of banks but here too they have been found to be lacking as the recent crisis has exposed the ALM mismatch that generated the problem.

Hence, while there is a lot of talk on how much money will be required for funding infrastructure, the real challenge is in finding the institutional framework for supporting the same. This will probably be the factor dominating future thinking. We have to move to a market-oriented solution and keep banks away from such lending. One option is for the RBI to specify tenures of lending which banks can undertake, though this could be interpreted as being an intrusion in their commercial decisions.

24

CEO Tenure

Too Short or Too Long?

In the banking system, the tenure of the CEO has become an issue of debate. While the age of 60 is recognized as being the end of the road for the CEO, it is different for private banks which have had the history of fielding long-serving heads. The CEOs of all banks need to be approved by the RBI and hence there is nothing incorrect in a banker holding the post for an extended period of time which can go up to 70 years. This does not happen for the PSBs but for the private bankers the choice is made by the shareholders and hence it is supposedly a transparent process. Normally at the annual general meeting (AGM), such recommendations that are made have the support of all institutions which sort of close the issue. The RBI only needs to ratify the same and the extension comes through. If there are no cases of serious wrongdoing, the approval is more or less assured.

Table 24.1 gives the tenures of some of the bankers who have headed their organizations for a long period of time. The tenures of some of the PSB chiefs are also put down to draw a comparison between the two.

The debate on the tenure of the CEO has come to the fore for a variety of reasons. The present situation in Indian banking typified by increase in the NPAs and requirement for capital for

Table 24.1. Tenures of Heads of a Sample of Banks

Bank	CMD/Chairman/ MD/CEO	Tenure
ICICI	K. V. Kamath	1996–2009
		2009–2015: Non Ex Chairman
	Chanda Kochhar	2009–2018
HDFC Bank	Aditya Puri	1994–present
IndusInd Bank	Ramesh Sobti	2007–2008 onwards
Kotak	Uday Kotak	2003 onwards
SBI	Rajneesh Kumar	2017 onwards
	Arundhati Bhattacharya	2013–2017
	Pratip Chaudhuri	2011–2013
Bank of Baroda	P. S. Jayakumar	2015–2019
	S. S. Mundra	2013–2014
	M. D. Mallya	2008–2012
PNB	S. S. Mallikarjuna Rao	2019 onwards
	Sunil Mehta	2017–2019
	Usha Anantha Subramanian	2015–2017

Source: Annual reports and websites of banks.

PSBs has also brought in focus some private banks where the central bank had raised certain issues. There is the issue of vested interest which builds up or could come in where there will be no opposition from within because the stature of the CEO is larger than life.

The arguments for having a flexible tenure for a banker are the following. First, the banker has been tested for over a long time period and has continuously delivered superior results for the shareholders. Therefore, there is no reason to put a brake here on account of the age factor. In fact, as experience builds up, it adds value to the bank as the person in charge has seen everything and knows exactly how the company should respond.

Second, shareholders and other investors always look at the top management and get a lot of comfort from the name of the

CEO. Very often a change in the leader when things are going just too fine can make the foreign investors nervous. The fact that the Board which represents the shareholders has given an extension reflects their views and hence cannot be contested. This becomes the main factor driving extension of tenures as the name of the CEO or head spells stability when it comes to private banks. The same does not hold when one is investing in SBI or BOB because here it is accepted that the bank is larger than the Chairman or CEO and given the government setting does not matter as investors know the limitations of the head in such an environment.

Third, the strategy of a bank has to be long term as banking is a staid business. For the strategy to be carried out successfully continuity is required and if the CEO is performing well, they can be the right person to execute such a strategy. Getting a new person at this time can create chaos because it is human tendency to always bring in change in the approach of the bank as every new CEO has a new pack of ideas. This can disturb the equilibrium and also make the earlier plan less relevant which involves a cost. This is precisely the reason why it has been argued that the PSB heads need to have a longer tenure as often they get a term of just two to three years which does not give them space to do anything meaningful and often they are doing more cleaning up operations. This argument has also come up in the context of the RBI Governor where there is a school of thought which believes that tenure of five years is what should be awarded to begin with and not just three years which has been the case of late.

Fourth, in case of private banks, normally a MD and CEO who has served a long term also has a very strong team at the senior level who have been with him for a very long time. Often when a MD or CEO comes in the person, tends to create new team which can consist of insiders or those who have worked with her/him in the past. The comfort level is higher for such teams. In case of a disruption of getting in new CEOs after a tenure of five years, one cannot rule out the entire team moving out.

This will be quite unsettling as the cycle continues when a new MD and CEO takes over the person and would like to bring in a new set of senior management especially in areas of risk and business operations. Such a conundrum does not arise in case of PSBs as the tenure and seniority are protected almost till the end. At any rate, a person cannot lose the job which is possible in private banks when a new CEO takes over where the old management personnel become less relevant.

Interestingly, there are strong counterarguments here on most of these justifications which have been put across the table.

While it is true that a bank chief has done very well for an extended term, the fact remains that fresh ideas do not come into play. This holds anywhere and banking is no exception. Every human being tends to think in a certain manner and when the chief rules the bank for a very long period of time, there is stagnation in generation of new ideas. This leads to the bank actually doing the same things all the time. The fact that the senior management has been with the CEO for a long time only reinforces the argument that new ideas will never come in and hence there will be limited progress. Hence while such banks have done very well continuously, the question is would they have done better in terms of approach and strategy had the management team changed over the period of say a decade or two decades? There is no definite answer here but the question is relevant.

Second, there has also been the case where the CEOs have run the bank in a manner which never helped groom the second line, which is again a problem in a number of non-banking organizations too. The explanation given every time is that there are no capable people who can take over, which becomes a justification for further extensions which is easily accepted by the Board. It did happen in case of a leading private bank when an outsider was finally brought in as no one from within was considered to be good for the post for the simple reason that no one was groomed for the same. This is where the personality of the CEO makes a difference as well as the confidence of the board members. There is a perverse incentive to keep the other seniors in the shadows till the person gets frustrated and leaves.

One can look at some of the new private sector banks and their history to ascertain the truth in this argument. Critics argue that in some of these banks, we would never have heard of the second in command because practically speaking the power has gotten concentrated at the top with little room provided to the next in command. This problem results from the fact that some of these CEOs have been appointed at an early age and have a long term by virtue of the fact that the retirement age is 70. As is the case with anyone in power, a strong fortress is built around this position that cannot be dodged with the Board also buying into the continuity story since the banks continue to deliver higher value on a continuous basis.

Third, when there is a fixed tenure for all employees who perforce have to retire at the age of 58 or 60 as the case may be with the bank, the same rule should hold for the chief too. There cannot be two different rules for staff members. This is a valid enough argument as there are several qualified and experienced personnel who could have worked for a longer period of time if permitted. It is only when they are close to the CEO that they retire and re-enter through the door which is euphemistically called 'consultants' or 'advisors'.

This is really a decision which has to be taken by the RBI on whether or not such extended terms should be provided for bank heads. The rules should be clear just like they are for PSBs where there is an age factor and a term that are well defined. It's true that for the PSBs things are tilting towards the absurd as there have been several cases where the Chairman or Managing Director have terms of just two years and cannot really do much for the bank. Often, they could be in due to a political push or out of sheer gravity and hence would also not be interested in taking any critical decisions. At times because of uncertain decision-making process, the post is given just to ensure that someone is the captain.

Ideally, there has to be an age limit which should be 60 years and a term of 5 years if a person is nominated as chief at the age of 59. Otherwise it should be not more than 8 years with an initial term of 5 years and extension of 3 years. This will ensure that the person has a good time period to actually bring about change and improvements without letting it move the way towards closure of new ideas.

In the case of PSBs, the tenure should be fixed at five years irrespective of the age at which a person is selected for the post. This will be an incentive to actually work better and try and bring about improvements. This would work better for the person as well as the bank and can be potentially a win-win situation.

25

CEO Compensation

Compensation is a tricky issue when it comes to comparing the two sets of banks. In case foreign banks are also added, the situation can be quite bizarre as at times they are dollar-denominated. However, given the dominance of PSBs and private banks, it is worth examining how different are the pay scales of the CEOs. The numbers have been taken from the respective annual reports and may be assumed that the components are similar. Stock options which are given or exercised where specified separately have been excluded from the packages which include also bonuses and retirement benefits. Table 25.1 also presents the size of the balance sheet as one does tend at times to link compensation to the size of the business with the argument being that a big balance sheet deserves higher compensation to the leader.

The difference in pay packets for the two sets of banks is quite stark and even within the private banks there is substantial difference in the compensation of the heads. This calls for a discussion considering that the range of activity carried out by the two banks is the same as it is pure commercial banking. Investment banking is not permitted and hence there is homogeneity in terms of overall business while there can be differences

Table 25.1. Compensation of Some Bank CEOs

Bank	Size of Balance Sheet FY19 (₹ Lakh Crore)	Compensation
ICICI	9.64	4.90 cr
HDFC Bank	12.44	13.67 cr
Kotak	3.12	3.25 cr
IndusInd	2.77	5.34 cr
Yes	3.80	6.48 (partial) cr
SBI	36.81	29.54 lakhs
Bank of Baroda	7.81	33.45 lakhs
PNB	7.75	28.08 lakhs
Federal Bank	1.59	1.34 cr
IDFC Capital First (summing two heads)	1.67	5.81 cr

Source: Annual Report of banks.

in strategies and focus areas. This is important because once the discussion goes to investment banking, the risk–reward matrix is different and the compensations can be different.

The compensation of PSBs is more or less fixed by a rule which means that there is limited flexibility for change. These salaries tend to be linked with the central bank implicitly and unless the pay scales change, only then will this move. There is also a tenuous link with the salaries of government officials but the Pay Commission affects the latter but not the former. Pay structures are negotiated periodically and IBA plays an important role here.

Nonetheless, this is an interesting question on whether or not there should be parity in pay scales. As can be seen, the salary of the head of a PSB could be as low as 2 per cent of the highest-paid CEO of a private bank and around 25 per cent of an old private bank CEO. A multiple of 40 looks too high at the limit for the same work being done.

The size of the balance sheet of the banks has also been put in Table 25.1 which can be reflective of the responsibility being carried by the CEO. SBI has a size of three times that of HDFC Bank while the next two big PSBs, Bank of Baroda and PNB, have a size which is a little over 60 per cent of the largest private bank. With the mergers being announced and implemented, the size would increase substantially and come closer to that of the large private banks. This means for handling a similar, if not bigger balance sheet, which is indicative of the size of the business, there is wide disparity in the pay packages of the heads.

In fact, if one looks at the risk of PSB chiefs it is far higher. First, there is the constant threat of being ill-treated in case political calls are not adhered. There is in a way a sense of subservience attached to these posts in the public sector irrespective of the industry. Second, there can be transfers at any stage in case they are seen to be non-compliant. Third, they are subject to the scrutiny of the CBI, CAG and CIC which do not affect the private bankers. Therefore, from the point of view of risk, there should be additional compensation.

The private bankers are not normally answerable to anyone but the Board and in the absence of what looks like major financial impropriety, are generally insulated against failure. High NPAs can lead to the non-extension of contract but rarely goes with the investigative agencies gunning for them. Therefore in terms of risk, private bankers have automatic insurance.

How about performance? There does seem to be an automatic insulation here too, where there is a difference between the salary which is very high and the performance bonus which can be pruned in case the bank does not perform. However, for a PSB head there is a fixed salary of not more than ₹30–35 lakhs per annum which does not change even in case the bank performs very well. This has led to two consequences. First, the incentive to excel comes down and often the banker is happy to run the tenure without any negative mark. In fact, talks with senior bankers reveal that they prefer not to change or take decisions when times are tough like in the last couple of years as there was a risk of being hunted down post retirement. They openly say they prefer to come to office have their tea and go home. Second, there has also been the case of some bankers giving into the temptation to taking bribes or favours when disbursing loans. While there can be no justification for doing so, it is understandable that they fall into this trap. Human beings are fallible and tend to compare their standard of living with their peers. The lifestyle and media coverage of the private bankers could stoke a modicum of envy leading to temptation. While private bankers are in the midst of media glare with regular interviews on their life, children (foreign-educated), holidays (foreign locales), the same rarely holds for PSB chiefs who have struggled all their lives.

Private bankers put forward the argument that PSB chiefs have a different set of perquisites such as spacious residence, a retinue of staff, liberal entertainment and furnishing allowances which do not enter the pay package and so on. However, even if this is added the packages vary a lot as the ₹30 lakhs mark fixes the limit.

There is also an aura about private bankers where there are interviews in the media and regular membership on various panels on banking. While some of the largest PSBs also do qualify of late, but the attention is always on the private bankers. The media wants to know where the children are studying and what the favourite food of the private banker is. But rarely do we get to know the same of a public sector banker. Hence there is definitely a class difference in the way in which these bankers are treated.

Now if one looks at the private bankers, there is also a large bonus which comes with the pay package which in a year can be higher than what a public sector banker has earned all through the tenure. The question is should such a topping be provided to only private bankers? This has been debated before and it is agreed that PSB heads too should get similar packages based on performance. But it is yet to be implemented.

Hence, it is free-market capitalism which has brought about this distortion in pay scales across the private sector and cannot be controlled. All these pay packages get the approval of the RBI and hence are not being done outside the system. The issue gets highlighted especially so since the pay packages of some chiefs have hit the roof.

It is true that on a like-to-like basis there is a big difference at all the levels of staff where private sector employees in say the treasury or risk department earn substantially different packages. In fact, in private banks, a person at the age of 25–30 with two to five years of experience can be earning what a PSB chief does. Hence, such an argument may not lead to any meaningful conclusion.

Assessing the performance of any banker is difficult. So far the tendency is to gauge how the bank has grown, innovated, made profits and so on during the year. Blowing up the balance sheet is very good because it means getting market share. High profits improve the EPS and hence market price which is evidence of top performance. Opening new subsidiaries or taking over other banks sounds good and progressive and credit is given for all such good work. However, the developments in the last few years show that this may be a myopic way of looking at things. Banking decisions taken today have repercussions if any several years down the line. By the time the backlash is experienced, the management would have changed and there is nothing that can be done. An example here is that in the period post financial crisis several bankers rode the wave of aggressively lending to large infra projects and steel. The benefits came in immediately and the CEOs showcased their success. Subsequently, they left after their term/extended term and the management changed alongside. The bubble of infra lending burst and the bank/s was left holding an adverse portfolio which today is called poor judgment in retrospect. In such cases, the incumbent CEO faces the crisis, while the one responsible for this upsurge is forgotten. Therefore, it is hard to really evaluate bankers in the business of banking!

Of late, however, another interesting issue has been put forward by the RBI regarding the compensation of bank CEOs. This relates to clawing back of rewards after a time period in case it is found that the banker did not work in the interests of the bank. This has also raised ideological issues of the central bank interfering in the pay packages of the private banks. When a company is in the private sector, it is the Board which decides on the pay and it is true that the Boards tend to be controlled by the CEO who forces them indirectly to assign higher salaries. Both these issues need to be addressed in the new policy put forward by the RBI.

In October 2019, the RBI has issued the final directives on the compensation package of not just the MD and CEO, but also the other senior management whose decisions are considered to be crucial especially in the area of risk. The rules now are that the payment comes in several parts. There is a fixed pay and a variable component that is capped as a percentage of the former. The variable pay comes mainly in stock options of which a part gets deferred over time so that there is a phased payment. To top it all, non-performance would mean claw back of pay which in a way is a kind of punishment for taking excessive risk.

For private banks, the idea put forward is that first certain part of the compensation paid to the heads would be deferred for a period of say three to five years and be paid provided there is nothing untoward found out during this term. Second, in case of a misdoing, there will be the provision of a claw back of the payment made at a later date. These ideas have been in vogue post the financial crisis when investment banks went overboard in taking risk which helped to enhance business levels and profitability in the short run. However, post the crisis time, it was found that these decisions were incorrect and that the damage done was immense. There was then a call for a claw back of the benefits that had gone to them which became difficult because it was hard to prove that it was deliberately done or there was carelessness involved.

Besides, their contracts did not specify the same, and hence legally the CEOs could not be penalized. At no stage are CEO compensations linked to the future as the pay is based on meeting certain targets for the year. Once they are met, the compensation is through hefty bonuses and stock options. The idea of stock options is to have management skin in the game as it helps the team to feel incentivized all the time to perform better as when the bank does well, the share price would go up thus rewarding shareholders.

The view now taken by the RBI is that there is a case of also penalizing CEOs who finally are responsible for the performance of the bank as they are also paid the highest packages and hence have to also be penalized in an equivalent manner. This thought has come up in the wake of the irregularities witnessed in some of the private banks which were attributable supposedly to the CEO.

How far is this right? No other regulator interferes with the performance of the CEO and the pay packets and hence this may be considered to be quite unique. Further, if the regulator is okay with approving the pay packages, the error is at this point if at all. Third, taking back money is neither possible nor right and hence holding back the pay makes more sense as it is feasible. Critics here argue that regulators should not interfere in business affairs of the regulated as often they are nudging them to do certain things instead of letting them do their own business. Therefore, logically this should stop.

On the other side, why should this hold for only the private banker? Should not the regulator also punish the public sector banker who is responsible for the mess of say NPAs? Merely because the compensation is low does not mean that the banker can be exculpated from blame. Also, the argument that the investigative agencies are anyway in the loop is not strong because technically if a fraud is committed even private bankers can be investigated. There cannot be two different laws of the regulator for two regulated entities merely because the pay scales are different.

While on moralistic grounds having some control on the disbursements of pay cheques of CEOs sound all right, there are always counterarguments that regulatory intervention may not be the right thing as it does not happen elsewhere in other sectors. However, the banking system is quite different because banks use the money of deposit holders and hence have a different kind of responsibility. Bankers take decisions today which have a bearing on the outcomes which materialize several years later. Rarely do CEOs take bad decisions consciously meaning thereby that they do not give loans which they know will not be repaid. Even in some cases where of late there has been governance lapses with interconnected lending being the course followed, it was never expected that the assets would fail. Hence, in the quest for growth and better valuation in the market, bankers may enlarge their balance sheet size through some aggressive lending which leads to high growth. However, when the assets fail, it has a backlash on the performance of the bank as it leads to larger provisions, erosion of profits and net worth and in the worst-case scenario a collapse of the organization.

The problem is really that in the private sector, there are asymmetrical payoffs for the top management which have gotten the approval of the RBI. The boards tend to be subservient to the CEO that often is a very strong 'name' who commands the respect of the corporate world. The directors get the best treatment which in turn creates a symbiotic relationship that results in such pay packets which includes also stocks. The value of these stocks depends on the growth of the bank and if top line and bottom line show accelerated upward movement, the market rewards the shareholders and hence the top management which always have a disproportionate share of stocks.

This perverse incentive has caused the RBI to review the system and come up with a new template which first identifies the material risk-takers of the bank, ensures that the compensation is reasonable, fixes perquisites, bonuses, stocks and so on. Further, the RBI has fixed the variable part of the salary which increases with designation and cannot exceed 300 per cent of fixed pay. The important aspect here is that a part which could be 60 per cent of the variable pay would be deferred. And more importantly, there is a clause for claw back of pay in case of any misdemeanour. This model would be in operation and it needs to be seen as to how it works going ahead.

What is the stance taken here? Ideally, the RBI can have guidelines about what should be the approach but the regulator should ideally not be getting into commercial decisions of the bank. Fixing limits is probably a better option but issues like clawback which though makes sense should be a Board decision taken and not one by the regulator. The Boards should ideally be more effective and this issue should be taken up later on the subject of corporate governance. Such ideas should be coming ideally from the Board which should also look at the compensation curve of the entire staff and see the dispersion.

At a broader level, a fundamental question that can be asked is whether at all for banking is a steady business where one deals with deposit money rather than shareholder money. This is a different kind of business where it is not shareholder but deposit money that is used for business. The idea is to protect the deposits and make money and not take extraordinary risk for flying returns. This argument will be turning around the ethos behind stocks for the staff!

Extending the same argument of evaluating the performance of a bank, critics argue ask whether the same should be done for the regulator? This opens up a very controversial and unexplored field because logically if everyone in the system is accountable for what they do, it should hold for the government and regulators too. Governments can be voted out of power theoretically (though it is rarely the case when economics brings them down), but regulators are never questioned. That is an interesting thought for sure.

26 Bankers on Interest Rates

Narrow Views Always

The Indian banking system is so structured that bankers too are always advocating for a cut in interest rates from the RBI. This has become a habit as banking is always looked at from the pure lending standpoint and the belief is that merely lowering rates people borrow more. Ironically, when the RBI cuts rates, banks are slow to change their lending rates and have their own explanations on why it cannot be done, which in a way is justified.

Today, it is the prerogative of banks to decide on their interest rates and while the basic lending rates which are the base rate and marginal cost lending rate (MCLR) is determined by a formula, the rest of the rates can always move in a random manner if the bank so chooses. Of late, the RBI has mandated banks to link their retail and SME loans with a market benchmark.

Let us see how the interest rate mechanism works in the commercial banking sphere. The RBI first lowers the repo rate and signals to the market that the central bank is keen on all interest rates coming down as this is the goal of monetary policy. The main thrust is to spur growth because when interest rates come down, companies would borrow more and individuals would buy more homes and so on.

The repo rate affects the bank in a limited manner. Until February 2020, credit policy was a cap on the amount of funds that can be borrowed through the liquidity adjustment facility (LAF). This was 1 per cent of NDTL which can be around ₹1.5 lakh crore. Quite clearly, 25 bps cut in the repo rate is unlikely to really move the overall cost of funds for banks and hence has a limited impact on the benchmark rates.

Here, initially it was the base rate which was brought in which was defined as follows.

The components of base rate will include cost of funds, negative carry on CRR/SLR, un-allocable overhead costs and average return on net worth.

1. The marginal cost of funds should be used for computing the cost of funds. The marginal cost should be arrived at by taking into consideration all sources of fund other than equity. Cost of deposits should be calculated using the latest interest rate/card rate payable on current and savings deposits and the term deposits of various maturities. Cost of borrowings should be arrived at using the average rates at which funds were raised in the last one month preceding the date of review. Each of these rates should be weighted by the proportionate balance outstanding on the date of review.

2. Negative carry on the mandatory CRR arises because the return on CRR balances is nil. Negative carry on SLR balances may arise if the actual return thereon is less than the cost of funds.

3. The unallocable overhead costs should comprise solely of costs incurred for the bank as a whole and, hence, not allocable to any particular business activity/unit. These components would be fixed for three years, subject to review thereafter.

4. The average return on net worth is the hurdle rate of return on equity determined by the Board or management of the bank. It is expected that the component representing 'return

on net worth' will remain fairly constant and any change would be made only in case of a major shift in the business strategy of the bank.

As can be seen, the plain repo cost of 25 bps, change will be too marginal to move the overall cost of funds and the main factor, that is, deposit rates have to change. Therefore, banks have to first change the deposit rate as almost 80 per cent of total funding comes from this source. Here, there is a puzzle. The deposit rate change can be invoked only when a deposit comes for renewal or a fresh one is placed. The existing deposits cannot be touched as they are contracted at the earlier rate. Therefore, while banks announce the lowering of the deposit rate, the cost of funding will not change immediately while the lending rates change immediately in the direction of the rate change. They have to change across the board for all loans. Hence, as the cost of funds component does not change significantly to the base rate or marginal cost, the lending rate too will not change much. This is the reason for slow transmission even though over a longer period of time, the two do move in the same direction.

There is hence a reason for the stickiness in interest rates when it comes to transmission from the RBI to the banks and the formula tries to strengthen the same but has its limitations. Banks can however still lower the rates which are charged that are above the base rate but are hesitant to do so as rates are aligned with the benchmark. Therefore, the stickiness gets further entrenched in the system.

The transmission conundrum is quite typical of India and this has not been spoken of in other western economies where the pivot rate is stronger and the market forces ensure that the transmission is smooth. It is not surprising that there is an obsession on interest rates and it is taken that lowering the rate is the panacea for all our problems. But the issue is that just lowering the rates will not get people to borrow. Let us see how this happens.

For lower interest rates to lead to an increase in demand, an individual will weigh certain factors. Chief among them is the cost of the object that is being procured. Suppose it is a mortgage which involves property, the decision to buy will hinge on the price of the house as well as the expectation of price movements. In a bull phase, one would buy a house when prices are rising, but when prices move down, there would be a tendency to wait and watch as expectations are formed. This does not hold for vehicles where the prices rarely come down and therefore festivals or other occasions work well for the lending institution. Here, the rate of interest per se may not matter as the vehicle loan has to be repaid in five years' time unlike a house which can stretch to 15 or 20 years.

Also, the income prospects of an individual matter. When there is a slowdown in the economy and wage increases are minimal, there is a tendency for people to defer any loan as it becomes onerous to service. Therefore, the overall financial health of an individual matters a lot.

When it comes to a company, lower rates do help to reduce costs and hence prop up profit. But it ends here at the working capital level. For investment to take place, companies normally look at their capacity utilization rates and then take a call on whether conditions are ripe for expansion. Various industries have different threshold levels of capacity utilization which prompt them to go for fresh investment. Normally a thumb rule is that 80 per cent is the level which should trigger fresh investment. Investment at lower rates and lower capacity utilization may not make economic sense as the cost of servicing is higher and there may not be a corresponding flow in revenue. This is why investment reacts more to demand conditions. If one looks at the average capacity utilization rate in India in the last five years or so, there has been a range of 70–74 per cent maintained on a quarterly basis which has not induced higher investment and hence borrowing. Depressed demand conditions which started off as lower rural demand due to successive droughts was followed by demonetization and later GST which affected the income of households as they had a bearing on job creation.

Also, companies which are already deep in debt like in the infra space may be reluctant to take on more leverage and often their demand for funds at lower rates is more to repay old loans rather than take on fresh borrowing for investment. This was noticed in the last couple of years that companies preferred to repay old loans that were expensive with cheaper loans where there were fixed rates.

On the supply side too, while banks were lowering their MCLRs they were not willing to lend given the NPA overhang. Hence while the MCLR is only an indicative rate they tended to charge a very high-risk premium on lower rated companies which acted as a deterrent. At times when the banks were still not willing given the large sectoral exposure already taken, companies had reached out to the NBFCs for such loans.

Therefore, the picture is quite complex and lowering the rates is only part of the story which has to be followed up by buoyancy in economic conditions to keep the chain moving.

The new rule brought in by the RBI is to link retail and SME loans to a pre-decided benchmark which can be the repo rate or a market rate like treasury bill or G-sec. This ensures that when these benchmarks change, the ending rate too would move in tandem. This is definitely a more effective way of transmitting rate changes though poses some challenges for banks which have to change return on assets without having similar control over the cost of liabilities, that is, deposits. How good is this idea?

A view here is that the idea of benchmarks is good, but can it be forced by the RBI as a matter of principle as it is a commercial decision which banks have to take. Any involvement in fixing rates even if it is the base rate makes the regulator part of the commercial activity and decision of banks which is not really desirable.

27 Relevance of CRR

The CRR is quite unique and a tool of monetary policy for the RBI. By statute, banks have to keep a certain amount of their NDTL in the form of cash with the RBI. The earlier logic was that this was meant to be a safety buffer to ensure the solvency of the bank. It came to be used as a tool of monetary policy as any change in the threshold level of these balances would lead to resources of banks being increased or decreased. Hence, the quantum of lendable funds can be increased or decreased by changing the CRR. It is universal in the sense that it applies to all banks and not just to specific banks, and hence is a superior form of monetary management compared with say an open market operation (OMO).

OMOs are called durable liquidity mechanism because they also give a permanent sum of money to banks or withdraw the same. But they are inferior to the OMO because the banks involved would be those who own the security that is being purchased as the RBI announces which ones they would be buying. Hence, it is possible that the bank which has a liquidity crunch does not have a security that is being purchased that it can sell. Therefore, CRR is more universal in nature and effective.

The issue with the CRR is that the balances do not earn any interest and hence the money lies idle. The average cost of deposits is, say, 6 per cent, and a small part of 4 per cent of the sum is held as idle balances with the RBI. Is it fair? Bankers would rather make this impounding not be there or that the RBI pay an interest on the same. There is an implicit loss of revenue for the banks as at 4 per cent, the total cash balances held by the RBI is around ₹5.2 lakh crore which on an annual basis will mean a cost of ₹30,000 crore which can go up to an opportunity cost of ₹40,000 crore in case it were to be deployed as lending, which is quite significant. These are absolute idle balances that lie with the central bank and are hence not put to any use.

Does this exist in other countries?

As can be seen in Table 27.1, not all countries follow this principle, but the same is in force in some major countries too with the range going up to 12 per cent in Philippines and China. Even USA had CRR of 3 per cent which has been reduced to nil in March 2020. Therefore, having a CRR is not an odd regulation.

Table 27.1. Cash Reserve Ratios in Some Countries: An Illustration

Country	Central Bank	Date	Ratio
Argentina	Central Bank of Argentina	28 September 2018	44%
China	People's Bank of China	January 2020	12.5 from 13
Euro Area	European Central Bank	18 January 2012	1% from 2%
India	Reserve Bank of India	March 2020	3% from 4%
Indonesia	Bank Indonesia	November 2019	5.5% from 6%
Malaysia	Bank Negara Malaysia	March 2020	2% from 3%
Philippines	Bangko Sentral ng Pilipinas	March 2020	12% from 15%
Russia	Bank of Russia	27 June 2016	5% from 4.25%
South Africa	South African Reserve Bank		2.50%

Country	Central Bank	Date	Ratio
Turkey	Central Bank of Republic of Turkey	16 February 2019	7% from 8%
United States	Federal Reserve	March 2020	0% from 3%

Source: http://www.centralbanknews.info.

Interestingly, the CRR has also been historically very high in India and it was only in recent times in 2013 that has been reduced to 4 per cent. Table 27.2 gives the more inhibitive CRR rates when the concept of incremental CRR also was in existence.

The CRR has been looked at as being onerous because of the number of conditions which are put by the regulator. Of every ₹100 kept as a deposit, banks have to keep CRR and SLR aside in cash or government securities. Of the balance that has to be lent, 40 per cent goes as priority sector portfolio which really

Table 27.2. CRR Changes in India

Date	CRR
5 July 1935	(a) 5% of DL
	(b) 2% of TL
5 June 1979	6.00
24 October 1987	10.00
1 July 1989	15.00
1992	15.00
28 March 1998	10.25
16 November 2002	4.75
10 November 2007	7.50
30 August 2008	9.00
3 November 2012	4.25
9 February 2013	4.00
April 2020	3.00

Source: www.rbi.org.in.
Note: DL, demand liabilities; TL, time liabilities.

constrains banking operations. The thought behind solvency was logical but considering that we have travelled a long distance and the BIS norms now talk of liquidity ratios where government paper held is considered to be a part of the portfolio sounds anachronistic.

However, on the other hand as seen in case of bank failure, theoretically a bank cannot sell its portfolio of securities if it is sizeable as it will create turmoil in the market. That's why having cash to save a bank run in the initial stages can still be justified. A solution is to actually pay some interest on the CRR so that banks are able to cover their cost. The average cost of funds for the system can be calculated for the system and be paid partly by the RBI. Alternatively, the reverse repo rate can be paid which is what banks get for their surplus liquidity which is parked in these auctions. This will also help banks to lower their MCLR as they are allowed to put a cost of carry for CRR balances when reckoning their overall cost for determining this benchmark. Is the RBI willing to pay this cost?

28 Banking Costs

They Really Hurt

The business of banking is quite unique and works on building liabilities through deposits rather than the shareholder money. In fact, the so-called share-capital is very low for an industry which has a balance sheet of ₹15,000,000 crore. It works on collecting deposits from the public and lending the same at a higher cost with the spread being the gain after adjusting for their operating costs. The bank hence makes money on the deposit holders' money. The deposit holder does not know how to evaluate customers who want to borrow and hence entrusts the same with the bank which plays the role of an intermediary. In this process, there are certain costs which are incurred which is called the cost of intermediation. The important thing is that without the deposit holders' savings, the banks would not be able to do business and is hence dependent on them.

Yet banks pay scant regard to the customer mainly due to the fact that they are a large number of such account holders who require the bank to park their savings as much as the bank requires these funds to do their lending. It hence is a banks' market where the reins are held by them and the customer has to follow. In a competitive set up, customers do have a choice of banking with a number of banks and can theoretically move from one to another where the terms are favourable. However, the same does not happen as there tends to be stickiness in human behaviour. Also there tends to be a convergence to an oligopolistic structure where the choice could be having to bank with say 50 entities but practically speaking the same language as they all behave in a similar manner. With heightened competition, there is a convergence in behaviour of banks when it comes to dealing with deposit holders and this is manifested in the charges levied.

There was a time when most banking services were free for customers who could withdraw money any time they wanted, and while withdrawals were constrained by the number of cheques that could be issued were quite generous in scope. But things have changed now and customers have to pay their way through all processes if they are not special customers who get so classified if they are part of a corporate deal or a high net worth individual.

First, there are charges for entering the bank and carrying out transactions. Too many cash deposits invite a fine and the same holds for depositing money. It has to be done at the ATM or online. Asking for statements would invite a charge for the printout. Also, there are limitations on the use of an ATM and beyond the maximum stipulated would invite a charge. Similarly, while there is flexibility in using other bank's ATMs there are restrictions on the number of transactions. Online transactions are encouraged but there can be charges hidden depending on which mode is used. When bank accounts are opened, a debit card is forced on the customer with an annual charge being a recurring expense. Hence we end up paying for using all banking facilities.

The justification given is that the bank is providing convenience in terms of allowing technology to permeate our lives. But this helps banks to save on human resources as technology involves a capital cost to begin with and a low recurring operational cost which is lower than having individuals at the teller. This has made banking an onerous affair.

Table 28.1. Illustrative List of Some Bank Charges for Customers

Cheque Book	First 10 Free in a Year, Pay Subsequently
Non maintenance of minimum balance of ₹1,000–3,000 depending on location	Penalty
Passbook	First free, duplicate chargeable.
Account closing	Less than one year, penalty
Signature verification	Chargeable
Photo attestation/record verification	Chargeable
Collection of outstation cheques	Chargeable
NEFT/RTGS in branch	Chargeable (free at home)
Cash deposits	More than three transactions chargeable
Cash withdrawals	Chargeable based on times and amount
Debit card	Free issuance but annual charge with no option of not going for a card
Exchange of soiled notes	Chargeable based on quantum

Source: From various banks websites.

Some of the charges of banks can be looked at in Table 28.1.

The above is just an illustration of various charges levied by banks when a customer puts money as deposits. Banks always argue that their cost goes up when these services are rendered which is disingenuous to say the least as withdrawing money from an ATM multiple times does not really have a cost. Similarly, making cash transactions should not be an extra burden for banks which use their existing staff anyway. If debit card is the way to make a person withdraw money from a bank, there is no running cost. But banks charge annual fees of ₹150 per year (it is waived if the terms of having a salary account provide for such exemption). There are around 80 crore debit cards in the country which at an average fee of ₹150 yield ₹12,000 crore to the banking system. It does look exploitative. Besides if banks feel stiff about such services, then they do not take any responsibility for the mismanagement of funds which cause high level of NPAs. Deposit holder's money is finally mismanaged for which there is no penalty for the bankers who continue to draw their salaries as the blame is normally passed on to others.

The RBI would need to really look into these charges again. All these costs have been approved by the central bank in the name of freeing charges. But the fact that banks have not performed well in terms of doing an efficient job of intermediation raises questions of ethics. As mentioned earlier, banks run on the basis of deposits and should not be charging them for services. Already savings deposits are being reckoned at a low rate of 2.5 per cent by some banks which are virtually fixed deposits as the average balances of most account holders remain constant. These accounts are used for receiving salaries and, with virtually a fixed amount being withdrawn, the balance continues to lie with banks at this low cost.

In this context, the following data needs to be examined. First is the spreads of banks, that is, difference between cost of deposits and return on advances. This has not come down as Table 28.2 shows where it is around 3.65 per cent which is very high given that these funds are not even managed well given the governance issues as well as creation of NPAs which is a reflection of limited credit risk assessment ability. Second is

Table 28.2. Select Performance Ratios (%)

Parameter	2008–2009	2018–2019
Cost of deposits	6.24	5.00
Return on advances	9.89	8.68
Spread	3.65	3.68
Share of savings and current deposits	33.20	40.00
Mismanagement of deposits (NPA ratio)	2.25	9.10
Operating costs as % total assets	1.87	1.93

Source: www.rbi.org.in.

the share of savings deposits in total deposits. Third are the operating costs of banks. Here too the ratio has not really changed. The idea of intermediation is that banks have superior skills compared to individuals and hence need to be paid for that. Clearly this is not revealed in their performance. Lastly, the mismanagement of deposits can be gauged by the probability of creating NPAs. Here the gross NPAs to total deposits can be used as an indicator. Related to this are the bank failures which take place or the revelations of the inspection reports of RBI which show that they have not been compliant with basic regulation. This will help to gauge whether banks have actually used their oligopolistic power to extract higher income as charges from customers.

Select performance indicators of banks.

The irony of the situation is that most of these charges are removed once the account is under the financial inclusion bracket. The Jan Dhan account gives a free debit card and is free from encumbrances. The minimum balance rule does not apply and hence banks are quite happy with the scheme while charging other customers who keep larger balances for all services rendered.

There is definitely a pressing need for the RBI to revisit these charges and ensure that deposit holders get a better deal and are not charged for all services which legitimately have to be provided to them. Alternatively, deposit holders should also have a say in the functioning of banks especially so as there has been talk at the government level (which is not yet up for active discussion), that risks of banks have to partly shared with the deposit holders. Also, with limits being put on deposit insurance, these holders must have the right to dictate some policies of the bank and have their representatives on the Board.

Priority Sector Lending

Will We Ever Get Out of It?

Priority sector lending has been a goal of our banking system post nationalization in 1969. The aim was to ensure that the banking system made available credit to vulnerable sections of society which was defined to cover agriculture, small industry, socially underprivileged groups, education, housing and so on. Over a period of time, the components increased to include more claimants based on the evolving political scenario. The limit however has been restricted to 40 per cent of total credit (or to be more specific Adjusted Net Bank Credit or Credit Equivalent Amount of Off-Balance Sheet Exposure, whichever is higher). Within this level of 40 per cent, there is a sub-limit of 18 per cent for agriculture, 7.5 per cent for micro enterprises, 10 per cent for weaker sections and so on.

There were however several allowances made in terms of including direct and indirect finance so that it was more doable. This also includes buying priority sector lending certificates so that the target is met. Further, if banks did not meet the target by the end of the year, the balance had to be transferred to the RIDF fund of NABARD. Here the bank receives a lower return which varies from bank rate minus 2 per cent to bank rate minus 5 per cent depending upon the shortfall in priority sector lending.

There are some ideological issues which have to be discussed. Priority sector lending is something that is forced on banks and hence even if a NBFC wants to convert into such an institution, these prerequisites have to be met. This cannot be compromised. Priority sector lending norm of 40 per cent means that of every ₹100 of lending ₹40 has to be lent to the segments that are included in this category. The rate of interest on bank loans will be as per directives issued by the Department of Banking Regulation of RBI, from time to time. Priority sector guidelines do not lay down any preferential rate of interest for priority sector loans. The rate of interest would vary. For agriculture it is fixed at 7 per cent with a subvention being provided by the government in the Budget of 2 per cent with an additional discount of 3 per cent if paid on time. Therefore, the effective rate can be 4 per cent. (This can change based on budget considerations).

SMEs on the other hand do have a grievance of being charged higher rates which makes it onerous. There is however MUDRA loans which come under this category where the amounts are fixed but not the rates. These rates can vary from 10 to 20 per cent. Hence, this may not be very attractive for the borrowers. Interestingly, it should be pointed out that MUDRA loans are not a new dimension which has been added to the financial system but a reclassification of SME loans that were already being disbursed by the banks under this umbrella. There is some refinance which is provided to banks but that is minimal.

The first question is whether or not such a scheme called priority sector lending can be run after 25 years of financial sector reforms. Globally, priority sector credit is linked with those segments that need to be given a push for growth like exports. In the Indian case, it is more a case of financial inclusion where lending is a part of the package besides providing a deposit account. The difference is that while normally such preference is given to specific sector which can grow and add value, in our case it is more a case of providing credit to the vulnerable section of society which does not have access to other sources of finance. Also, simultaneously these sections would not have the wherewithal to service these loans as their income streams are uncertain as they would be susceptible to weather interventions (in case of agriculture) or performance of customers (in case of SMEs). Therefore, the focus of banks is more on meeting targets than actually ensuring that the funds lent are effectively used. It is a kind of affirmative action being taken by the government through the banking system. The cost of keeping these accounts has to be borne by the bank. Should there be a time frame for such lending? Ideally less, though it will be hard to do so as the farmer community in particular is vulnerable and requires such support every year. Hence it becomes an ongoing process.

The second is whether or not banks really find this profitable? While all bankers aver that they are committed to inclusive banking and lending, they never cross the statutory limit which is indicative of the fact that it is more of a regulatory requirement and compliance. Counterintuitively, it can be argued that if banks were really committed to such lending or found it more profitable, they would definitely have lent more to this sector which is not happening. To make this avenue profitable, there are major agrarian reforms which have to be undertaken by the state governments in particular so that farmers have a viable ecosystem where they are linked with supply chains as well as marketing so that an end to end solution is there. In the absence of such a linkage, there would be a tendency for bank credit to operate in isolation from the rest of the activity which makes it vulnerable to defaults.

Here some progress has been made, though the loose ends need to be tied up. Farmers have to be provided with crop insurance which should be mandatory so that in case there is any failure, the insurance company will compensate them which in turn can be used to pay the bank. Similarly, provision of high yielding variety seeds and other inputs like fertilizers and pesticides should be made available to them so that they productivity improve and they are able to earn more on their land. This includes access to irrigation which protects against monsoon failure. Northern states like Punjab and Haryana are good examples of how such an ecosystem can be created. Similarly, for marketing farmers should be provided access to two systems. The first is marketing facility either to mandis (it is there but often they sell to middlemen because of the access in terms of roads and transport) or the future market so that the price received is fair. Second, the backend infrastructure needs to be created so that warehousing and transportation issues are addressed. This way farmers would be able to have an end-to-end solution for their problems. While scattered attempts have been made at different points of time in different states, it has rarely been comprehensive as a package. In fact, if such a solution is created, farmers would be less vulnerable to market forces and would be able to service their debt on time.

Third is whether priority sector lending is feasible for banks. While the IBC cases are the big-ticket ones and catch attention, priority sector lending involves more vulnerable sectors which have higher propensity to turn adverse. Hence a weak monsoon would mean that farmers' crop can get affected, SMEs are always at the risk of being adversely affected when the business cycle turns negative. As their fortunes are linked with the larger companies, they are hindered by growing receivables or decline in demand when the main customers get affected by the business cycle. And considering that typically they tend to borrow at higher interest rates, their cost of servicing debt is also more onerous. Their debt service ability came down when demonetization was introduced. It was exacerbated with the introduction of GST which was a second disruption for them. To tackle both of them, there had to be intervention from the government and RBI to give them more time to repay their debt as loans were restructured. With the COVID pandemic creating another major distortion across all countries, this segment becomes more vulnerable with units closing down due to the shutdown leading to unemployment as well as bankruptcy as they are unable to repay loans at a time when payments from their customers get blocked.

A thought which comes to mind here is whether one can think of a solution in the realm of a CDS for bank loans which hitherto has been made available for debt instruments only. Having a swap writer makes sense for banks because is loans are backed by insurance, the spreading of risk becomes easier and banks will be better placed to disburse loans. This idea needs to be germinated now. Just like how there is deposit insurance with limits for deposit holders, can loans also be guaranteed by an insurer in return for a premium? This model needs to be examined and implemented at least for priority sector loans where often it is not possible to do the same due diligence that can be done for large ticket size loans in the formal sector where annual reports and projections are available. Crop insurance should be a part of the deal with the premium being paid from the loan directly to the insurer or the government providing the funds under the PM Kisan Fasal Bima scheme.

The Narasimham Committee had actually recommended that this level of priority sector lending should come down to a level of 25 per cent over a period of time. However, this is probably the only recommendation that has not been considered actively and with there now being political undertones it is unlikely that any government is willing to actually lower this limit. Therefore, this will continue for a longer period of time.

A question raised has been whether lending for infrastructure should also be included in the priority sector as this is very much an important focus area for all governments. While there have been strong arguments in its favour, in the present situation where a large amount of NPAs are concentrated in this segment, it looks unlikely that it would be considered for such a classification. But including infrastructure would widen the canvas for banks to deploy funds and there could be sub-limits placed on the same. Further a single infra project would be large enough for banks to take one which can lead to chunky NPAs being built if there is failure unlike for farm loans which is of a much small ticket size.

These ideas are worth examining because priority sector lending should be used to bring about improvement in productivity which will eventually lead to higher growth. It should not be targeted at just about bringing about the sustenance of the weaker sections. The social programmes of the government should instead be more active here. At any rate, there is need to revisit this programme and bring about the necessary modifications in the light of several schemes of the government being announced, especially for the farming sector which should get integrated into this regulatory requirement.

30

Benchmarking of Interest Rates

Who Should Decide?

From 1 October 2019, banks entered a new world of setting interest rates where the basis of doing so changed as the RBI brought in a new framework for specific loans. While the new regime will be holding for retail and SME loans to begin with, it may be expected that all lending could eventually be shifted to this system. It is all about using benchmarks for setting interest rates on the lending side. Banks have to move away from the present system of MCLR and follow the benchmarking process. Why has there been a change in the system?

It is almost clear that one of the goals of banking is to ensure that lending rates are down which means that the market forces are to be skipped and investment to be given precedence over savings. Interest rate direction is a curious concept as while low interest rates are good for investment, savings get retarded as the earnings come down which in turn can affect consumption as often savings are used to finance consumption for the fixed income earners. This being the main objective of the RBI, efforts have been on to fix the basic lending rate of banks. In the past, there was a minimum lending rate (MLR) which was specified by the RBI below which one could not lend and remained uniform across all banks. This system prevailed between having an MLR and a ceiling rate till 1980–1981 to one of only a ceiling rate till 1987–1988. Subsequently, the MLR took over. This was followed subsequently by the prime lending rate (PLR) which was left to banks that had to be transparent in disclosing the same on the website. The PLR was the rate offered to the best clients and resembled the new base rate or MCLR except that the interest rate was decided by the bank and not by a formula as was dictated by the central bank.

The PLR gave way to the base rate when the RBI got into the act of getting banks to specify their base rate based on a formula which included cost of funds and other components. The motivation was both to get in transparency and also ensure that there was good transmission of monetary policy decisions. Hence, when the repo rate was lowered, the base rate too should have gone down. However, this did not happen as banks were slow to re-price their credit as deposits had to re-priced first which would work with a gap as only new deposits or those renewed would be subject to these rates. Also, at times banks would be reluctant to lower deposit rates or would do so selectively to ensure that new deposits do not move away based on their ALM requirements. Hence, the base rate was not too effective.

At the next stage came in the MCLR which worked on marginal cost pricing. However, here too the sluggishness has been evident as rate changes have not been transmitted. It is not hard to guess the reason as using the marginal cost pricing for pricing average assets is complex and banks continued to be slow in transmission. This has led to the change in stance of the RBI which had gotten in the benchmark system.

Here, the banks are supposed to adjust their lending rates on retail and SME loans to a pre-decided benchmark which is driven by policy changes. Hence if a benchmark like the repo rate is chosen, the bank can price these loans at say 200 or 300 bps above this rate. Hence if the RBI lowers the repo rate by 40 bps, all such loans get cheaper by 40 bps. Similarly, if the benchmark chosen is the Tbill rate or the 10-Years G-sec rate, as these rates move, so would the lending rates. The rules also say that this re-pricing would take place every three months while the rates chosen by the bank in terms of the spread above the benchmark would be fixed for a period of three years. From the point of view of the RBI, this is a foolproof system and hence will make policy work faster and smoother and achieve the desired goal of ensuring that the monetary policy transmission process is seamless.

The problem would arise in case the benchmark does not change which has happened when the RBI lowered the repo rate by 35 bps and the 10 years yield went up by 20–30 bps due to a different set of factors. In such a case, it would be contrary to what the central bank is driving at and could defeat the purpose. Here the RBI would be quite helpless if the market does not support the RBI decision. But this may not be very frequent and it has been generally seen that the market rates to go in the same direction as the repo rate changes.

Banks however would be in a quandary. First, they have to contend with the fact that while their assets or rather some of their assets are being re-priced, their liabilities continue to bear a fixed cost in terms of deposit rates. This part of the architecture has not been changed. It would also be hard to do so as all deposit holders pitch for this avenue of savings due to the fixed known return. Making them variable would be a disincentive and expose them to market forces which are not the purpose of such deposits. Therefore, any decision taken by the banks on these benchmarks must weigh in the fact that the deposit rates would not be changing simultaneously. Also, they would not be in a position always to physically alter these rates for new deposits as these benchmarks would tend to change every three months as per the rules of the game.

Second is which benchmark to use? The repo rate is the safest in terms of being known for a specific period of time. Other instruments like treasury bills or G-secs are market-driven and would vary depending on the market conditions. At times they could go in the opposite direction or could even fall faster than the policy rate which can affect the earnings significantly. Hence, they will have to scrutinize whether they will like to use a benchmark which is more or less sensitive to the changes in repo rate and based on their appetite pitch for the same.

The third question relates to the spread chosen. Should it be 200 bps or 300 bps or 100 bps? This would be the base lending rate that has to be made available to the best borrower. Often they will not be able to discriminate between individual borrowers like can be done for corporates and would be fixed to the tenure and amount of loan. This would be fixed for three years. While there will be scope for SMEs where some kind of rating score can be taken, it would otherwise be a base case nonetheless.

Therefore, the concept of a benchmarking system is interesting and challenging for banks. But at the broader level some issues remain. First, should the central bank or even the government be dictating at what rate the bank should be lending? In a free system, the choice is with the bank to charge any interest rate and there can be no compulsion to transmit the repo rate change if it is not warranted. Banks have to look at different factors before altering their rates which includes the flow of deposits, the ALM issues, the overall economic environment, the credit risk perception and so on. It is rare to come across instances where the central bank is a free market system, which forces banks to lower their rates by dictates that are what this system is. Banks have to be transparent and reveal their PLRs or base rates or MCLRs. But the way in which they determine their rates should ideally be left to the banks because at a certain level, the RBI would be party to the setting of rates. This means that in case the bank's business model goes wrong, the central bank has to take some responsibility for forcing them to fix their lending rates in a certain manner as these benchmarks are subject to market risk on a daily basis. This holds especially for SME loans as this sector is quite vulnerable to economic cycles which can mean a higher possibility of default. By not giving banks full flexibility at the time of lending, they would be at a disadvantage when these loans go bad or give lower returns.

The second is that does such a system, which smells of some desperation, also indicates that monetary policy is not effective. Ideally the repo rate should work well through the LAF window as well as influence all the other rates which should influence the base rate. Quite clearly, the rate cuts which are based on the inflation targeting is isolated from the banking reality which makes policy measures less relevant. This is important because while the RBI today is working to lower rates, it can become pernicious once the rates start going up due to rising inflation when the lending rates could scale new heights. At an ideological level it can be said that if the central bank is creating a system of determination of interest rates for better transmission, then the idea of monetary policy as the tool to control money supply in the economy becomes less potent.

Lastly, the Lehman episode can be brought in to highlight the pitfalls of such a system, especially for the retail segment. Giving teaser loans had led to an increase in retail lending in mortgages which also coincided with the housing boom. The advent of financial engineering meant that banks which originated loans did not have to hold on to them and they were sold and repackaged into securities which were then marketed as CDOs and MBS. The problem erupted when interest rates moved up and individual borrowers were unable to repay or service their loans which were under variable interest rate regimes. As these defaults mounted, they were forced to leave their homes which led to a crash in the market. While this is an extreme situation which probably will not be enacted again, the fear of providing such low interest rate loans is palpable.

It has been noticed that there is pressure of servicing debt in the retail segment in 2019–2020 mainly due to the stagnant income conditions with an economic slowdown. While defaults are not the case, there has been some skipping of payments due to slowdown in the flow of income to service such debt. With all banks now systematically reorienting their policies to the retail segment ostensibly due to lower delinquency, the continuous lowering of the repo rate could just be igniting a larger portfolio which can become difficult to service in tough times. An example here is any event like the coronavirus which had led to lockouts and job losses, and pay cuts can in turn lead to delinquencies on repayments. Therefore, this factor should be kept in mind when the twin policy of lowering interest rates is combined with linking home loans with benchmarks.

From a banking perspective, however, the benchmarking of retail loans along with SME loans can be seen as being a precursor to the wider policy of linking even corporate loans to the same. It may be assumed that the RBI is experimenting with the small ticket size first before moving on to the larger loans which has to be done in a calibrated manner so as to ensure that the overall risk in the system is continuously monitored and kept under control. At any rate this will be a new chapter in a way in which bank lending is conducted and would have to be kept in mind as we move along. It may not be the most ideal way to go about as normally the market, which includes demand and supply conditions and economic environment led risk factors, should drive such decisions.

31

Don't Use the Small Savings Argument Please

Bankers are known to always put forward the argument that they are not in a position to lower deposit rates even when RBI lowers the repo rate because if they were to do so, customers will withdraw their deposits and put them in the small savings accounts offered by post offices. Small savings interest rates have tended to be higher than bank deposit rates. This has also been supported by the policy statements of the MPC where there is reference to the same thought and often mentioned with a touch of sympathy. The government on its part is also in agreement with this argument and keeps asking for the same. Just what is this argument all about?

Small savings is a different set of savings schemes directly floated by the government and organized through post offices mainly, though banks also come in when mobilizing funds under the Public Provident Fund (PPF). The thought process was that savings had to be mobilized from everyone especially in smaller places and hence post offices were given this role. The National Savings Organization was created post independence and gradually the savings deposits got expanded to include certificates, different kinds of deposits, special schemes (senior citizens, girls) and so on. Therefore, there were, broadly speaking, two sets of savings under this umbrella which are deposits and certificated. PPF comes somewhere outside as it has a different nature.

These funds were kept in a fund which in turn was used to finance government expenditure. Intuitively, it can be seen that such funds were more expensive than market borrowings which could generally be lower by 50–100 bps. But as these funds came in exogenously to the system, they were useful in so far as that the deficit could be financed without upsetting the market. The government could draw from this fund at a premium to cost of these funds which could be in the region of 50 bps. States did not want to use these funds and some of them have moved out of this circle. The central government continues to leverage this source and has over time found it convenient to use them to finance the fiscal deficit besides providing buffers for other finances such as subsidy for short time periods.

As of November 2019, total small savings summed to ₹9.99 lakh crore as outstanding amounts in all forms of which total deposits were ₹6.81 lakh crore. There were ₹2.38 lakh crore in certificates and ₹0.80 lakh in PPF. There is a need to make a distinction between these three sets because the motivation behind each one of them is different. The deposits are analogous to those offered by banks and are strictly comparable as they include savings and term besides recurring accounts. The certificates are different in the sense that one invests money in a certificate and gets a fixed sum after a defined tenure. There could be tax breaks on amounts invested in some of them. PPF is an annual contribution made by holders who have to invest a minimum every year with limited withdrawal facility but have the benefit of tax breaks all through as the maximum amount that can be withdrawn is defined along with the minimum tenure of holding.

Total bank deposits as of this date were ₹129.6 lakh cr. The ratio of post office deposits to bank deposits is just 5.3 per cent. Even in incremental terms for this period bank deposits had increased by ₹11.45 lakh crore while small savings deposits increased by ₹0.64 lakh crore. The ratio here for incremental post office deposits to incremental banks deposits is 5.6 per cent. Hence, either way the ratio is just around 5.5 per cent and it is hard to believe that this small proportion can move the larger number. This means that the argument that lowering deposit rates will lead to large scale migration is quite far-fetched because if it were remotely so, people should have shifted in large numbers because the difference in rates could be as high as 100–150 bps. But this has not happened.

It has been reiterated elsewhere in this book that all banks charge different rates on loans and offer different deposit rates. But yet, customers are there for all banks for various reasons. Therefore, even though some private banks offer higher rates on savings deposits of above 4 per cent, we do not see people earning less than 3 per cent rushing to the other banks. There are reasons behind such behaviour.

Customers first tend to be inclined towards the bank they have been with for a long time. It is always a challenge to wean them away and while the entry of a new bank can make a difference for incremental deposits existing customers rarely exit their existing bank.

Second, often they are not aware of the higher rates offered because of the comfort with the trend. Third, there is inertia because opening accounts may not be easy, given the location differences even in case it is possible to do online banking after opening an account. Fourth, there is always scepticism that while the rates offered today could be higher, they could go down later in which case they would be losing out at a future date. It is assumed that things even out over a period of time as rarely does any banks continuously offer higher rates at all times. Fifth, there is a cost involved when moving out of a bank as there are several penalties which can be levied for premature withdrawal.

Therefore, interest rates for deposit holders would seldom be the clinching factor. In fact, the decision to choose a bank initially is linked with the location of residence after which it becomes mechanical and more of a habit.

Now when one talks of post offices, the situation is even more glaring. No one likes to go to a post office as there are always negative connotations. It ranges from the physical look of the post office to the staff and the perceived ease of transaction. It is always assumed that post office savings are for the lesser privileged people, which is what it was to begin with. Therefore, there is a certain level of apathy for going to a post office even though rates offered may be comparable if not better. Also, it is assumed that they are not technologically savvy and hence are inferior to banks in terms of offering online facilities and ATM access.

Hence, it can be said that post offices do not really compete with banks for deposits based on interest rates as tradition drives a lot of our savings habits. Just like how customers with PSBs never shifted to private banks due to better rates offered, the same holds for post offices too. Substitution has never been seen between post office deposits and bank deposits. In fact, at times the more market-savvy customers could shift incremental deposits to debt mutual funds or even company fixed deposits.

Hence this entire argument of higher deposit rates being offered on small savings being a barrier to banks lowering their deposit rates is not convincing and more of an excuse. Lowering their deposit rates could lead to migration to the market instruments at the margin as was witnessed in FY19 but the movement to post offices has definitely not happened.

32

Are Your Deposits Really Safe?

A notion that is widely held is that bank deposits are safe unlike other savings instruments in debt as there can never be a default by a bank. This belief is reinforced when one looks at PSBs where even declining profits and erosion of net worth does not evoke fear of loss of deposits. This sentiment is supported by history as post nationalization deposit holders have never really lost their deposit money if put in commercial banks. It has been taken for granted that the government would step in to ensure that the deposit holders are protected even in the worst of times when it comes to PSBs.

The failure of PMC Bank has however brought to the table the issue of safety of deposits. The sudden shutdown of a bank on grounds of unethical lending practices in 2019 has raised the issue of whether bank deposits are really safe. The shutdown of the bank overnight was accompanied by announcements of how much money one can withdraw from the bank which resulted in panic across the state of Maharashtra as several retired persons as well as funds (provident and pension funds) had kept deposits in this bank. The withdrawal limits were gradually raised over time but the sense one got was that, technically speaking, there was limited guarantee for deposit holders that their money was safe.

Failed banks have been merged with stronger ones which ensured continuity and while deposit holders did face uncertainty and a modicum of inconvenience due to shifting of deposits from one bank to another, the savings were secure. If one looks back at say the Global Trust Bank in the private sector which failed, the merger with the Oriental Bank of Commerce ensured that while the staff may have lost their jobs in course of time, the deposits remained firmly secure. The same holds for other private banks which were bailed out by the RBI.

This belief is supported by the concept of deposit insurance in the country where deposits up to ₹1 lakh per account was actually insured by the DGCIS as of 2019 as all banks have to take membership and get such cover. There is a catch however in that there is a limit of ₹1 lakh which covers all accounts held in the name of the person in the bank. Therefore, it is not without limit as is assumed and technically a bank which goes under without a bailout will mean that deposit holders with large banking relationship with the failed entity will receive not more than ₹1 lakh. Hence, the umbrella of security is very much limited in the extreme case.

It is true that banks will not be allowed to fail as it involves the deposits of several small account holders and retired persons whose savings are invested in such deposits on the premise that the money is safe. Few are aware of the risk factor that technically exists here and assume by default that there will not be a bank failure. But going ahead, there is a need to revisit the approach to bank deposits.

Table 32.1 is interesting as it gives a picture of the proportion of deposits which finally get covered under deposit insurance at two points of time. In 2008, 56 per cent of total deposits was covered while in 2018 it halved to 28.1 per cent. This ratio has been falling which is significant as the cover provided was for ₹1 lakh per customer and quite evidently most of the customers over the 10-year period were those who had deposits of a higher value. This held for all kinds of banks and even in case of RRBs

Table 32.1. Proportion of Deposits That Are Insured

Bank Group	As on 30 September 2018			
	No. of Insured Banks	Total Assessable Deposits	Total Insured Deposits	Percentage of Insured Deposits
2018–2019				
1. Public sector banks	19	7,201,100	2,224,400	30.9
2. Private sector banks	38	3,017,200	526,000	17.4
3. Foreign banks	46	558,600	16,600	3.0
4. Regional rural banks	51	378,300	225,100	59.5
5. Co-operative banks	1,941	849,200	377,500	44.5
6. Local area banks	3	700	400	57.1
Total	2,098	12,005,100	3,370,000	28.1
2008–2009				
1. SBI and its Associates	7	756,100	514,500	68.0
2. Nationalised banks	18	1,485,900	972,200	65.4
3. Public sector banks { (1) + (2) }	25	2,242,000	1,486,600	66.3
4. Private sector banks	24	655,200	149,800	22.9
5. Foreign banks	31	161,800	27,100	16.7
6. Regional rural banks	86	98,000	83,000	84.7
7. Co-operative banks	2,137	241,000	162,100	67.3
8. Local area banks	4	600	300	50.0
Total	2,307	3,398,600	1,908,900	56.2

Source: www.rbi.org.in.

which would tend to have low-income customers, the cover came down to 60 per cent from around 84 per cent. For foreign banks the cover is just 3 per cent which means that most of the deposits kept by customers are well over ₹1 lakh and get a lower insurance cover on this score. Even PSBs are secured up to 30 per cent as of September 2018, which gives an idea of how low the coverage is even for these entities. Quite clearly, the limit of ₹1 lakh is outdated and needs to be revised.

Banks are unique organizations which do their business on other people's money and not that of shareholders. For the maintenance of the system, it is essential that the deposit holders should be protected fully or else there would be uncertainty and retail holders would be at a disadvantage. These deposits would be no different than those kept with companies or NBFCs which are called unsecured deposits. The Budget for FY21 has addressed this issue and raised the level to ₹5 lakhs from the existing threshold of ₹1 lakh. This was quite timely considering that just a month after the budget was announced, Yes Bank has gone down under and the ₹5 lakh limit has provided comfort to an extent to the deposit holders. But the aim should be to provide full protection rather than partial to make bank deposits different from other savings forms. In fact, similar facilities are offered by post offices which belong to the government of India and hence are completely safe. It would make sense for households to shift their term deposits to these post offices and only maintain savings deposits with banks which can be used for daily requirements. Post offices also provide the facility of similar tenures and would be a very good substitute for bank deposits. In fact, often the structure of interest rates offered on long-term deposits in post office savings is higher than those offered by banks.

Such migration of bank deposits to post offices would also be a concern for the government because these are deposits which do not have limits and have to be accepted by the P&T department. They are transferred to the NSSF and drawn by both the central and state government as per a pre-decided formula. The issue of course will be that hypothetically if large amounts flow in the cost of funds for the government, it would go up as they are typically higher than the cost of market borrowings. Also, such an occurrence would also distort the bond market as there will be fewer market borrowings leading to shortage of government paper. Therefore, it is necessary to maintain the sanctity of bank deposits and ensure that there are no major swings due to issues related to credibility.

WHAT IS THE FUTURE OF BANK DEPOSITS?

Bank deposits have always been considered as the most secure form of savings historically as they were generally owned by the government and one could feel assured that savings were safe. In fact, households preferred these deposits because of this reassurance as even though the interest earned was lower compared to what was offered by corporates with high credit rating, the security aspects was the clinching factor. Small savings provided an alternative but have never really managed to catch on as they catered primarily to the non-metro regions and were associated with the lower- to middle-income levels. This is why their size remains limited today.

However, with these recent developments on the safety of bank deposits coming to the fore, the absence of higher guarantees would definitely make households reconsider their options. Debt mutual funds would compete with unsecured bank deposits and could offer higher returns with the benefit of capital gains if held for over three years. The recent development of the issuance of Bharat bond ETF is another step that could pose serious competition to bank deposits as the money collected is to be invested in only AAA-rated PSU bonds. This is again analogous to the small savings from the point of view of the savers. They do not have the flexibility of withdrawal before the term and unless such ETFs are listed, will an exit route be available.

Banks have not quite performed well in the past on managing their assets and the build-up of an adverse portfolio has been witnessed periodically. With several cases of mismanagement of assets by banks, the level of deposit holders' confidence has been maintained on account of the implicit guarantee assumed by everyone. Once this trust is questioned, there will definitely be a flight to safety as banks would be viewed differently.

An interesting question raised is that of how deposit holders would react to a situation where there is limited guarantee or no guarantee on deposits. Presently all banks are placed on par especially the commercial banks. If differentiation has to be made, it would work against those who do not perform well. Hence, all the periodic problems that afflict banks like NPAs or capital will actually accelerate the panic level in the system. Just think of a situation where a bank is categorized as being under PCA. The risk of failure looms large and the deposit holders would shift to other stronger banks which will automatically weaken a weaker bank. In fact, there would be a need for deposit ratings of a bank just like it is necessary for a company deposit or NBFC deposit. The redundancy of such a rating stems from the fact that there is an implicit guarantee that deposits would always be repaid when called for and that there would never be a run on a bank.

This issue has to be decided by the government along with the RBI because there needs to be certainty when it comes to the security of a deposit with a commercial bank. The public has to be educated on these nuances so that an informed decision is taken by the household when allocating savings across different avenues and within deposits across carious banks. The RBI has already been emphasizing the importance of inclusive banking which includes putting money in deposits. People have to be clear about where they stand on the security of a deposit and hence a White Paper on the same is called for. In fact, with differentiated banks in the system which now have small banks and payments banks besides commercial banks and cooperative banks, the customer has to know how they are different from the point of view of savings which are deployed as deposits. Not highlighting the possible risks would be mis-selling deposits to customers. There has to be clarity on the guarantee that is provided because even for a PSB today, which may become a private bank tomorrow, the assurance of government ownership will be missing.

NBFCs and Shadow Banking

The Next Frontier

It is not unusual for countries to have a parallel banking system as part of the organized financial system. This goes beyond the concept of informal lending which is prevalent in developing economies as the formal system is unable to reach a large section of the population. This is why it is referred to as the shadow banking system which offers financial facilities to the public which are similar to banks without being these institutions. In India, one part of this system which is partly regulated by the RBI is the set of non-bank FIs.

The NBFCs have grown in size and importance over the years to now be around 20 per cent of the size of bank lending. They are divided into two categories based on whether or not they accept deposits. If they do then they are very much regulated by the RBI. If they do not, then while regulatory standards are present in terms of capital adequacy, they are not subject to the same stringent regulation.

The evolution of NBFCs is interesting because they have all specialized in certain activities. They can be looking at home loans in which case they are called housing finance companies but are under NHB and technically are not classified as NBFCs by the RBI. Others deal with say auto finance or consumer finance while others can deal with all kinds of loans. They generally borrow funds in the market through bonds or loans from banks and lend the same for various purposes. Some of them specialize in gold loans or loans against property where they lend to individuals or small units based on pledge of such physical security where good margins are maintained. If the price of the collateral which is say gold comes down, adjustments are made accordingly. These loans are expensive but carry relatively lower risks for the lending institution.

Intuitively, it can be seen that their cost of borrowing would be higher as they do not raise funds through deposits like banks where there is some implicit guarantee of safety to market sources or banks. Therefore, in a way there could be double inter-mediation wherein banks take deposits from the public and then lend to NBFCs who in turn lend to various customers. Hence, the final borrower from the NBFC will normally pay more than what a bank charges, though there could be exceptions. At times the NBFC can borrow from the bond market which would tend to be higher than the MCLR of banks and then lend to the customer with margin that can be competitive. But at any rate, it will tend to be higher than a bank. Hence, their standards of due diligence when lending could be less conservative as they cover the risk with a higher charge.

The structure of NBFCs in terms of their size and classification is provided in Table 33.1 for FY18.

Table 33.1 shows that the major beneficiary from credit from NBFCs was 'industry' with a share of 54 per cent in FY18. Within 'industry', the large industry had the highest share of 26.8 per cent. Within services, the real estate sector was a major recipient of credit from NBFCs which is understandable as banks are more cautious when lending to this sector as it is considered to be a sensitive sector which constrains the flow of credit. Within the retail segment, auto loans were dominant as a large part of auto sales is driven by such loans.

Table 33.1. Structure of Lending of NBFCs

Items	March 2017	March 2018	Share in Total
Gross advances	1,485,782	1,764,317	100.0
Non-food credit	1,485,770	1,764,074	100.0
Agriculture and allied activities	40,104	47,051	2.7
Industry	868,864	953,303	54.0
Micro and small	48,133	55,736	3.2
Medium	17,645	24,483	1.4
Large	428,644	472,926	26.8
Services	234,485	317,197	18.0
Transport operators	15,161	19,437	1.1
Trade	31,567	34,454	2.0
Commercial real estate	96,256	125,101	7.1
NBFCs	20,535	24,196	1.4
Retail loans	259,668	361,701	20.5
Housing loans	16,080	13,330	0.8
Consumer durables	5,475	8,670	0.5
Credit card receivables	12,932	17,525	1.0
Vehicle/Auto loans	106,056	165,300	9.4
Other non-food credit	82,650	84,822	4.8

Source: www.rbi.org.in.

In this context, a comparison can be made with o/s bank credit for the same sectors.

- For credit to real estate, bank loans were ₹1.85 lakh crore which is marginally lower than that of NBFCs which were ₹1.25 lakh crore.
- For auto loans, banks had exposure of ₹1.90 lakh crore compared with ₹1.65 lakh crore for NBFCs.

Interestingly, a number of corporates that deal with certain lines of business do set up finance companies which while being open to all business lines would tend to get linked with the sales of the parent company. Hence, if the parent company sells cars, the finance company would focus on car finance, and buyers of cars from the company would have the option of taking finance from this company. Hence, in a way it is a fairly well-defined circle which makes the end-to-end solution possible with the finance company being a part of the supply chain where the part concerned is finance.

SMEs in particular have been quite active when borrowing from NBFCs as they have a wider reach as often their branches or touchpoints could be a small office room from where loans are given. This helps to lower operating costs as well as opens scope for wider reach. They also work on the concept of outsourced staff which may operate from homes but do business for the NBFC. In this manner, overheads are kept to the minimum with remuneration being linked with business obtained.

The NBFCs are an important part of the financial ecosystem, not just in terms of their lending but are also linked strongly with the banking system. Loans given by banks to NBFCs as of March 2019 were ₹6.41 lakh crore which is quite significant for the RBI to be worried about. They become systemically important because any showdown in a NBFC becomes a banking problem as loans not serviced become NPAs of banks. This is why they are important.

NBFCs of a certain size and performance have been looking to become banks and this holds also for the category of FIs of which IFCI is a glaring example. The reason is that these institutions do have a tough time in running a high-cost business as the lending charges are higher with more risk appetite being a part of the deal. However, the reaction to this move has been not very positive.

IDFC, which was set up essentially to finance infrastructure, got permission to become a commercial bank when the RBI gave permission to two institutions to turn into banks. However, IFCI was not given permission nor any other NBFC. The former is significant because IFCI is owned by the government and could have justification just as IDBI got permission in 1993 to set up its bank. The rationale for both ICICI and IDBI and more recently IDFC was that their original model was not sustainable and hence there was merit in turning into a bank.

NBFCs turning into a bank would have to follow all the banking guidelines from Day 1. This includes CRR and SLR. Capital adequacy norms have already been specified and may become less onerous once they get converted into banks. Similarly, priority sector lending would be mandatory, which again could be a challenge for some of them as while there is lending to agri-culture, SMEs and affordable housing the target of 40 per cent would still be quite high. The benefits of being bank would be compelling like getting access to deposits.

NBFCs came back into focus first during demonetization and later when the crisis erupted starting with ILFS. Growth in their business was quite impressive as they were able to fill the gap left by banks which were overwhelmed with the entire demonetization process. The party lasted until the fissures showed in their models. This included the conventional NBFCs as well as HFCs that followed similar strategies. The approach was simple. To keep costs down, they borrowed in the short-term market especially CP which had a duration of up to one year. This was rolled over continuously so that there was backup of long-term assets which could be for housing or even infrastructure. Normally these institutions should have been taking long-term loans from banks or borrow from the debt market by floating bonds and debentures so that the tenures of the assets, that is, home loans in particular. However, this would have pushed up costs and in order to compete favourably with banks which had access to demand and savings deposits that helped to reduce costs, the route chosen was the CP market. It was not surprising that this market flourished due to these institutions which accounted for 55–65 per cent of total issuances. The ILFS crisis ignited crisis of confidence as mutual funds started selling paper of NBFCs which led to a crisis where they were unable to raise funds through the CPs and this had a ratchet effect on several such companies.

Therefore, there is a sound reason for the NBFCs to turn into banks as they have the reach and expertise to do what banks also do. Regulatory flexibility is what is required to keep this model viable or else the lending would always be high cost which would be acceptable only to the lower-rated companies.

34

RBI versus Government

Is It a Healthy Relationship?

The idea of having a central bank which is also the monetary authority is that there is an independent organization which is in charge of conducting the affairs of the monetary sector which sets benchmarks in monetary policy as well as oversee the operation of banks. Therefore, the role of a central bank is manifold and includes printing currency, conducting monetary policy, being an agent of the government and hence a banker for the same, managing the forex reserves of the country and hence the exchange rate besides being a banker to banks. While this is what all standard textbooks say, the role gets expanded when one looks at the attention paid by the central bank to all issues which pertain to banking which includes the controversial case of NPAs. The monitoring of capital which is an intrinsic part of banking ever since there is a universal pursuance of the BIS norms, means that the central bank also has to guide the banking system to being compliant with the global best practices. The scope of the central banks stretches to cooperative banks, NBFCs, RRBs and so on which makes the role all encompassing.

Besides conducting these operations, the role is also one of bringing about development so that there is growth in all segments in an orderly manner. This basically involves introducing various reforms in different segments of banking and financial markets so that they are aligned with the times and provided with specific incentives or safeguards depending on the situation. This is why the central bank has dedicated teams for monitoring and administering policy for each and every segment.

To accomplish these goals, there is a great deal of independence that is required for the central bank to operate efficiently. It is assumed that the central bank is equipped with a team of professionals and the job is to ensure that all activities are carried out as per the rule book so that there is no conflict of interest. This is one reason why the central bank is not a commercial entity and if it earns profit, it is more an outcome of its activities rather than a goal that is being pursued. As the central bank is agnostic to ownership or profit, it is really not concerned with which entity gains or losses as long as the system is in order. With this in mind, the conflicts between the RBI and the government which has erupted in the last few years may be discussed.

The first issue is of the RBI talking on government issues. Is this the right thing or is there something fundamentally amiss? There is no answer here as at the theoretical level there should be a healthy debate on each authority talking on other issues pertaining to the other entity. Therefore, the RBI should be in a position to talk on the fiscal situation just like how the government should talk on the monetary situation. The government gets involved because thought processes and hence policy action like those relating to interest rate affect the fiscal position of the government as costs go up. Also, the government would like interest rates to be low so that companies can borrow and bring about growth which in turn will boost government revenue. The RBI is worried about the fiscal deficit as it means that monetary policy has to accommodate the same to reduce volatility in the market and hence there is reason to be overly concerned on this issue. Higher government borrowing leads to greater claim on limited bank resources which in turn can crowd out the private sector. Therefore, the RBI is concerned with government spending and does send signals continuously to rein the same as it can upset all monetary policy actions.

Now things can get stretched further which leads to a situation of conflict when the tone changes. The problem with economists is that they tend to comment on everything which tends to stoke controversy. Hence, there have been cases when Governors with an academic background have spoken on political issues which lead to potential situations of conflict. This rarely happens in other countries where the lines are clearly drawn, though of late this has been seen in the USA too where the President has not minced words when commenting on the actions of the Federal Reserve. In fact, there have been clear innuendos to claim that the President can dispense with the Governor if the person is not performing in accordance with the wishes of the government.

But in terms of views on the economy, traditionally there has been variance with the government always being overly optimistic and the RBI being cautious. This can be expected as the former has to face a political audience and is always gung-ho on everything in the economy. The same does not hold for the RBI which takes a cautious view and in a way is more pragmatic.

Connected to providing opinion is the issue of monetary policy. Government interference in the conduct of monetary policy is not uncommon with the most overt case being that in the USA where Mr Trump has been more than vocal in his view on lowering of interest rates. The government thus has a voice in opining on monetary policy but the central bank has the prerogative of heeding to the advice or command. This is one of the reasons why there is a MPC for most central banks which have been adopted by India too. The idea of having a committee is to ensure that the view taken is not by an individual but by a group of learned men and women. This makes sense because, practically speaking, when the Governor takes a view it is unlikely that there will be dissent from within the Bank and having independent members act as a check.

In India too, there is now a MPC which consists of six members of experts, three from the central banks and three from outside and in case of a tie in opinion, the Governor gets to decide. Ideally this could have been made seven members—an odd one so that it becomes more transparent. But interestingly, there never has been the case where the Governor had to use his power as there seemed to be consensus on every occasion. This may sound surprising considering that the three independent members are economists who normally tend to differ on everything. There is a view that the RBI should ideally not have three members on the committee as they would tend to move towards the Governor's or Bank's view and there should be more independent members. In fact, even among the independent members there has to be representation from various constituencies and having three academicians would not bring in this diversity. This argument is extended to support having someone from industry, the liabilities side of banks, bankers, government, retired bureaucrats, fund houses and so on, so that all views would be presented. Probably in course of time when there is a review of the concept of MPC, these views could be considered.

The irony is that when the government chides the RBI for being standoffish on interest rates, it is misdirected because the committee has been constituted by the former and has taken the decision and hence it is not that of the RBI. Also, the main goal for targeting has been specified by the government at 4 per cent and hence there can be no blame put on the RBI for being intransigent. When the view is on how to interpret inflation direction, the call is taken by six members and not the RBI. Hence, there should actually be no complaint directed at the central bank.

The third issue which comes up often in this case that pertains to government decisions on banking. Here the one which is often debated is bank loan waivers. This is more ideological but the central bank has always spoken against this scheme as it sets a precedent. Besides it vitiates the spirit of banking if waivers are given as they create a moral hazard. The broader issue should the RBI be talking on this issue if does not mean any loss for the banks as the money should be paid by the government?

The same holds albeit in a different manner when the government tries to force certain programmes on the banking system like the Jan Dhan scheme or even the MUDRA loans. These are rather elaborate schemes of the government under the umbrella of financial inclusion which have been introduced that serve wider goals of development. A Jan Dhan account is useful for enabling cash transfers for various schemes. MUDRA loans are targets set for banks so that the SMEs are able to get loans. The schemes are good in scope and are driven through the PSBs. Here the RBI really has no say as the government can defend these moves as being driven by virtue of being the owner of these banks. Therefore, it is not really the RBI to say anything on the issue.

Fourth, the NPA issue has been controversial in terms of its resolution. The 12 February 2018 circular on NPA resolution of large accounts clearly stated that a one-day default would mean that the bank will have to start off the resolution process with the client in the next 180 days failing which it would be referred to the IBC which can mean the sale of asset. The move was applauded by the industry and even the government had to clap since the RBI was only drawing up a scheme to ensure that the insolvency law got teeth. And the insolvency Act was moved by the government in 2016 and spoken off as being the solution to the problem of NPAs. Therefore, the rules and implementation looked fine. However, once the truth dug in it was realized that several large loans got stuck in this abyss and there were several representations made to the government. This is turn made the government ask the RBI to reconsider the notification. But the RBI was unrelenting which led to another major difference of opinion that escalated into a clash of personalities.

Can it be said that the rule was all about the RBI and the banks and that the government had no right to interfere? Prima facie economists argued that this was the case as the resolution was now getting diluted significantly on this score as companies could get away once again. All the distance that the RBI had travelled to solve the NPA issue had gotten vitiated with any dilution in norms. With the Supreme Court subsequently ruling that the RBI notification was void, it was a victory for the government in a way.

The government on the other hand was justified in its view though had little power of coercion on the RBI. In fact, the only way it showed its dissatisfaction was by constantly putting pressure on the central bank which did not work. Now the government has to see the larger picture and while the RBI can look at NPAs, the former has to look at sustainability of the sector and hence economy and was within its right to lobby with the RBI. At no stage was the RBI asked to withdraw the circular.

Therefore, it can be seen that the so-called conflict of opinion between the two has been exaggerated to an extent and while the government was well within its right to be caustic on the RBI actions, it has never really forced the RBI to change regulation. On the other side it was also argued that such constant criticism of the central bank had led supposedly to the resignation of a Governor which was definitely a blow to the system as the wrong signal was sent to the outside world. It was interpreted as being more than a coincidence. Also, as this act came in just after demonetization when the general belief was that the RBI was not in favour of the move, the issue was sensationalized. Therefore, from the point of view of perception building such differences of opinion do tend to present a picture where the government seems to be dictating terms which is not the case. One may recollect that even in an earlier regime of the UPA, the FM had stated with a touch of sarcasm that he would have to walk the road alone if the RBI was not helping out by lowering interest rates.

The question really is as to what should be the ideal relationship between the central bank and the government? The central bank is finally a part of the system and in a way is connected with the government. The government should ideally, for the sake of prudence, not comment too much on the RBI policies as it would vitiate the perceived independence of the central bank. The government has an interest in certain decisions while the RBI does not as it is concerned with the overall stability of the banking system. But as the appointment of the Governor as well as Deputy Governors is by the government, there is an implicit understanding that the central bank is, in a way, part of the system.

Ideally, there should be a dotted line which should not be crossed. Governments come and go and the overruling of the central bank's decision in one regime can backfire in the next and there would be no one to apportion the blame. This is what the government should ideally keep away from interfering in the RBI actions as it can be detrimental in the long run. One can see a number of cases where the central banks of countries in Africa and Latin America have pursued ultra-liberal policies and brought the country to ruin. Treating NPAs lightly can win votes in the short run but can be deleterious in the long run. This is why systems collapse; and that is why prudence is the way out.

This is where there should be respect shown to professionals who run the central bank. Statements made by politicians always give a different meaning to the situation as against say a similar remark made by the Finance Secretary as the latter is a professional and would be speaking in this capacity. Therefore, the mode of communication used and the language involved can send different signals on the same issue.

Central banks have to be independent and cannot be used as a tool to run political agendas. The rules of the game should be laid down which define the perimeter within which the central bank operated. The role in terms of controlling certain targets has to be spelt out and it should be left to the experts to sort them out. In this way, an objective definition of the inflation concept for the MPC was significant because it made the process more transparent as prior to this structure, the central bank always spoke about growth with stability with no definite numbers put down which left it open to interpretation. On other aspects too there should be clarity such as currency so that there is nothing left in the open.

Quite interestingly, even here there has been a different interpretation given by the MPC to the concept of linking interest rates with inflation. In the earlier regime under Dr Patel, it was clearly stated that the legislative mandate was to target only inflation while the present regime has looked at growth too at times when taking a call on interest rates. However, given that these debates are across professionals, it only adds to the intellectual content which would sound like an order if coming from the Finance Minister.

35

Handling Public Debt?

The RBI has traditionally been the banker to the government and the role means managing the debt of the government which involves both the enabling and maintenance of the same. This is an agency role and the idea of the central bank handling the same is to ensure that it maps well with the overall liquidity situation in the country. Being the monetary authority, the RBI is abreast on a real-time basis on the monetary situation in the country and is best able to manage the debt to be raised. The timing is always important so that there is no untoward pressure on the market given the state of liquidity. This involves not just the central government but all the states. The government needs money to spend and if it were to borrow independently in the market, there can be chaos. This is why the two entities jointly issue a calendar of securities to be raised every six months so that there is no surprise sprung on the market. Also, for temporary mismatches which can lead to liquidity issues for the government there are facilities like WMA (ways and means), overdraft, and so on, so that work does not stop.

Is there a conflict of interest in the RBI handling government debt? The answer is an emphatic 'no' because the central bank is an independent party which manages debt to ensure the stability in the system. It has no view on the rate at which the government borrows as the borrowing is based on the necessity of the government when the income and expenditure do not match. Beyond this the market decides on the interest rate. Hence, while the government would like the cost of borrowing to be kept down, the RBI is agnostic to the cost and would ensure that the auction goes off successfully. In fact, at times other measures are used such as term repos or OMOs in case liquidity is tight and comes in the way of such borrowing programmes of the government. In fact, the controversy in the last couple of years on the RBI not lowering the rates as much as the government would have liked supports the view that the central bank is really not concerned with the cost of borrowing for the government.

There has been a case made that the two functions of central banking and debt management should be separated and a new debt agency created which looks after the borrowings of both the central and state governments. This may not be a sound idea as it will create another structure which has to work with the RBI or else there can be a major misalignment. Let us see why this may not work.

A separate public debt agency would be entrusted with the job of managing all the auctions of the government. As there are also state governments involved, this will mean that it would necessarily have to handle all of them as it cannot be just the centre and not the states. This will mean handling around ₹10–12 lakh crore of issuances every year which will normally tend to only increase. The problem with issuances is that presently there is no system which ensures that if bonds are not bought, they can be absorbed by the RBI. Hence, matching the two becomes important. The PDA has to be fully aware of the liquidity situation for timing these issuances.

The RBI presently is in charge of monetary policy which is not just announcing monetary policy measures but also monitoring the market. The market is interconnected and is not just the market for securities. It involves the call market, the G-sec market, the CBLO market and so on. Add to this the forex market where there is constant monitoring of the dollar movement with interventions at the right time to ensure that the state of liquidity is maintained. This also ensures that rates remain stable and volatility is reduced to a large extent. While the RBI maintains that it has no particular exchange rate in mind, it is definitely against speculative forces driving the rates and hence works towards lowering volatility in the market.

Can the PDA be aware of all these factors? While theoretically monitoring the same may not be onerous, no action can be taken by the PDA as it would be within the realm of the central bank. Therefore, taking a 360-degree view of the markets at large and bringing about selective effective intervention is the forte of the RBI and cannot be that of the PDA if so created.

Further, the market is driven also by the RBI when other monetary policy measures like the OMO or LAF are conducted. These are two very critical measures of monetary policy that happen on an almost real-time basis. There involves the sale and purchase of government paper by the RBI to maintain the liquidity situation as well as influence rates. Such actions have a bearing also on the primary issuances both in terms of interest as well as pricing. This is why the RBI seems to be in an advantageous position to handle the market for government paper.

Under these circumstances, having a new organization for managing debt does not make too much sense as the idea of debt management has to be in accordance with monetary policy powers. It cannot be that the PDA handles debt while in talks with the RBI as the latter takes decisions based on what the MPC feels. Therefore, having a separate agency will only create administrative work and will lead to interference with the functioning of the RBI as the PDA will have incentive to keep rates low while the government would prefer market forces to be the deciding factor.

A related suggestion made is that the public debt department of the RBI can be hived off instead of creating a new set
of staff. This too does not make sense as the basic argument is
that managing debt is part of the entire system of liquidity and
monetary management which should be under the central bank
to make things robust.

36 RBI Reserves

Leave Them Alone

One of the most controversial issues that have surfaced in 2018 was the transfer of reserves of the RBI to the government. Transfer of surplus is acceptable as any profit made by the central bank through its operations belongs to the government, even though the profit earned is quite unique because the central bank can print 'n' number of notes or create 'reserve money' as and when required and lend the same and make money.

This was quite singular as there has so far never been a verbal debate fought on the subject with there being strong cases put forward on both sides. It has since been clarified that such a possibility as legal and provided for by statute and hence when the government first made the pitch for the transfer of reserves of the RBI, it was perfectly within the rules of the game even though it was never considered before. To resolve this debate, a committee was set up to decide on how best to use the reserves of the central bank.

The central bank of any country is quite unique in the sense that it has a balance sheet which is different from that of the other entities which run such a statement. By virtue of being the central bank, the RBI has control over the size of the balance sheet and can print currency at will—at least theoretically. Most central banks are judicious and do not do so. But there have been instances where dictators of countries like in Zimbabwe or Venezuela have made the central bank print tons of currency which has led to inflation in the range of million per cent. Therefore, central banks have to be discreet when they build their balance sheets. But still it is different as there is no law that stops the central bank from increasing the domestic currency especially if it is not linked to gold which is the case now for almost all countries (some may still have a link with forex reserves).

There was a time when the currency in circulation was a function of the amount of gold held by the central bank which was the gold standard which got linked to the currency rate too. But this was abandoned after the Great Depression and while some countries tried to live with a link to the dollar, it is now virtually free float in most countries where the decision is taken internally.

The liabilities of the RBI can be seen in Table 36.1. They comprise mainly currency and other liabilities. The other liabilities include a contingency fund of ₹2,321 billion and currency and gold valuation of ₹6,916 billion. As can be seen, these reserves get created when assets accumulate on the other side of the balance sheet. These are investments in foreign and domestic securities. As the RBI keeps buying government securities and holds them, the assets keep adding up while the liabilities will be through the creation of reserves. The deposits held are those kept by the government and banks (CRR claim) and are hence exogenous.

When a surplus is earned by the RBI during the year, if it is left untouched, then it is transferred to the reserves. Income is earned on forex assets and G-secs. The latter accrues when gains are made when selling securities as well as interest paid on the holdings by the government. The sale is more when OMOs are conducted when securities are sold to absorb liquidity which can yield a gain or loss for the central bank. The compulsions are hence not like those of a treasury of a bank or company but more due to monetary operations. Therefore, a central bank is a healthy entity which earns as it goes. When the RBI lends in the LAF channel (that is the repo operations which is overnight, term or the now more novel long-term repo operations), banks pay the repo rate. In a situation of deficit liquidity in the system, there would be a tendency for the RBI to increase its income. Further, when the RBI buys securities from banks through OMOs, then the securities that are purchased earn an interest for the central bank. A liquidity shortfall in the system is a profitable venue for the RBI. On the other hand, when there is surplus liquidity in the system, the RBI will be paying interest to banks and will earn less income. And in case of a deficit, when the RBI provides liquidity it creates money which is the prerogative of the central bank by getting in more 'reserve money' or 'high powered money' and thus increases money supply in the system.

Being the RBI, there is really no cost of matching these assets through liabilities even if it means printing them.

The question raised by the government was whether or not the RBI should hold such high reserves or should it transfer a part to the government. The logic is straight forward. The RBI

Table 36.1. Balance Sheet of RBI

Liabilities	2017–2018	Assets	2017–2018
Capital	0.05	**Assets of Banking Department (BD)**	
Reserve fund	65.00	Notes, rupee coin, small Coin	0.09
Other reserves	2.28	Gold coin and bullion	696.74
Deposits	6,525.97	Investments-foreign-BD	7,983.89
Other liabilities and prov	10,463.04	Investments-domestic-BD	6,297.45
		Bills purchased and discounted	0.00
		Loans and advances	1,638.55
		Investment in subsidiaries	33.70
		Other assets	405.92

(Continued)

(Continued)

Liabilities	2017–2018	Assets	2017–2018
Liabilities of Issue Department		Assets of Issue Department (ID)	
Notes issued	19,119.60	Gold coin and bullion (as backing for note issue)	743.49
		Rupee coin	9.26
		Investments-foreign-ID	18,366.85
		Investments-domestic-ID	0.00
		Domestic bills of exchange and other commercial papers	0.00
Total liabilities	36,175.94	Total assets	36,175.94

Source: www.rbi.org.in.

for all purposes is an arm of the government. When the RBI earns a profit or surplus, the amount is transferred to the government. This is legitimate. An extension is that the balance sheet of the RBI belongs to the government, and hence, the latter can claim what is on it. Therefore, the argument has been made that a part of the reserves can get transferred to the government and a committee is to decide on the same.

The curious anomaly is that a part of the balance sheet of the RBI gets created due to the central bank holding on to government securities which are required for conducting monetary policy. The same set of assets in government paper has matching reserves that are created as per the accounting norms. This will mean that as the government will keep borrowing more in the market and as liquidity tightens, the RBI will buy paper from banks and then hold on to them. When this happens, the reserves will increase automatically and if the RBI was to pass on an equivalent to the government, then the latter gains both ways. This is the genesis of the puzzle.

Also, when a liability is reduced, the asset side too should witness a decline. Suppose the RBI was to offload G-secs which it is holding, this will create excess supply of paper in the market and the prices will move down and yields up. Therefore, a physical reduction of securities is not a feasible option. A possibility is that debt can simply be written off by the stroke of the pen just like how the liability was created. This can be done which will shrink the size of the balance sheet.

The other way out is to lower the reserves which have been kept against forex assets. But if that has to be done, the forex assets have to be lowered on the assets side. This can be done by either selling in the market, which is against the idea of holding reserves. Alternatively, it has be kept in a special off-balance-sheet account and not used for any purpose. This will be more of an accounting issue.

Therefore, any way one looks at it, the concept of transferring reserves of the RBI to the government does seem like an accounting procedure. This is analogous to the bank recapitalization procedure where money is created by an accounting entry wherein the government issues bonds that are subscribed by banks and no money is transferred as there is a simultaneous entry made in terms of the government increasing its capital in the bank. Here it will also involve crediting the government account with money which will in turn increase the volume of reserve money and hence money supply.

The resolution of this issue was done by the Bimal Jalan Committee which recommended a formula for sharing the reserves with the government. The more fundamental issue is whether the government should be even looking at such options or instead rely on its own resources which are generated in the ordinary course of activity. The novel idea to lay claim on reserves of RBI, it was argued by critics, was a desperate measure invoked at a time when expenses were high and revenue was just not increasing. This should not be the spirit it was further argued. This seems quite a valid argument and ideally the contribution should stop at the level of surplus transfers even though going beyond is legally tenable.

Also once done, such a measure can be invoked again as there is a precedent and this is something which needs to be monitored.

37

What Should Be the Tenure of RBI Governor?

The tenure of the Governor of RBI has been an issue of discussion as it is often felt that every Governor needs to get an extension, especially if the view is that the Governor has done some exceptional work during the tenure. The tenure is normally for five years but there have been cases where it is for three years. At times there are extensions while on other occasions there are none. Let us look at the arguments.

Normally it is felt that with the RBI occupying a pivotal role in the banking system, there is reason for the Governor to have long enough tenure to carry out an agenda which is normally spelt out when stepping into the office. This makes sense as in a dynamic set up one would require a reasonably long period of time to really make a difference. This is so because a shorter tenure or uncertain tenure will restrict the game plan as the Governor is aware that the next Governor could have a different view and accordingly a different set of priorities. Alternatively, there could be a rush to do a lot which can be challenging for the system as any change made needs all payers to play along as they have to adjust to the environment. It is for this reason that a five-year term appears to be quite appropriate.

A three-year term when given looks more like the government not being sure of the candidate or just preferring to take a shorter-term view. At times, the tenure of the RBI Governor may cross over two governments in which case there may be support for the tenure to be of a shorter duration.

The argument for a shorter duration can also be that the Governor is supposed to address only issues of short term in nature and with the possibility of an extension, can be drawn ahead if it is required. Therefore, five years can lead to some degree of closed-mind while three will keep the doors open for a change. But a shorter term creates controversy as the market always feels that the absence of an extension has something more diabolic behind the thinking and opens the door to controversy. Today irrespective of whether or not it is true tags are attached to various Governors. So, one Governor may be independent or too independent while another may be compliant. These are evidently creations of the media which is absorbed in the market and then gives rise to speculation when extensions are not given.

In fact with too much media attention, it is assumed that Governors should always take a tough stance and ask the government to back off. But this is not how it works as a collaborative effort is required all the time as it is a team effort involved at all stages. We do not expect employees to defy the CEO or the CEO to defy the Board which represents the owners. But for the RBI it is assumed by the media that a defiant stance is taken which is actually quite absurd.

Table 37.1 gives the tenures of various RBI Governors since financial sector reforms were introduced.

The issue of tenure of the RBI Governor has come up in the recent past on account of Dr Rajan not getting an extension as it was widely believed that there would be one consideration that the term was for three years. His predecessor was given a two-year extension. There was speculation that his approach to running the RBI was not in alignment with that of the government which led to an extension not being given. Also, the fact

Table 37.1. Tenures of Various RBI Governors

Governor	Tenure	Number of Years
S. Venkitaramanan	22 December 1990 to 21 December 1992	2
Dr C. Rangarajan	22 December 1992 to 21 December 1995	3
Dr C. Rangarajan	22 December 1995 to 22 November 1997	2
Dr Bimal Jalan	22 November 1997 to 5 September 2003	6
Dr Y. V. Reddy	6 September 2003 to 5 September 2008	5
Dr D. Subbarao	5 September 2011 to 4 September 2013	2
Dr D. Subbarao	5 September 2008 to 4 September 2011	3
Dr Raghuram G. Rajan	4 September 2013 to 4 September 2016	3
Dr Urjit R. Patel	4 September 2016 to 11 December 2018	2
Shri Shaktikanta Das	12 December 2018 onwards	

Source: www.rbi.org.in.

that he was appointed by a different government fuelled such speculation.

But as Table 37.1 shows, there have been instances of Governors having multiple terms which summed to five years. Dr Rangarajan had a term of three years which was extended by two years. Dr Subbarao too had a 3+2 combination.

However, the concept of a three-year term now seems to be the norm as Dr Patel too was given a three-year term as has Mr Das. It does look like that this could be the practice going ahead where the term will be kept to three years with the prerogative to extend it if required. This will be a break from the past where after Mr Venkataraman the term has tended to be five years with an extension for Dr Jalan.

There can be no clear answer on whether the term should be three years or five years but it would always be better to have a fixed term stated in general so that the incumbent knows exactly how to plan the agenda during the tenure. For a developing country, a longer term is desirable as there are lots of things that have to be done. This holds for India where there is still a large unorganized sector and a financial system that operates outside the regulated perimeter. The evolution of these alternative modes of finance was linked with the inability of the banking system to be accessible. Also, the formalization of norms or criteria for dealing with a bank as a deposit holder or a borrower has made the unregulated system easier to use. With the RBI trying to integrate the other parts of the system it becomes necessary to take a longer view of five years which supports such tenure. In fact, the movement towards a more integrated system requires a lot of fine-tuning in terms of structures as well as regulatory systems that call for a longer-term view.

Also keeping the term fixed without an extension can be argued for as there needs to be certainty in the time period that is offered to the Governor. Often the Governor of RBI would supposedly be having a different view from the government on various issues which in turn leads to conflict. As long as it is a healthy debate, there is nothing amiss. But once the perception spreads that the two are not in sync in spirit too then it leads to widespread speculation in the market which increases volatility. Normally such perceived conflicts peak while the term is coming to a close, and this leaves room to further speculation on whether the term will be extended and whether the Governor becomes more complaint. This issue can be addressed by making it clear that the term will be five years with no extension.

Also, for a body like the central bank, there must always be a churn for new ideas to come in. This probably holds for any organization and hence the tenure must be fixed so that a new incumbent has scope to bring about the inflow of new ideas.

Let us see how other countries address these issues. The Federal Reserve gives a term of four years which can be extended based on the prevailing line of thinking of the government. The Bank of England gives a term of eight years normally and hence offers opportunity for a longer term for the Governor. In case of ECB, there is a now renewable term of five years. For Japan, it is five years. Hence it does appear that three years may be too short a tenure for a Governor and should be extended to five years.

There are also issues regarding the background of the Governor of RBI. Let us look at all the questions that have been raised over the years given the pivotal role of the head of the central bank in India who has to work closely and smoothly with the Government of India. First, is whether the Governor should be an Economist or not. Historically, the Governors have tended to be economists though this is not a necessary condition. Besides, there is no clear definition of an economist. Normally all incumbents from the Ministry have been dealing with economic issues and hence have a very practical sense of economics. In fact, economists can be very theoretical and dogmatic especially if they are wedded to an ideology which is often the case. Therefore, they tend to be more intransigent in their views and would prefer to go by the book.

A background of economic functioning is desirable so that the interlinkages are understood of various sectors as most policies impact not just banking but all other segments. This is where probably career commercial bankers may lose out as their focus is always on banking and the larger picture is often not seen as it does not matter in terms of their job of being a CMD of a bank. Also, pure academic background may not be suited for the reason of not being able to marry the practical reality with theory. All economic theory or rather monetary theory is filled with jargon and modelling today. While these fancy models are good for ex-ante behaviour and effect, extrapolating the same for the future and living in tis tower could be impractical as the world is dynamic and results have to be in the short term. This is why pure academicians will not be suited for the role.

Second, does experience in the government matter? The answer is yes, as if the incumbent has worked in the government and has the background of the Civil Services, then there is a broader view of things. They would tend to know how the government works which is very important considering that whether or not we like it; the RBI is an arm of the government. Knowing how the government works means knowing how the politics works in the economic frame. Working in the Ministry gives one the tact to deal with politicians who do not understand economics but are good at ensuring that their party comes to power. The practical side is hence addressed by the person from the Ministry. While the central bank is an independent authority it has to work within a framework where there is harmony with the aspirations of the government. Dialogue and reconciliation are important factors that have to be considered along the way and here professionals from the Ministry have an edge.

Third, should the incumbent be from outside the country? This was the case with Dr Rajan who came with the background of an Indian citizen who had a qualification of engineering and management to begin with but topped it with a doctorate and is an acknowledged expert in finance and economics and worked as Chief Economist of IMF amongst other assignments. Does having a pure non-domestic experience give an edge? Those in favour say that it does as there are no preconceived notions and the best practices globally followed are brought into the frame. The case of Mr Mark Carney is one where a non-Englishman became Governor of the Bank of England. The counterargument is that the same can be imbibed in the globalized world and almost every top bureaucrat has considerable global exposure in the form of assignments in various multilateral agencies and hence cannot be a major advantage. In this context, it is pointed out that being from within has the advantage of knowing how to work within the system which ensures smooth functioning.

At times this is interpreted by the media as being more complaint which is not the case. Also, an outsider would not be aware of systems work in any country and would have a challenge communicating with the government. This is critical because monetary monitoring is the mirror image of all other government policies that require funding support for the constituents.

Fourth, should the incumbent have experience with the country? This ideally should be the case because the two main functions of the central bank in India are monetary policy and regulation of banks. The former requires knowing how policy measures work within the framework of the governance structure of the country and the latter is important because the complex system needs to be understood before applying any policy. But surprisingly the presence of commercial bankers stops at the level of Deputy Governor and all Governors have been from the Ministry or academia. This issue came to the fore when the country had demonetization imposed. It was announced that cash would be available in the ATMs after 48 hours. But it did time to sink in that the new notes were not compatible with the ATM machines which had to be recalibrated. While this may not exactly be what a RBI Governor should know, there could be several such processes on which policies are formulated that would require some knowledge. Here it is assumed that the experienced commercial banker serving as Deputy Governor would be better ·placed to advice on the matter. But the issue nonetheless is important for consideration. Besides, today with the dissemination of information and the sharing of best practices due to the BIS, one need not work outside to have knowledge of how the world works. While a couple of decades back working in international organizations offered an edge to the prospective Governors, this no longer holds as there is constant dialogue with global peers all the time.

Lastly, should there be a cut-off age for the Governor? This is pertinent in India because running an organization which has to continuously have an ideological dialogue with the government and other stakeholders require a high level of maturity. Governors cannot be speaking their minds in public as it sends incorrect signals. Conflicts are bound to be there when dealing with the government which have to be addressed with maturity and tact. Therefore, an age criterion is required and ideally 55 years may make sense. The argument for youth which goes for private enterprise does not hold here as RBI is not a commercial enterprise running to earn profits. We do not need risk-taking ability to be the criteria for selecting Governors (which holds for business and commerce) and hence age matters.

The appointment of the Governor of RBI is hence quite an interesting one as it does raise issues of varied nature that are not just connected with the subject knowledge. There have been instances like the Bank of England where an outsider from Canada was made the Governor which had worked smoothly. Therefore, there is nothing to exclude such persons from being appointed. However given that in India the maturity levels are not the same as in some of the western developed countries (the USA has also had the President imposing on the Fed Chairman while countries like Turkey have virtually ordered the central bank for action on interest rates), an insider is less likely to be rigid in the political sense.

38

MPC
Time to Go Back to the Textbook

The MPC is a foreign concept that has been brought into the process of monetary policy formulation. While such systems exist in several central banks, the one in the USA probably is most publicized as the Committee meets for two days before a decision is taken on interest rates. The same has been pursued in our context.

The concept of monetary policy is that the central bank meets periodically depending on the mandate. It used to be twice a year which got expanded to eight times and year and then reduced to six times a year. Therefore, presently there is a monetary policy review every two months when a call is taken on interest rates. The mandate comes by legislative action and hence the contours are really fixed. The MPC is to decide on the changes in the repo rate and have been mandated to target a CPI inflation number of 4 per cent. A band of 2 per cent has been fixed on both sides and hence the ideal situation is that the inflation number must be between 2 and 6 per cent. The Committee consists of six members, where three are independent experts and the other three are from the RBI. The members from RBI are the Governor, Deputy Governor and Executive Director where the latter two are involved with monetary policy. The decision on interest rates will be based on a majority vote. If there is a tie, then the Governor's decision will be final. The job of the MPC is to ensure that inflation remains within the range specified and in case this is not adhered to, there would be an explanation that has to be given.

Is this something unique for India ever since it was brought in 2016? The answer is yes and no. Yes, because the MPC per se did not exist earlier. No, because there was a technical committee which was existing doing a similar role. It was more of an advisory committee which had external members and some from the RBI. The difference was that the technical advisory committee was not in the nature of a decision-maker and the RBI Governor had the last word. Hence even if the Committee felt that rates should be lowered, the RBI Governor had the overwhelming power to go ahead with his view. The MPC hence is different because all the six members have the voting power and the Governor can overrule only in case of a tie.

There are different views on what should be the ideal composition of the MPC. One view is that all the constituencies must be accommodated in this effort and hence there should a representative from industry, academics, government and other regulators. A point missed is that monetary policy has an impact on savings, which is a very important part of the economy there should be a representative of households who can express views from this end. In such an event the MPC would become a lobbying forum. Therefore, it was decided apparently that it would be best to get experts from the academics to deliberate on these issues. Hence presently there are three economists from very reputed institutions on the MPC.

Having academicians on the MPC has its set of issues. They tend to get theoretical and hence the decision based on such views would tend to be slanted. While they would definitely also be looking at the practical side, the ideology they carry on their shoulder cannot be wished away. Therefore, the views could get tilted. Economists tend to carry badges with them and could be a monetarist or a Keynesian or a neo-Keynesian or a follower of New Classical Economics. Also, with economists normally always having differing view there could be multiple opinions put forward. Probably, this has been eschewed by having a single variable to be targeted, that is, CPI inflation. And surprisingly so far there has been a tendency for the Committee to have a similar view on most occasions. Therefore, this has not really created a chaotic situation.

How about targeting just CPI inflation? This is probably unique to our system because prior to the MPC being constituted the RBI policy always spoke about maintaining a balance between growth and inflation. This made a lot of sense because theory always draws trade-offs between the two which can then be driven by varying perspectives on the future of the economy. But the MPC directive is cast in stone and it is just the CPI inflation number that has to be targeted. This is significant because in one of the press conferences post policy announcements, the RBI Governor made it clear that their mandate is to target inflation and nothing else. Hence, even though growth, global developments, exchange rates, investment etc. are all part of the deliberations and enter the statement, the final decision is based on inflation perspective. The unique factor is that the minutes of the discussion of the MPC are released subsequently and contains the reasons given by each member on the decision that they have stood by. This makes the process transparent.

Is CPI inflation the right target? This question has been asked often because if one looks at the composition of the index it is heavily tilted to food items. There are some components that are quite different from normal calculations like house rent, health and education. Here the movements in the sub-price index are based on factors that do not change on a monthly basis. For example, the house-rent index is based on what government employees pay which is actually not the best proxy as rents in the country are diverse across cities, towns and villages. But it is hard to get these numbers and hence the central government HRA is being used. Now the thing about these numbers is that they change only periodically when the Pay Commission recommendations are invoked. Therefore, there would tend to be a jump in these numbers when reckoned this way after which they remain flat subsequently. This is not how the real estate market really behaves where rents move up and down. Further for items like health and education too, these charges change periodically when fees are revised upwards (never down) as are health charges. Therefore, there would be a bunching of costs in one year when the revisions are made. After this point, the price index would tend to be flat and show no change in inflation.

How about the number of 4 per cent? The Committee in its wisdom chose the target of 4 per cent which may have been bold though through a string of coincidences has been very much on the mark as the CPI inflation number has rarely strayed out of bounds. Table 38.1 gives the inflation rates in the last eight years gauged by both the new series which is being used that came into force post 2012 and the CPI for industrial workers which was the benchmark for all practical purposes before the advent of the new index.

But, is CPI inflation a valid index to target? This has become an issue for debate if one tries to trace how policy can control inflation. Theory says that if interest rates are increased, there would be less demand for funds in which case overall demand would come down and inflation will decline. The assumption really is that demand is being funded by bank credit

Table 38.1. Movement in WPI and CPI Inflation Indices

	2012–2013	2013–2014	2014–2015	2015–2016	2016–2017	2017–2018	2018–2019	2019–2020
CPI New	10.1	9.4	5.8	4.9	4.5	3.6	3.4	4.8
CPI-IW	10.44	9.68	6.29	5.65	4.12	3.08	5.45	7.53
WPI	6.9	5.2	1.3	–3.7	1.7	2.9	4.3	1.7

Source: www.rbi.org.in.

Table 38.2. Structure of CPI and Linkage with Borrowing

Category	Weight in CPI	Do We Borrow to Pay for It?
Food	45.86	Unlikely except credit card
Pan and tobacco	2.38	No
Clothing and footwear	6.53	Unlikely except credit card
House rent	10.07	No
Fuel	6.84	Unlikely except credit card
Miscellaneous	28.32	
Household goods and services	3.80	Unlikely except credit card
Health	5.89	Unlikely except credit card
Transport and communication	8.59	No
Recreation	1.68	Unlikely except credit card
Education	4.46	Possible for higher education
Personal care	3.89	No
Total	100.00	
Proportion that is leveraged		

Source: CSO: www.mospi.nic.in.

and other borrowings which get impacted when the repo rate is changed. Here one can look at the composition of the CPI index (Table 38.2) and link the same with the funding theory as if it cannot be established, there would be a question mark posed.

Therefore, it can be seen that only when credit cards are involved would the borrowing concept be applied. Out of a total outstanding credit of around ₹90 lakh crore, the outstanding credit card dues are just about ₹1.1 lakh crore, which is slightly more than 1 per cent, Education loans are around ₹70,000 crore. Combining the two, the leveraged based consumption would not be more than 2 per cent of total credit outstanding and hence change in interest rates will not really be able to drive credit decisions.

The other interesting point is that an increase in most of these components is not due to demand-supply imbalance but pure cost side factors. When the international price of oil goes up, fuel and transport costs move up. When onion crop fails, prices go up and increasing rates will not help to bring down prices. Similarly, when telecom companies increase their tariffs prices go up which cannot be related to excess demand.

The question really is whether higher rates deter students from taking loans for education or a patient for treatment? These are necessities. Similarly, loans are rarely taken to pay rent or electricity bills. Cards can be used for filling the vehicle with fuel more for convenience and not affordability. Hence, higher repo rates will not curtail the use of cards which tend to be used more as debit cards.

This raises the question of whether or not an increase in repo rate will actually affect demand. It normally works on investment where corporates are involved and not individuals. Individuals also can be affected when it comes to say housing where higher rates will lead to less demand for housing which lowers the demand for cement and steel which in turn can lower prices. But this does not work that easily.

Ideally, a producer's index would have been better because if the MPC targeted the WPI, it would directly affect industrial goods which are based on credit that would in turn lower the price increase. In fact, the RBI used to make reference constantly to WPI inflation earlier when targeting growth and inflation. But the new framework ignores growth and targets CPI inflation. Therefore, there is an anomaly here. At that time, often the critics view was that it was CPI which was important when calculating the real interest rate and this was the time the CPI inflation was higher than WPI. Hence, there tended to be a swing to the CPI in terms of impact through real rates. In a sense, the central banks kept changing the goal post by shuffling between the WPI and CPI as the anchor inflation number.

In this case, the interpretation of the CPI being targeted is more from the view of tempering inflationary expectations which get built into producers' plans.

How about the growth objective? While the mandate talks expressly on targeting CPI inflation it does not dwell on growth. The MPC in some of the statements has made it clear that there is no reason to focus only on inflation as growth matters. Hence with inflation within range and growth low, there is reason to lower rates. This sounds reasonable and should ideally be in the mandate. Probably it was felt that to begin with it should be unequivocal and target inflation only. This is something that can be taken up so that there is clarity in the concept of the MPC mandate.

Another concept that merits discussion is the concept of stance. The stance has become important in terms of what the market expects and interprets. However, no one is sure what it means. There was a time when the stance was an interpretation and terms like dovish and hawkish were used. However, things have changed and it is more like 'neutral', 'accommodative' or 'calibrated' tightening being used. This has added to the confusion as interpretation is not straight forward.

If rates are not changed but the stance is neutral, does it mean that things are not expected to change in future? If the rates do not change, but the stance is accommodative, does it mean that the RBI will ensure that there will always be liquidity to maintain stability? This also is unclear because liquidity management is another function which goes on in parallel and not dependent on the stance taken. For if there is a liquidity crunch the RBI has to intervene irrespective of stance. If the rates are not changed but the stance is calibrated tightening, does it mean that the next step is likely to be the hardening of rates? This sounds logical though may not always be true especially if the next step ends with a rate cut, which has happened. Does this mean that even though the stance was for future tightening, the next action was actually a rate cut because conditions changed so dramatically? Therefore, there is considerable ambiguity in terms of interpretation of the concept of stance. At some point, the press call did have the RBI say that accommodative meant that the possibility of rates going up are low.

Interesting possibilities that arise are the following. As growth cannot be separated from the policy framework it must be included somewhere in the signposts to make it transparent as that is the idea of casting the 4 per cent CPI target in stone. The market will then know if the growth path is on course. The ambiguity comes in when the government says that growth at 7 per cent is robust but the RBI maintains that with inflation being stable at less than 4 per cent a thrust has to be given to growth which is lagging. By quantifying the growth rate, the action of the central bank or rather MPC can be anticipated.

Also, as the MPC keeps recommending rate cuts as inflation comes down, the question is when will this chain stop? Suppose inflation keeps moving below 2 per cent, will the repo cuts extend to say 4 per cent or lower? Alternatively, if inflation goes up from 4 per cent towards 6 per cent without touching the limit, should the call be to increase interest rates or keep them unchanged? Therefore, the path of monetary policy will always be interesting. Going by how the MPC has taken decisions there is no fixed way of determining whether such movements in inflation will provoke interest rate action. This is where a subjective view comes in where the decision is taken based on the expert's view of the situation. Expectations on future inflation get combined with growth conditions and there is a judgment call taken on what should be done on rates.

Therefore, there are lots of unanswered questions in the way in which the MPC targets an inflation index and reacts to conditions. At times when the market expected a rate cut, there was a pause. On others even as inflation kept rising, the decision was to lower rates rather than take a pause. This is what will keep the market guessing and it will not be driven by any implicit algorithm.

Conclusion

This book has tried to be objective in presenting facts and added subjectivity in terms of views. The purpose was to answer the question on whether or not Indian banking has come of age. This is appropriate because we have been through over 25 years of financial sector reforms. As is the case with any set of reforms, they start off in a big way and have an impact by creating the necessary disruption. This is in terms of ideology and application. But then there is a period of consolidation when everyone has to reconcile with the situation, and a number of tenets that have been put forth do not seem to be entirely workable. This is when there are lines drawn and systems move backwards as the practical reality leads ideology and no longer the other way. Some may call it compromise, but it is necessary as all reform packages have limitations when it comes to dealing with political economy.

Yes, political economy is important because as much as we try and steer clear of politics, it can never be separated from economics as all governments come to power based on promises that have to be fulfilled and in so doing, prudence is given a skip. While in the puritanical sense the critic is right in her criticism, practically speaking, one cannot separate the two and politics has to dominate when it comes to crunch time.

So, if we look at banking this is what is the case. Governments just don't want to give up control of PSBs as these institutions were so created for serving a social purpose and while Basel II and Basel III norms hold for ensuring that banks follow prudential norms, the owner which is the government tends to dominate the functioning of the banks. This is the irony here as the RBI is against corporate ownership of banks for this reason. There is suspicion that funds will flow to their own interests which should be avoided. But for PSBs, it is accepted that the owner can run programmes which require backup from banks even if they are not prudent. Banks do not have a say here.

What have we witnessed along the way? The book has looked at reforms as they were conceived based on the Narasimham Committee Report. This sort of sets the perimeter of operation with various goalposts being defined along the way. There can be no objection to any recommendation made by the Committee which definitely was in a way on par if not ahead of its time. The first part of the book was objective and descriptive and juxtaposed data over this period. Essentially the structure of banking over two periods of time was examined in some detail. Some of the observations were quite revealing.

First, having new private sector banks was not an unmixed blessing. While access and experience improved with the effects spilling over to PSBs, quite a few of them were not sustainable and were merged with others. But for sure, the market share of PSBs had to come down which was expected as more players joined the fray.

Second, there was also a shift in terms of location of branches which moved more to the metro and urban areas which was driven by purely business concerns. Post nationalization banks per force had to open more rural branches which got reversed once the arena was opened up.

Third, the structure of deposits showed some interesting changes. Metro and urban branches dominated in terms of share in total because this is where savings were high. Financial inclusion which continued to be our goal brought in an increase in a number of accounts, but the actual savings came from the business centres. Also, the maturity pattern of deposits changed and while the longest term of above five years changed, the shorter maturities dominated which reflects the savings preferences of savers. A part of this explanation can be found in the ownership of deposits where the share of government and corporates increased as these entities typically keep deposits in short-term maturities. Surprisingly, the top 10 states in total deposits remained virtually unchanged reflecting the static pattern of financial savings in the country.

Fourth, the structure of bank credit also underwent some significant changes. The metro region dominated in terms of disbursement of credit which can be attributed to the fact that most borrowing from head offices tend to move to these regions. Also, loans of higher denomination would have to be approved in the head offices which are metro-centric. The pattern of distribution of credit changed with retail gaining at the expense of industry and services. This can be attributed more to the progressive sophistication of households where borrowing became the norm. Earlier there was a stigma attached to being a debtor. But with the acquisition streak increasing with rising incomes individuals have never shied from borrowing for a house, vehicle or even durable good. Further, while the share of use of credit cards in overall credit is low, it has grown quite rapidly as these habits have caught on. Banks have been adept to catch these tendencies fast at a time when they have had to compete with NBFCs and HFCs which are alternatives that have grown at a rapid pace over the years. Lastly, interestingly, loans with size of over ₹1 crore account for 60 per cent of total credit and less than 0.1 per cent of total accounts! This gives a clue as to why banks like to go after big tickets loans as it helps them meet their targets with less effort, albeit with higher risk attached.

Fifth, in terms of structure of income, interest income is the mainstay and while treasury operations have improved, the same has not been seen in fee income. Hence, here there has not been much of a shift to non-fund-based activity. Here the foreign banks dominate in terms of such income which is also reflected in their domination in the contingent liabilities of the system.

Sixth, there has been some distinct change in the staffing pattern of banks which has moved towards having more officers and less support staff. This is a major change in the outlook which was brought by the private banks and got imbibed in the PSBs too over time. The focus is on higher productivity which has been enabled by technology as the concept of paperwork and passing of files has been reduced and made less relevant progressively. There has also been a smart increase in the average compensation of bankers across all segments. Here while the foreign banks are way above the average, PSB cost per employee is actually higher than that of private banks which comes as a revelation. This is against the generally held belief but can be explained by the relative less egalitarian structure in new private banks and substantially lower pay scales in old private banks which are fairy niche in nature and conform more to tradition in terms of structure with conservative pay packages.

The section on controversies in Indian banking is definitely more thought-provoking as there are always two sides to the issue. There is clearly no straight answer on whether or not government intervention is right in PSBs, given that it is the owner. If a private sector owner can call the shots in an owner-run company, which holds also for banks, then there is a strong justification for the government to interfere especially so as it is done in the name of the 'larger good'.

As far as possible, the treatise looks on both sides of the argument and then opts for one of them which may not always be against what has been adapted by the system. The reader is free to choose what appeals to her the most. One may find the approach 'two handed' which is the route most economists opt for as they prefer to be balanced and conclude that a stance is not being taken. This has been attempted at the end of the discussion when the stance is unequivocal.

Some of the issues raised have deep implications. We should not go slow on IBC if we are serious about NPA resolution and the government should be the last entity to ask for dilution, given that the initiative came from here. Even the concept of PCA which stops weak banks from performing certain business activity until they are back on their feet became controversial when implemented. If a system has been approved, it needs to be followed and this should be the spirit. True having such a rule running impedes the landing activity of the concerned banks but provides the guidelines to move out of the weak position and improve going forward. We need to look at the medium- and long-term gain as against short term travails.

Second, the merger of PSBs does not make too much sense if the public nature of the bank is not going to change. If the government does not want to ease it grips on the system, then merging balance sheets is a summation of numbers without a change in character. Similarly, the government needs to be more responsible when it comes to capitalizing banks as weak governance is a result of too much interference. The usual explanation for lapse in governance is in the area of turning the finger to previous political regimes. But this is not a solution. Also doing book entries to capitalize banks is not the best idea as recapitalizing banks should be in the right spirit.

Third, the tenures of heads raise a dilemma. PSB heads have too short a term to make a difference and carry the risk of being haunted post-retirement. Private bankers at times have too long a tenure which should not be allowed by their shareholders howsoever good they may be as it comes in the way of grooming new talent which can lead to seniors seeking jobs elsewhere. Also, there is no flow of fresh ideas.

The same has been discussed for the RBI Governor too where the tenure should be known in advance and kept at five years so that one can manage change. At any rate, politicizing the post and the renewal of terms does not do good to the office of the Governor, which is one of the most respected positions in the country.

Fourth, the debate on use of RBI reserves is quite unnecessary and gave the impression of trying to use the argument to fulfil the Budget. The policy already allows for 100 per cent transfer of surplus to the government which was being done. The controversy brought in a debate which was quite unnecessary. In the same vein the difference of opinion between the government and the RBI though good when it leads to meaningful debate, should not deteriorate to one-upmanship. This means sending signals that the central bank can be overruled is not the right one for the market.

Fifth, the discussion on RBI intervention in interest rates is not favoured as commercial decisions are to be taken by the bank and by imposing a formula, the central banks become part of the process of interest rate determination which should not be the case. On the other hand, the RBI has given too much freedom to banks to charge high rates on services to deposit holders which should be controlled as they have become quite exploitative.

Sixth, monetary policy formulation needs to also look at savers as the discourse is on borrowers and never deposit holders. The MPC needs to relook at the appropriateness of targeting the CPI. Bankers too seem to have only demand which is lowering of rates. Their argument is that small savings rates come in the way of deposits rates being lowered is very weak and it is shown that there is really no relationship between the two.

Seventh, loan waivers should ideally not be the rule as it comes in the way of damaging the credit culture on both the sides—banker and borrower. This is another of the several compromises which PSBs have to make given their ownership and governance structures. But if one looks at the issue with equanimity, if loans of corporates are rescheduled or written off by the banks which affects the profit and loss account, there can be no harm in the government paying for the waiver. Clearly there is an ideological tussle in thought here.

Eighth, the episodes of PMC Bank and Yes Bank has brought to the fore the question of whether or not our deposits are safe. Clearly the limits for insurance has to be increased and people should be told about the security of their savings. Technically one can lose their money if deposits cross a limit (₹5 lakhs presently). This should be made known before putting money in a bank. A suggestion is that all deposits should be rated so that the public is aware of the risk factor in various banks.

Ninth, compensation of some private bankers has made headlines and spurred the debate on how high can the pay be. It is a private enterprise where the shareholders decide, but the entire process is convoluted that it becomes self-fulfilling. This needs to change for sure and while RBI laying down rules of limits and claw back may not be strictly speaking right when private enterprises are concerned, it may be deemed to be necessary to ensure that CEOs don't take excessive risks for immediate gains which can have repercussions later for the system as a whole.

Lastly, is the issue of governance which is quite interesting at both the private banks and PSBs. There is clearly need to improve on the governance structures and the controversies generated in several episodes of failure is not a good sign for a financial system which has prided itself in being one of the best in the world given the rather strong regulatory and supervisory structures that were set up.

If the reader has tended to disagree with the views presented, it would be considered to be a success for the author as the purpose of fomenting debate is to provoke discussion and criticism as these are the bedrocks for future policy formulation.

About the Author

The author is a practising corporate economist for 33 years, starting his career in the erstwhile ICICI Limited in 1987. He has worked with ICICI Bank, Larsen & Toubro, NCDEX and is presently working with CARE Ratings as Chief Economist. A postgraduate in Economics from the Delhi School of Economics, Sabnavis holds a degree in BA (Honours) in Economics from St Stephen's College. While his objective was to join the civil services and serve the nation, his inability to do so coincided with his bid to impress his fiancée (who became his wife); he began freelance writing in business newspapers in 1988 where he made a mark by being critical of every policy that was passed. This contrarian streak struck the right note with editors of various business newspapers which have helped him cross the 2,500 articles mark which is still ticking. This was a strong foundation for having three books also published by him where publishers were willing to take a chance, *Macroeconomics Demystified*, *Eco Quirks* and *Economics of India: How to Fool All People for All Times*. He can also be seen on business TV channels where the contrarian streak has worked yet again!

He is on various committees of SEBI and Indian Institute of Banking and Finance. He has also served as Co-Chairman and Chairman of Committees of Indian Merchants' Chamber and Bombay Chamber of Commerce and Industry.

His interests are in English literature, cricket, music—western classical, Hindustani, rock and new age (Yanni) music. He reviews books on economics, management, biographies, sociology, politics and so on, mainly in the *Financial Express*. Such reviews were also done earlier in *Businessworld* and *Business Standard*.